*The publisher and the University of California Press Foundation gratefully acknowledge the generous support of the Simpson Imprint in Humanities.*

THE CALIFORNIA WORLD HISTORY LIBRARY

*Edited by Edmund Burke III, Kenneth Pomeranz, and Patricia Seed*

*Potosí*

"I am the support for your columns." The Cerro Rico of Potosí as depicted by Felipe Guaman Poma de Ayala in Martín de Murúa, *Historia del origen y geneología real de los reyes Incas del Pirú,* f.141v (1590, private collection of Seán Galvin). The Andean artist Guaman Poma applied silver leaf to the cross-hatched entrails of the mountain, which once shone but now appear as a tarnished gray. Image courtesy of the Getty Research Institute, publication permission courtesy of Seán Galvin.

# Potosí

THE SILVER CITY THAT CHANGED THE WORLD

*Kris Lane*

UNIVERSITY OF CALIFORNIA PRESS

University of California Press, one of the most distinguished university presses in the United States, enriches lives around the world by advancing scholarship in the humanities, social sciences, and natural sciences. Its activities are supported by the UC Press Foundation and by philanthropic contributions from individuals and institutions. For more information, visit www.ucpress.edu.

University of California Press
Oakland, California

Library of Congress Cataloging-in-Publication Data

Names: Lane, Kris E., 1967- author.
Title: Potosí : the silver city that changed the world / Kris Lane.
Description: Oakland, California : University of California Press, [2019] |
    Includes bibliographical references and index. |
Identifiers: LCCN 2018048203 (print) | LCCN 2018059652 (ebook) |
    ISBN 9780520973633 (Epub) | ISBN 9780520280847 (cloth : alk. paper) |
    ISBN 9780520280854 (pbk. : alk. paper)
Subjects: LCSH: Silver mines and mining—Bolivia—Potosí—History.
Classification: LCC HD9537.B63 (ebook) | LCC HD9537.B63 P674 2018 (print) |
    DDC 984/.14—dc23
LC record available at https://lccn.loc.gov/2018048203

Printed in Canada

28   27   26   25   24   23   22   21   20   19
10   9   8   7   6   5   4   3   2   1

*To the memory of Julian E. Lane (1895–1991),*
*Colorado miner*

I am Rich Potosí
Treasury of the World
King of Mountains
And Envy of Kings

*—Motto from Potosí's Coat of Arms,*
*Granted by Holy Roman Emperor Charles V*

# CONTENTS

# ILLUSTRATIONS AND MAPS

## ILLUSTRATIONS

MAPS

# ACKNOWLEDGMENTS

I owe a mountain of debts, first to the many kind residents of Potosí who stopped to chat with me about mines, mills, reservoirs, lost treasures, Faustian pacts, mass graves, the weather, llama breeding, UFOs, the CIA, and much more since my first visit in 1995. Terry Burke encouraged me to write this book one snowy morning in Washington, D.C., and the following people helped me do it: Peter Bakewell, Allison Bigelow, Kendall Brown, Zephyr Frank, Raquel Gil-Montero, Luis Miguel Glave, R.E. Lane, Jane Mangan, Kenneth Mills, Daniel Oropeza Alba, Matthew Restall, Diego Rodríguez de Sepúlveda, Federico Sartori, Masaki Sato, Heidi Scott, Tatiana Seijas, Shefa Siegel, and Steven Topik. Anonymous readers for the University of California Press helped as well, and my editor, Niels Hooper, kept me focused. Paul Tyler edited the typescript with clarity and grace, and Bradley Depew and Sabrina Robleh patiently sorted mislabeled images, maps, and diagrams. Emilia Thiuri piloted the barge across the river. Ximena Lane executed two essential diagrams and generously aided with manuscript transcriptions and photographs. Rick Britton mapped my world. As always, my wife, Pamela Johnson-Lane, provided moral support, priority reminders, ticket information, hydrocortisone, and all the homemade biscotti and granola I could eat.

The School of Liberal Arts and the Roger Thayer Stone Center for Latin American Studies at Tulane University supplied "la plata" necessary for research over three summers when it should have taken two, and the SLA Dean's Office generously subsidized the maps. I was also helped by a John Simon Guggenheim Memorial Fellowship in 2015–16, for which I owe another book in addition to my soul. Thanks also to the staffs of Tulane's Latin American Library, the John Carter Brown and Hay Libraries at Brown University, the Huntington Library in Pasadena, California, and the Lilly

Library in Bloomington, Indiana. I wish I could deliver silver certificates to all the wonderful archivists who helped me in Spain, Bolivia, Chile, and Argentina as well. In Bolivia, I thank the staffs of the Archivo y Biblioteca Nacional de Bolivia, the Archivo Histórico de Potosí, and the Archivo Histórico Judicial de Oruro. In Chile, I thank the staffs of the Archivo Histórico Nacional and the Biblioteca Nacional. In Spain, I thank the staffs of the Archivo General de Indias, the Biblioteca Nacional, the Real Academia de la Historia, the Archivo Histórico Nacional, and the Archivo General de Palacio. In Argentina, I was aided by the staffs of the Archivo General de la Nación in Buenos Aires and the Archivo Histórico Provincial in Córdoba. I blame remaining errors on hypoxia, silica dust, mercury vapors, the Evil Eye, and bad singani.

# PREFACE

Two years before local farmers led him to Peru's great Inca site of Machu Picchu in 1911, American explorer Hiram Bingham visited the legendary Imperial Villa of Potosí. He was captivated: "By the time we had been here a week we agreed with those who call it the most interesting city in South America." And: "If it were not for the great expanse of ruins and the very large number of churches, it would be difficult to realize today that for over a century this was the largest city in the Western Hemisphere."[1] Bingham estimated Potosí's population at 15,000, or one-tenth of what it had been at its height around 1640.

Bingham may not have grasped it, but the discovery of the world's richest silver deposit in highland Bolivia in 1545 marked a turning point in world history. Perhaps prefiguring the discovery of gold in California in 1848, Potosí's great silver bonanza prompted land invasions, brutal work regimes, disease epidemics, ethnocide, political corruption, and rapid destruction of the natural environment. Yet the discovery also vastly expanded the world's money supply and led to the creation of new and lasting cities, employment for thousands of migrants, the development of agriculture and manufacturing, the rise of lending institutions, and the growth of world trade. Both discoveries fueled and helped realize imperial aspirations.

Gold and silver rushes are a touchstone of modern world history, and we may compare the Potosí and California bonanzas with those of Brazil, Australia, the Klondike, or South Africa, yet the story of Potosí, much like that of California, is of a different order of magnitude, approaching that of Mexico's great silver boom of the later eighteenth century.[2] Potosí's fabled Cerro Rico, or "Rich Hill," cast a long shadow in part because it appeared so early and so prominently on the global horizon. For this reason, the dramatic rise of Potosí in the sixteenth century, coupled with its survival to the turn of the nineteenth century and beyond—indeed, until today—demands analysis and reflection.

Beginning in the 1970s, world-systems analysts saw the Cerro Rico as a classic example of a peripheral supplier of raw materials to an industrializing center, namely Western Europe.[3] It is clear that much Potosí silver flowed to Europe, mostly through Spain, and its effects were profound. Spurred by the silver of the Cerro Rico, textile production took off in France, Italy, the Netherlands, Ireland, and England, even as Spain's own cloth industry was pinched off by price inflation. Many other European industries, including iron founding, shipbuilding, and gun manufacture, were stimulated or disrupted by this early American mining boom.

Eurocentric assumptions limited early world-systems analysis, and the architect of the model, Immanuel Wallerstein, was taken to task for failing to reckon with contrary evidence from the so-called periphery, which, as this book shows in some detail, could be quite "industrial" or capital-intensive, its workers skilled, well paid, and often innovative.[4] World-systems analysts are now more subtle and varied in their approaches, and their interests go beyond explaining global patterns of capital accumulation, the international division of labor, and the origins of industrialization, although these remain pressing concerns for many scholars.

In the early 1990s, historians traced the rise of so-called merchant empires by taking a fresh look at how world bullion flows interacted with mercantilist desires, but still with a Europe-centered view.[5] As in the case of Wallerstein and most world-systems analysts, there was a tendency to acknowledge Potosí's obvious importance while still treating it as a remote, technically backward satellite or dependency of Spain, its silver a brute commodity produced by unskilled workers. It was left to economists to sort out how American silver bullion became money and afterwards how it transformed global credit structures.[6] Scholars of early modern empires have lately "decentered" Iberian hegemony, such that places like Potosí are no longer seen as simply peripheral, but much remains to be explained.[7]

World historians zoomed out in the late 1990s to trace where most of Potosí's and the rest of Spanish America's silver went, and what effects it had on places other than Europe. We now know that Potosí silver did not tarry long in London, Paris, or Amsterdam, much less in Lisbon or Seville; the lion's share was traded away to Asia. This was no secret to historians of China or India, or of the Dutch or English East India Companies, but it has taken a while for the global implications of Spanish America's great silver bonanzas to come into focus.[8]

In *ReOrient,* Andre Gunder Frank took a modified world-systems approach to argue for a China-centered global economy.[9] Historians of the Middle East and North Africa had long tracked the effects of Spanish American silver as it made its way east and ultimately into the massive, quasi-industrial economies of India and China, but telling the full story requires a lot of cooperation and digesting of complex economic data. Other scholars have reminded us of the importance of the transpacific silver stream, the so-called Manila galleons that transported Mexican and Potosí silver to Asia beginning in the early 1570s.[10]

Scholars of early modern Asia dispute the particulars, but it is now clear that the effects of Potosí silver, as in Europe, varied considerably from place to place. Much like Spain, the Ottoman and Safavid Empires suffered ruinous price inflation and other monetary problems in the seventeenth century, whereas Mughal India seems to have absorbed American treasure, including millions of debased Potosí coins, in stride.[11] Larger than Mughal India and more famously fond of Potosí silver, China under the Ming and Qing dynasties suffered repeated economic shocks in the seventeenth century. Even so, world bullion prices stabilized around mid-century and China remained a long-term silver sink.[12]

What China and India had to offer the world in exchange for Potosí silver was a little bit of everything, but most profitable were fine artisan goods, especially textiles. Just as it had spurred towns like Rouen (France) and Leiden (Netherlands) to produce more linen and flannel cloth, Spanish American silver drove Chinese silk producers in Nanjing and other coastal cities to innovate and expand. The southern Chinese town of Jingdezhen, in turn, produced massive amounts of blue-on-white export porcelain, some of it made to order.[13] At opposite ends of India, silver-loving Gujarati and Bengali weavers produced huge quantities of print cotton fabrics, which found buyers worldwide, including sub-Saharan Africans.[14] From Senegal to Mozambique, Indian textiles bought with American silver were traded for African captives who were then sent to the Americas, some of them to Potosí, again in exchange for silver.

The more we dig into Potosí silver's role in world history, the more questions arise. Historians of Eurasia's so-called gunpowder empires have asked how the massive influx of American silver in the sixteenth and seventeenth centuries fueled military expansion, and therefore the consolidation or breakup of states and principalities. We have long known that Spain was a formidable global power in these years precisely because it could tap the world's richest mountain, but historians have also calculated the costs of Ottoman, Safavid, Mughal, Ming, Qing, and other imperial military projects hastened along by Potosí's silver flood.

Environmental historians have approached mining booms, including the one at Potosí, with very different questions. Many focus on destruction of fragile ecosystems, combining archival and scientific evidence to gauge local, regional, and global effects.[15] Others have treated nature as a historical force in its own right, placing humans in a different ecological perspective and time frame. At ground level, environmental scholars have calculated vegetation loss, erosion rates, and other unintended consequences of mining and related colonization. Others have studied lake sediments and riverbeds for evidence of contamination by heavy metals, altered pH levels, and other traceable effects of mining and refining.[16]

Still other scholars have focused on public health in and around mining communities, their subjects ranging from mineworker lung disease to mercury or lead levels in women's and children's blood.[17] A broader theme in many of these studies is environmental justice; how were the environmental and health burdens of mining distributed socially, and why? To this more locally oriented work one must add the broader inquiries of climatologists and other scientists focused on the effects of the Little Ice Age, volcanic eruptions, and cyclical variations in ocean temperatures.[18] Such scholars often seek to correlate these larger, long-cycle, global phenomena with crises recorded by mining societies, including droughts, floods, famines, and disease epidemics.

In all of these types of studies, mining boomtowns such as Potosí figure prominently, yet we often forget that these were cities in their own right, vibrant and changing urban ecosystems. This book aims to balance the local and the global by treating Potosí—city and mountain, mines and countryside—as an example of early modern global urbanism and extraction in action. It is interested in how disparate groups of people on opposite sides of the planet became connected by silver not only as victims and perpetrators but as human beings locked in a shared struggle for a better life, however brutal or misguided their efforts may appear in retrospect. If Potosí was an environmental disaster and a moral tarpit, it was also a monument to human ingenuity and survival. To examine Potosí's legacy today is to ponder the costs and benefits of globalization with more perspective and less romance than Hiram Bingham did over a century ago.

# TIMELINE

| 1532 | Spanish capture Inca Atahualpa at Cajamarca |
|---|---|
| 1538 | Spanish led to Porco silver mines |
| 1539 | Spanish establish regional capital at La Plata (Chuquisaca) |
| 1541 | Francisco Pizarro assassinated in Cuzco |
| 1542 | Charles V issues New Laws restricting *encomiendas* |
| 1545 | Diego Gualpa discovers silver on the Cerro Rico de Potosí |
| 1548 | Gonzalo Pizarro executed for treason |
| 1553 | Cieza de León publishes iconic image of Potosí |
| 1556 | Nicolao del Benino begins great adit to Veta Rica |
| 1560 | Fr. Domingo de Santo Tomás calls Cerro Rico "mouth of hell" |
| 1561 | Potosí designated Imperial Villa, Audiencia of Charcas created |
| 1563 | Mercury mines of Huancavelica discovered |
| 1572 | Viceroy Francisco de Toledo introduces amalgamation, formal *mita* |
| 1574 | Royal mint opens in Potosí, Toledo issues mining laws |
| 1575 | Potosí jurisdiction extended, *corregidor* moves from La Plata |
| 1592 | Potosí reaches peak production, approximately sixty-five stampmills operating |
| 1597 | Potosí *cabildo* expanded to sixteen aldermen |
| 1598 | Death of King Philip II |
| 1606 | Oruro bonanza depopulates Potosí |
| 1612 | Alonso Yáñez sedition plot foiled |
| 1618 | Alonso Martínez Pastrana arrives in Potosí to collect debts |
| 1620 | Royal decree calling in payment for offices |
| 1621 | Death of King Philip III |
| 1622–25 | Basque-Vicuña conflict, ended by royal amnesty |
| 1626 | Kari-Kari dams burst, flooding Potosí, destroying mills |

| | |
|---|---|
| 1633 | Inspector Francisco de Carvajal y Sande reforms *mita* |
| 1635 | Carvajal y Sande recalled, inspection ends |
| 1640 | Alvaro Alonso Barba publishes *Arte de los metales* |
| 1641 | Inspector Juan de Palacios recalled, mint fraud expands |
| 1648 | Inspector Francisco de Nestares Marín arrives to solve mint fraud |
| 1650 | Execution of Francisco Gómez de la Rocha, chief mint fraud culprit |
| 1652 | Potosí coin devalued by decree, monetary chaos ensues |
| 1657 | Accarete du Biscay visits Potosí, writes account for Colbert |
| 1660 | Deaths of Nestares Marín and Bishop Francisco de la Cruz |
| 1674 | Antonio López de Quiroga introduces black powder blasting |
| 1680 | Baghdad Chaldean priest Elias al-Mûsili visits Potosí for alms |
| 1682 | Convent of St. Theresa opens in Potosí |
| 1699 | Death of Antonio López de Quiroga, Potosí millionaire |
| 1705 | Bartolomé Arzans de Orsúa y Vela begins *History of the Imperial Villa . . .* |
| 1716 | Archbishop-Viceroy Morcilla visits Potosí, painted by Pérez Holguín |
| 1735 | King Philip V lowers Potosí's royal fifth to a tenth |
| 1736 | Death of Arzáns, new tax rate takes effect |
| 1747 | Miners' savings bank opens |
| 1749 | Conspiracy of *kajchas* |
| 1773 | New Potosí mint opens |
| 1780–83 | Great Andean Rebellion |
| 1794 | Nordenflicht mission arrives from Buenos Aires |
| 1814 | Rebels from Buenos Aires seize Potosí mint and city |
| 1825 | Simón Bolívar climbs Cerro Rico, Bolivia established |
| 1829 | First British mining company fails in Potosí |

# Introduction

"If I were to pay you, Sancho," responded Don Quixote, "according to what the greatness and nobility of this remedy deserve, the treasure of Venice and the mines of Potosí would not be enough."[1]

SANCHO PANZA WAS UNABLE to disenchant his master, but he understood the value placed on his services. They were, to paraphrase Don Quixote, "worth a Potosí." In 1545, barely a decade after the Spanish toppled the Inca Empire, a native Peruvian prospector stumbled onto the world's richest silver deposit. Diego Gualpa testified in old age that while on an errand for his European master a fierce wind knocked him down. His hands sank into pay dirt and word got out. The "Rich Hill" or Cerro Rico of Potosí, a barren 4,800-meter (15,750-foot)–high mountain in what is today south-central Bolivia, instantly became a global symbol of wealth. By 1573, when Diego Gualpa testified, over 10,000 Andean draftees worked the Rich Hill's cavernous mines and mercury-soaked refineries, and by 1600 the adjoining city, the Imperial Villa of Potosí, fanning out below the mountain at 4,000 meters (13,200 feet) above sea level, was home to over 100,000 residents, making it one of the largest—and highest—cities in the world.

Native Andean women ran Potosí's open-air markets. African men staffed its royal mint. Proud Basques squared off against equally proud Extremadurans on the city's cobbled square. Portuguese, Flemish, and Italian minorities grew in the shadows, as did an increasingly mixed population. Women of rank snubbed rivals as they strutted the streets in platform shoes, sporting the world's finest jewels, in addition to velvets, laces, and silk brocades. From its inception Potosí was violent, and even in decline it retained its reputation for mayhem. Vice thrived. By 1600, Potosí had more brothels, taverns, and gambling dens per capita than any other city in the Spanish realm. Desperate for stimulants, the city guzzled wine and maize beer, sipped yerba mate and hot chocolate, chewed coca, and smoked tobacco.

Yet Potosí was also devoutly Catholic, its core a Baroque monument to Christian piety, to the belief in redemption from mortal sin. Some twenty churches and chapels dotted the urban landscape by 1600, growing more opulent with each deathbed bequest. Priests came from as far away as Baghdad to beg alms. Despite its lofty isolation, the Imperial Villa of Potosí was a polyglot and cosmopolitan city, a fountain of fortune, a consumer's paradise. It was also an environmental disaster, a cradle of technical innovation, a theater of punishment, and a hotbed of corruption and fraud. In short, it was a conflicted and contradictory harbinger of globalized modernity.

Built on mining, Potosí was a long-cycle boomtown. By the early seventeenth century it lurched toward decadence. Though inexhaustible, the Cerro Rico's ores grew harder to extract and refine. New silver strikes in the hinterland raised hopes, but most were ephemeral, gone bust within a decade. A major mint scandal in the 1640s crippled the town's already precarious financial sector, and from the wreckage there emerged one of Potosí's greatest entrepreneurs and richest men. The Galician merchant and mine owner Antonio López de Quiroga flourished after the mint crisis until his death in 1699, seen by some as the exception that proved the rule of Potosí's inevitable decline. Already by 1690, Mexico's many scattered silver camps—including the namesake San Luis Potosí—collectively outproduced the Rich Hill, and they continued to do so until Spanish American independence in the 1810s. Despite revival after 1750, Potosí never returned to its glory days.

Decadence was not doom. Cerro Rico silver production bottomed out in the first decades of the eighteenth century, and plague killed a third of Potosí's inhabitants in 1719, yet the city still shone as a beacon of hope and a center for opulent display. It was in this hard-bitten era that town chronicler Bartolomé Arzáns de Orsúa y Vela composed his million-word *History of the Imperial Villa of Potosí*, a vivid and engrossing narrative that survives in two manuscript copies. Since its publication in 1965, scholars have struggled to parse truth from fiction in Arzáns. It was also in these years that Potosí's most famous painter, Melchor Pérez Holguín, developed his inimitable style, celebrating the arrival of a viceroy on a wall-sized canvas for the new Bourbon king.

There were other forces at work in Potosí and along the coasts of South America in the era of Philip V (1700–45). During and after the 1702–13 War of the Spanish Succession, emboldened French traders sparked a modest revival in silver mining, much of it apparently untaxed. Contraband trade with the English, who had won the Spanish slave trade concession at war's end, also thrived through the 1720s and 1730s via Buenos Aires. Hungry for revenue to offset huge new military expenditures, Spain's Bourbon kings took notice, and soon royal ministers began drafting reforms aimed at reviving the fabled Cerro Rico of Potosí.

The crown halved taxes on gross silver production in 1735 to 10 percent, and although it took time, this and other incentives paid dividends. The *mita* labor draft was reinforced in the early 1730s despite over a century of criticism, and a savings bank was created in 1747. A huge new mint facility, begun in the 1750s, opened in 1773. This elegant structure remains the pride of the Imperial Villa, a temple to its secular pretentions. After the new mint came a European technical mission led by a Polish baron, but it failed to revive Potosí's mines and refineries in the 1790s. Throughout the eighteenth century, indigenous miners known as *kajchas* developed their own parallel silver economy, sometimes paying taxes, sometimes not. When independence struggles began in the 1810s, Potosí was still considered the pearl of the Andes. Rebels from Buenos Aires seized the city and emptied its mint, only to be driven out by equally cash-starved royalists. Simón Bolívar ended his long southward journey of liberation by delivering a speech from the windswept summit of the Cerro Rico in 1825.

This book offers a concise history of Potosí from its discovery in 1545 to the arrival of South America's Liberator in 1825, the year the Republic of Bolivia took his name. An epilogue describes what has happened to the Rich Hill and former Imperial Villa since then. The chapters work chronologically but also thematically, each one centering on a debate or controversy, as Potosí was always debated and always controversial. Not long after its discovery, the city and its mines were held up as an extreme example of Spanish greed and cruelty, an iconic emblem of what became known as the Black Legend.

Controversy continues. Potosí has been described variously as a marvel of renaissance technology, an environmental hellhole, a hub of regional development, and a worst-case example of an export enclave. Others have described it as a space for native self-fashioning and social mobility, a stage for outbursts of pathological violence, a surprisingly normal Spanish city in a high desert setting, and a baroque dystopia. Scholars of the eighteenth century have alternately called Potosí a rare Bourbon reform success story and a blatant Bourbon failure. Bourbon excesses helped spark the greatest rebellion in all of colonial Latin America. After independence, the Cerro Rico was an ungraspable object of foreign desires, a monetary base for a new nation, and a nightmare colonial inheritance for a weak republic. In all these contradictory views of Potosí, in every polemic or encomium, one sees how a mountain of silver inflated imperial dreams and distilled colonial nightmares. In the end, most agreed that the Cerro Rico was a mirage, and devotion to its exploitation led only to disenchantment and poverty. It was an object lesson in human weakness, meanness, and folly.

All was not darkness, however, and views from the outside could be deceiving. From the start, the city of Potosí was famous for its diverse, dynamic, and generous society. Thus, this book emphasizes the lives of native workers, market women, enslaved African laborers, mule drivers, and other ordinary folks, alongside the lives of elite merchants, mine and refinery owners, wealthy widows, cross-dressed swashbucklers, priests, soldiers, and crown officials. The city's terrible work conditions and contamination plus its notoriously high murder rate and numerous executions are also placed in the context of the times. Early modern life was often nasty, brutish, and short. But bonanza also prompted surprising innovations, and made fortunes for entrepreneurs at all social levels. Some of them gave as profligately as they gained.

It is thus important to remember that although Potosí was a site of considerable suffering and mischief, it was also a platform for personal reinvention, and not just for elites. Poor men and women gained wealth and status with surprising speed if they were clever and lucky, and many cooperated with one another even as they competed. Factions and clans proliferated, enabling some stars to rise while snuffing out others. At their worst, Potosí's factions fought like Guelphs and Ghibellines, but just as often they made pacts and alliances to defend themselves against crown and critics. Family dynasties could appear or disappear almost overnight, saved by a lucky match or doomed by a prodigal son. Potosí silver enabled second acts in life despite rigid social hierarchies.

Just as significantly, this book emphasizes the environmental consequences of Potosí's discovery and development, detailing what we know of deforestation, fouling of streams, waste mismanagement, and pollution with mercury, lead, zinc, and other toxic metals and chemical byproducts. Potosí's history in this period is nothing if not a cautionary tale, and the environmental legacy of its early modern bonanza remains evident in the city's air, water, and soil today.

Last, this book does not treat Potosí or its inhabitants in isolation, but rather links them to the rest of the world, both as exporters of a large portion of the globe's silver supply and also as voracious consumers of raw and manufactured products from as nearby as the Pilcomayo basin and as far away as the pepper groves of southwest India. Most slaves in Potosí were African, or of African ancestry; this book stresses their importance as workers and bearers of culture. The number of Africans arriving in Potosí each year both before and after the era of Spanish-Portuguese union (1580–1640) was higher than most historians realize, shaping the city's culture alongside tens of thousands of native Andeans who were either drafted or chose to call the Imperial Villa home.

Potosí was, in its heyday, a major player on the stage of world history. It was known not only to all the monarchs of Europe but also to the sovereigns of the Ottoman, Safavid, Mughal, Ming, and Qing empires. Many such monarchs envied Spain's great Andean fountain of fortune, and several, including Louis XIV of France, pondered capturing it. Like Don Quixote and Sancho Panza, envious kings knew what it meant to be "worth a Potosí." They could not help but covet what the Emperor Charles V had rightly labeled the "Treasury of the World."

## A WORLD HUNGRY FOR SILVER

At the time of Potosí's discovery in 1545 both Europe and Asia were undergoing what economists call a bullion famine. Population growth and commercial expansion in the centuries after the Black Death of the 1340s drove up demand for specie, the hard cash that crossed cultural and political boundaries. In Eurasia, along with North and East Africa, only gold and silver fit the bill. With some exceptions in sub-Saharan Africa and Southeast Asia, copper, bronze, and iron currencies were not accepted outside a prince's domain. Paper money was even less transferable, handled mostly by big traders who could enforce contracts.

Foreign exchange demanded precious metals, raw or coined. Similarly, soldiers demanded pay in specie. Many were mercenaries. Globally, gold was scarce, silver somewhat less so—yet far more so than today. Because of its *relative* abundance compared with gold, silver was used for most international or inter-imperial money transfers. The ever-shifting exchange rate between gold and silver, or bimetallic ratio, was key in directing global trade flows. Royal decrees usually did little to change this, but imperial demand for silver in China after 1570 was enough to reset the clock of the world's commercial economy just as Potosí was hitting its stride.

In order to understand silver, one must take a brief look at gold. In Antiquity, gold was associated with the hot tropics, cooked by the sun and thus most abundant in sub-Saharan Africa and parts of Asia. The Portuguese tapped into the gold of sub-Saharan Africa by way of the Atlantic coast beginning in the mid-fifteenth century and in southeast Africa about a century later. Tellingly, the Portuguese gold trade in Africa remained more valuable than the slave trade until about 1650. West African gold, most of it alluvial or scattered in streams and riverbeds, was mined with great effort, and not year-round. West African gold flowed mostly in the agricultural offseason, sometimes interrupted by wars.

As much as they desired it, Europeans never managed to monopolize West African gold or even to get close to its sources due to the power of local rulers and the prevalence of malaria and other tropical maladies. The gold of southeast Africa, partly tied to the Great Zimbabwe and the legendary kingdom of Monomotapa, remained almost as unreachable, at least at the source, although the Portuguese eventually tapped in at the edge. In sum, without African middlemen willing to deal with Europeans, gold from the African interior would have continued to flow mostly into the Muslim world, either across the Sahara or through the ports of the Swahili coast.

Native peoples of the larger Caribbean islands also used gold, as Columbus discovered in 1492 to the delight of his Spanish sponsors.[2] Conquest followed. Although the Spanish quickly seized mines on Hispaniola and elsewhere in the Caribbean basin, the goldfields of the early Spanish Indies soon played out. Even in Columbus's day, Spanish migrants forced native Americans and enslaved Africans to wash gold for them. This was not the world of the grizzled European prospector, but rather something more like ancient Rome: mining was the work of slaves and convicts. As would happen in Potosí, early American prospecting and mining were activities delegated to coerced dependents, most of them non-Europeans. As one result, the true discoverers of America's great gold and silver mines were almost invariably native Americans, Africans, and mixed people of color.

The Spanish conquests of Aztec Mexico (1519–21), Inca Peru (1532–34), and Muisca Colombia, or New Granada (1538), also yielded considerable gold, but as in the Caribbean islands the most obvious alluvial sources were spotty and prone to quick exhaustion. Alluvial gold deposits not already worked by native peoples were rare, although some hard-rock deposits remained untouched. Gold-bearing veins were followed underground with newly introduced iron tools in places like Chisquío, Colombia, and Zaruma, Ecuador, but this kind of excavation required big investments. Worse, Spanish masters mistreated and exposed indigenous workers to disease such that the conquistadors' gold mines were virtual death camps. Indigenous complaints went largely unheard, but Spanish priests such as the Dominican Bartolomé de las Casas howled in protest. Seeing Spain's American bonanza and the moral failings that followed, many in Europe used the writings of Las Casas and other internal critics of conquest to malign the Spanish as innately greedy, cruel, and intolerant. The Black Legend was born.

Sub-Saharan Africans suffered likewise. Clerical pleading led Spanish monarchs from the time of Isabella and Ferdinand to decree gold panning a job fit only for enslaved Africans, and thus in many gold-producing regions of Spanish America, particularly in lowland Colombia, Africans and their offspring became a majority. Gold production cycles tended toward quick peaks and precipitous declines, sometimes connected to the ups and downs of the slave trade. By 1600, abandoned gold camps dotted the Spanish American landscape from western Mexico to southern Chile. Only New Granada continued to produce substantial gold up through independence, yet even here the trend was for gold camps to flash and fade as new frontiers were opened, conquered, and exploited.

It was the discovery of massive silver deposits that sustained the core Spanish colonies of Mexico and Peru after conquest, and that also ended Eurasia's bullion famine after 1550. Potosí was not the beginning, nor would it be the end. The first major silver strikes were in Mexico, at camps such as Sultepec, Taxco, and Pachuca, but none of these deposits, first developed in the 1530s, were easily exploited. Flooding and refractory ores were common. More northerly mining districts such as Zacatecas and Guanajuato, discovered in the 1540s and 1550s, proved far more promising, but they were distant from indigenous population centers. Only the wealthiest or most creditworthy Mexican mine owners could afford African slaves and the Spanish crown was loath to subsidize the slave trade. Indigenous workers were drafted but most had to be recruited and retained. As a result, Mexican silver mining lurched and stuttered before beginning a long climb to world dominance around 1690, peaking shortly before independence in 1810.

Before Mexico's great age of silver came the heyday of Potosí. In the high Andes of South America, Spanish conquistadors in the late 1530s followed the Incas to their remote gold mines at Carabaya, in the hot lowlands

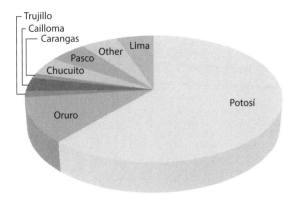

Potosí's share of Greater Peru's silver production, ca. 1545–1810 (based on tax records).

southeast of Cuzco, and to their silver mines at Porco, in what is today south-central Bolivia. Porco quickly became a bone of contention among conquistador factions, including men faithful to Gonzalo Pizarro, who rebelled against Charles V in 1544 to protest curbs on access to native subjects and their surpluses. In the midst of the fighting between royalists and rebels, indigenous mineworkers based in Porco, following the lead of Diego Gualpa, discovered the massive silver lodes of nearby Potosí. Within a few years, the word *Potosí* became a global byword for limitless wealth, and the Cerro Rico, or Rich Hill, a triangular icon of the Spanish Empire to match Charles V's Pillars of Hercules.

To get a quick sense of its quantitative importance, Potosí produced more silver, according to official tax records, than all of Mexico combined before 1650. In its first century, Potosí produced nearly half the world's silver. In the longer term, the amount of silver taxed between 1545 and 1810—again trusting official records and ignoring contraband—was 875.4 million pesos, each peso weighing about an ounce. This constituted nearly 20 percent of all the known silver produced in the world across 265 years. It was also more than twice the total silver production registered at Zacatecas, Mexico (401.4 million pesos), Potosí's closest competitor in the pre-industrial era. Despite an early bonanza, most of Zacatecas's silver was extracted in the eighteenth century, when Potosí was already in decline. The Mexican mining town of San Luis Potosí was founded in 1592 in hopes that it would live up to its namesake in faraway "Upper Peru." Notwithstanding a respectable output that also included gold, it never did.[3]

The kings of Spain, along with their enemies (who were legion), believed right up to the age of Latin American independence in the 1810s and 1820s that their fortunes were necessarily tied to the Cerro Rico. We now know that most of the Rich Hill's readily accessible silver had been extracted well before 1650, but even in decline Potosí was believed to be miraculous, unique, even capable of generating new metal deep within its own bowels.[4] It was an inexhaustible fountain of fortune that only needed priming, a new invention, another divine blessing.

## GLOBAL VISIONS OF POTOSÍ

Potosí was world famous soon after its discovery in 1545. After a 1553 woodcut was published in Seville, the Cerro Rico or Rich Hill became a secular icon. The image was made from a drawing by Pedro de Cieza de León, an early postconquest traveler in Spanish Peru who visited the bustling mining camp in 1549.[5] Within a few decades, descriptions of Potosí by Cieza de León and Agustín de Zárate, another early Spanish visitor, were translated into French, German, Dutch, English, and Italian. Cieza's description was the most detailed, and his 1553 woodcut was widely copied. As printers and other artists followed, the mountain's image grew more fantastic.

The 1553 woodcut depicts the Cerro Rico with five named silver veins near the summit, from left to right: the Mendieta, Rica, Centeno, Estaño, and Oñate. Two men, an apparently indigenous laborer with a pack on the left, and a Spaniard on the right with a hat and staff, make their way up the mountain on steep trails. In front of the Cerro Rico is the lesser hill of Huayna Potosí, and beneath it spreads the city—not yet known as the Villa Imperial— divided by a gulch, known as La Ribera. This creek seems to emerge from a circular lake or spring in the hills on the upper left side of the picture. Another smaller spring flows out from the right side of the Cerro Rico.

Cieza's woodcut depicts two churches: San Francisco and Santa Barbara, the first mistakenly set on the far side of the river, and both of them large given the early date. In the foreground is a haphazard-looking main square with a few human figures, including a clutch of helmeted soldiers with lances just beyond a severed head on a pike. This suggestion of deadly violence or rather, royal justice, is important. In the text, Cieza de León describes the key role Potosí played in the wars between Spanish conquistador factions that culminated in the execution of the rebel Gonzalo Pizarro in 1548.

After narrating Potosí's discovery, Cieza describes the widespread use of an indigenous wind furnace, or *guayra,* for silver smelting, the Castilian

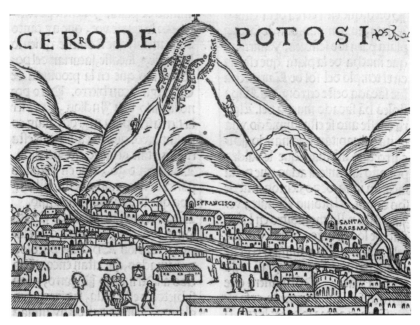

"Cerro de Potosí," Pedro de Cieza de León, *Crónica del Peru,* 1553. Courtesy of the John Carter Brown Library at Brown University.

bellows furnace having failed. These ingenious native ovens were so numerous in the hills around Potosí that at night, "they seem like luminaries." To smelt silver, Cieza said, wind was as important here as for sailors at sea. Cieza then suggests that because Potosí's mining and refining remained almost entirely in native Andean hands: "it is believed that many have become rich, and carried off to their lands a great quantity of this silver. And it was for this reason that Indians from many parts of this kingdom have come to this site of Potosí, to take advantage."[6] To trust Cieza de León, early Potosí was as much a land of opportunity for native entrepreneurs as it was for Spaniards. A mining town paradox was already evident: Potosí would be a pit of forced labor and mass suffering as well as a staging ground for personal gain.

Word of Potosí quickly reached the Near East, and by 1580 or so an Ottoman version of the iconic image of the Cerro Rico appeared in a compendium of writings on the Spanish Indies. Known as the *Tarih-I Hind-I Garbi,* this digest was reproduced in many versions over the centuries. One of the earliest ones includes a fanciful colored miniature of the Cerro Rico derived from the Cieza woodcut, or perhaps from an Italian copy.[7] The most striking difference is that the Cerro Rico has been rendered green by the

Ottoman illustrator, with lush vegetation in the foreground and spiked Mediterranean cypress dotting the lavishly built city. Ottoman-style architecture predominates, some buildings appearing to have lead roofs, and the city is surrounded by crenellated stone walls like those of Istanbul. The walls are on either side of the river, which originates in a circular lake or spring as in Cieza's original. Instead of soldiers, the Ottoman artist places two individuals in the extramural foreground, one white and one black, dressed in flowing garments and apparently standing among shrines or graves. The image is small but lovingly colored, evoking a "silver spring" in an earthly paradise.

The *Tarih-I Hind-I Garbi* text on Potosí is largely borrowed from Agustín de Zárate's 1555 *The Discovery and Conquest of Peru,* but the translation is not literal.[8] The Ottoman scribes refer to the rebel Gonzalo Pizarro's lieutenant who took over Potosí during the civil wars, Capt. Francisco de Carvajal:

> During the course of the campaign the afore-mentioned Carvajal saw on the skirt of a great mountain a prosperous city named Potosí by whose side a river flows. On whatever side they dug, if they fired the earth from one *kantar* [hundredweight] of it, fifteen *okkas* [19.2 kg or 42.3 lbs.] of pure silver flowed forth. (It seems that the afore-mentioned river was the source of the previously mentioned Silver River [the Río de la Plata].) Then Carvajal collected in the afore-mentioned place seven thousand Indians and laid down this rule: "Everyone is to deliver each week four gold [pieces] worth of silver and he is to keep the rest for himself."[9]

The Ottoman authors describe a city that precedes the mines. And they blend coercion and incentive, a departure from the free hand for enterprising native Andeans suggested by Cieza. Global tales of Potosí were already spinning, but one thing was clear: the Cerro Rico, as Cieza de León described it, was unique: "And from this, one may take as a great truth that in no other part of the world has there been discovered a hill so rich."[10]

In 1580, the Ottomans faced a powerful enemy in Habsburg Spain and its self-described Holy League of allies. Despite occasional victories, the memory of Lepanto, in which Ottoman naval forces collapsed in 1571, was still fresh. Stretched thin, the Ottoman Empire faced hard times under Sultan Murad II (1574–95) to whom this version of the *Tarih-I Hind-I Garbi* was dedicated. Spanish precious metals won by trade, plunder, and ransom had proved a blessing, then a curse, driving up prices throughout the Mediterranean and especially within the Ottoman realms. Yet Spanish American silver remained

طائفة مزبور، معادن مسفوره نك كيفيت استخراجنى بوطرتف اوزر

ايدرلرد بكد اقلاه برقلاه برفرقه عظيم سا ايدوب بعده خاك معدنى برمقدار

فحم ونريئا بلد خلطا ايدوب مزبور فرنك لجنله فضح ايدرلر •

دراونركاردن طرفنى نقبا ايدوب برترونن بيدا ايدرله بعد •

The Cerro Rico of Potosí, *Tarih-I Hind-I Garbi* manuscript, ca. 1582.
Courtesy of the Newberry Library, Chicago.

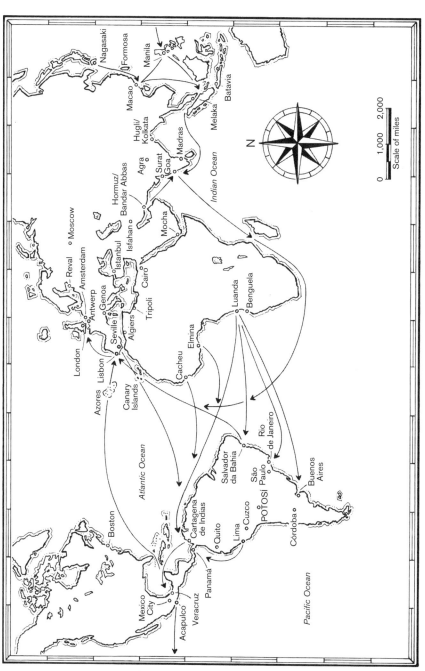

MAP 1. Global maritime trade routes in the age of Potosí silver.

the lifeblood of trade and the sinews of war, the only means of assembling and sustaining great armies and navies. Potosí, so lovingly rendered as an Ottoman city, could be imagined as a sultan's long-range objective or as a stubborn infidel's *pièce de résistance.*

By the time this illustrated dream of American treasure was floated before the Ottoman sultan, the streams emanating from the world's "fountain of fortune" in the high Andes flowed in all directions. Galleons laded Potosí silver by the ton at Arica, Nombre de Dios, Acapulco, Manila, and Seville. Production at the Cerro Rico grew rapidly, peaking in 1592. More than twice as much silver was shipped annually across the Atlantic to Europe than was sent across the Pacific to East and Southeast Asia, yet much of this "Atlantic" bullion and coin still ended up in India or China, often by way of the ports and caravanserais of the Near East and Central Asia.

Japan's silver, substantial but often forgotten in the shadow of Potosí, also flowed mostly into imperial China in the sixteenth and seventeenth centuries. Demand for silver in China has in turn masked the significance of India, which had a dense population, a diverse manufacturing sector, and a vibrant commercial economy. The Mughals and their neighbors soon joined the Ottomans and Safavids, using Potosí silver to finance their wars of conquest. In a world of only about 500 million people, half of them in Asia, the arrival of several million ounces of Potosí silver each year went a long way. The "piece of eight," the world's first truly global currency, crossed all frontiers, financing trade, war, and religious proselytization.

POTOSÍ IN THE WORLD AND THE WORLD IN POTOSÍ

As we have seen, news of Potosí's 1545 discovery spread quickly, spurring migration first from other parts of Spanish America, including greater Peru, Mexico, and the Caribbean, and then from Spain and other parts of Europe. Going the other direction, European merchants and priests announced the bonanza as they traveled to Amsterdam, Moscow, Istanbul, Cairo, Goa, and Melaka. Within a few short decades Potosí was known in India, China, and Southeast Asia. By 1602, the Italian Jesuit missionary Matteo Ricci and his assistant Li Zhizou marked "Potosí Mountain" (Bei Du Xi Shan) on their huge world map for China's Wanli Emperor.[11]

Under Wanli, China had suddenly turned to the outside world for silver, pumping out huge quantities of silk, porcelain, and other luxury commodities in exchange. The word "Potosí" was quickly displacing "Peru," made famous by the Inca Atawallpa's huge ransom of 1533, as the world synonym for imponderable wealth.

Just as Potosí entered world consciousness, worldly goods entered Potosí. As in gold-rush California, merchants selling tools, clothing, food, and stimulants were close on the heels of fortune-seeking miners. Necessities of all sorts poured in from Andean suppliers anxious to lay hands on silver, but Spanish wine, olive oil, iron, and luxury textiles arrived quickly, too. Newly rich mine owners' lavish consumption habits stunned early visitors, including Cieza de León, but he was equally impressed by native Andean market activity. Based on his 1549 visit, he called Potosí's marketplace the greatest in all of Peru:

> And I believe that no fair in the world would equal the trade of this market. I made a note of it several times, and once I saw stretched out along a plain towards the main square of this town site a long string of baskets of coca, so much that it was the greatest wealth of these parts; and on another side heaps of blankets and richly decorated shirts both thin and wide; in another part were great piles of maize and dried potatoes and other foods of theirs; not even mentioning that there were a great number of quarters of beef of the best sort available in the kingdom. And as they extracted silver every day, and these Indians are great eaters and drinkers, especially those who trade with the Spaniards, everything brought for sale was consumed.[12]

Competition was fierce, according to Cieza: "And as for the cost of things, there was so much merchandise that they sold Rouen woolens, broadcloth, and Dutch linens almost as cheaply as in Spain."[13] Potosí's early notary records back up these claims.

Ostentation grew over time, and by 1580 it was not uncommon for even poorer *potosinos* to sport garments blending the finest European woolens with the best Chinese silks. Spices and gems from all over the world were available in abundance, as were high-quality artisan goods such as eyeglasses, scissors, and even Venetian glassware. A barren alpine slope in 1545, the Imperial Villa of Potosí soon joined the world's cosmopolitan cities in terms of consumer goods and sheer diversity of inhabitants.

One of the Cerro Rico's most successful mine owners in the 1570s was Nicolao del Benino, a native of Florence and, according to his own testimony, a relative of the Medicis. Benino was one of several Italian immigrants. A Potosí homebuyer in 1549 was listed as Jácome Ginovés (Giacomo the Genoese), and in the same year one Francisco Caravaggio claimed a mine. In 1559, Flemish miners exchanged portions of their namesake vein on the Cerro

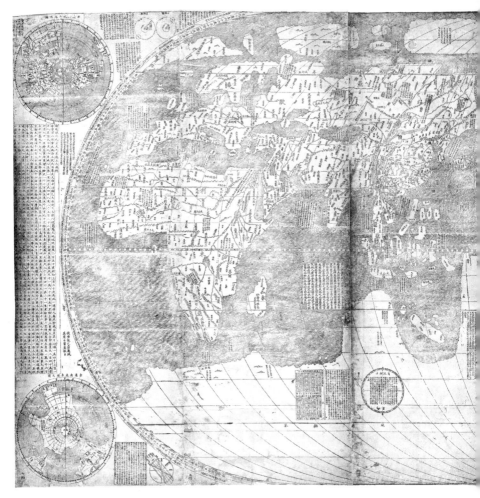

Chinese world map by Matteo Ricci and Li Zhizou, ca. 1602. Courtesy of the James Ford Bell Library, University of Minnesota (Potosí at right, near center of South America).

Rico, the "Veta de los Flamencos." Among the partners: "Juan of Brussels," "Levin of Antwerp," "Andrés of Louvain," and "Dionisio of Holland."[14] In addition to thousands of Europeans from all over the continent, and tens of thousands of multilingual native Andeans, Potosí was home to a rising number of sub-Saharan Africans. There were even a few Asians after 1570, brought in as slaves or servants via Acapulco and Lima.

Potosí thus joined a select group of early modern "world cities," its growth and development reliant on sustained connections to the rest of the globe.[15]

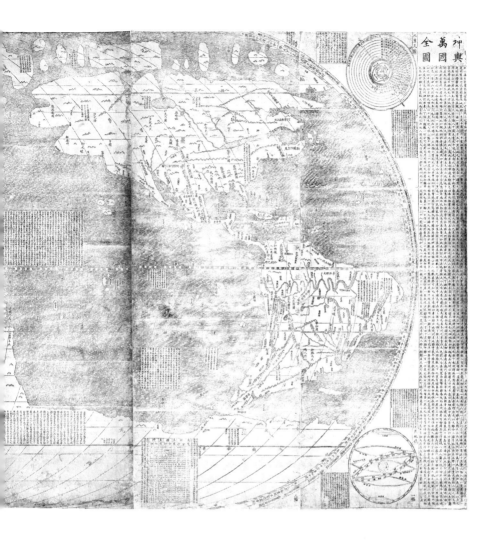

Potosí was unusual in that it was not a port or administrative capital but rather a completely new mining town, a lofty outpost that supplied the world with ready money. There was no place on earth quite like it, possessing a kind of alter ego, almost another city, adjacent to it and underground. As such, and with its iconic red hill towering above, Potosí seemed destined to become a symbol of a new global economic and political order.

Although several outspoken priests bemoaned the moral hazards brought on by bonanza, most Spanish commentators gushed at the good fortune of their Habsburg rulers to possess such unheard-of wealth. It seemed to bode well for the faith, which for the Spanish meant the Roman Catholic faith as they interpreted it. Potosí silver would fund far-flung missions and pay vast armies to "beat back the infidel" or "crush the heretic." Such providential explanations only fueled the myth of Potosí's inexhaustibility, tying its woes to human sin rather than to geology or the failings of early modern chemistry.

With the discovery of mercury in the mountains east of Lima at Huancavelica by 1563, Spain seemed to possess the necessary ingredients needed to support global empire. Mercury was used to refine Potosí's silver ores on a grand scale beginning in 1572, and some contemporaries wondered if God had not chosen Castile among all kingdoms and the Habsburgs among all dynasties as his most favored servants. What cures also kills, however, and it would not be long before commentators, including insiders, began calling Potosí silver a curse, the worst temptation ever placed before Christians. Huancavelica's deadly mercury mines, Potosí's Peruvian handmaiden, only drove home the point.

It is this moral ambivalence toward Potosí that has persisted, and yet the city's role as global silver supplier and significant market for global goods—and destiny of so many thousands of migrants—remains undisputed. Potosí was a site of technical innovation and industrial development in an age not thought of as industrial or particularly innovative. It was a site of enormous capital concentration and complex financial exchanges in an age not thought of as truly capitalist or financially sophisticated. It was an enduring battleground between private entrepreneurs and an increasingly absolutist state with mercantilist or monopolist pretensions. The following chapters aim to address some of these seeming contradictions or riddles of Potosí's early modern history, not losing sight of silver, but searching hard for the novelty of human experience in such a forbidding place, both above and underground.

Chapter 1 examines the disputed circumstances of Potosí's discovery and the importance of pre-Columbian mining and metallurgy. Why had the Incas not mined the Red Mountain? Chapter 2 treats the city's first boom, when Andean artisans dominated mining and refining. Why weren't the Spanish in control from the start? Chapter 3 details the revolutionary changes made by Peru's fifth viceroy, Francisco de Toledo, in the 1570s. Was Toledo's project an early attempt at state-managed economy? Chapter 4 examines the many marvels and miseries produced by Toledo's reforms. Who won and who lost out in the great bonanza? Chapter 5 relates a string of calamities that nearly destroyed Potosí between the 1620s and the 1650s. How did *potosinos* and outsiders reckon with natural and human-caused disasters? Chapter 6 treats Potosí's extended decline under the last Habsburg king, Charles II, and its partial recovery under the first Bourbon one, Philip V. Did indigenous miners and refiners again take over? Chapter 7 probes the great changes that occurred in Potosí after about 1750, when state intervention reached new heights. Would Enlightenment science revive the mines? The conclusion, "Summing Up," returns to the disputed significance of Potosí's early modern history, and an epilogue treats the city's fortunes since 1825. Despite nearly five centuries spent choking on its own dust, Potosí breathes eternal.

# ONE

# *Bonanza*

... and as several Indians belonging to a so-and-so Villaroel wandered among some mountains eighteen leagues from the Villa de la Plata, they came upon a very large peak seated on a plain, the size of which I cannot quite explain except to tell Your Mercy so that you may understand that it is as large as one might see in these parts. And they found in it signs of silver, and in smelting they found it so rich that wherever they took earth and fired it, it yielded almost nothing but silver, such that the least they got was eighty marks per hundredweight, which was almost half.

—ANONYMOUS,
possibly Lic. Polo Ondegardo, 1547[1]

AS ONE MIGHT EXPECT, Potosí's discovery generated legends. According to several Spanish writers it was early in the year 1545 that a native Andean man known either as Gualpa or Guanca happened upon an outcrop of silver ore while chasing a llama, a guanaco, or a deer up a conical red peak in the southern Bolivian highlands. The reddish mountain, possibly known as Potoc'chi, was not terribly high by Andean standards, but at just under 5,000 meters (nearly 16,000 feet) above sea level it did command an impressive view. The horizon was dominated by lumpy, barren *puna,* a high desert cut through by canyons topped with basalt cliffs, and with glimpses of vast salt flats framed by distant cordilleras.

According to most early accounts, there was little evidence of Inca or other pre-Hispanic mining activity on the red mountain's flanks. Not far off, about a half-day's journey southwest, were the former Inca mines of Porco, where Gualpa or Guanca was working as a *yanacona* or personal retainer for his presumably Spanish overlord, called "Villaroel" in the account above. Porco's silver mines were rich, but many had flooded due to the high water table, driving up costs and diminishing returns.

It was a moment of crisis according to the providentialist narratives, and in one of them Diego Gualpa became the Juan Diego of the Andes. The

Virgin of Guadalupe did not appear to him, but either the Christian God or the God of Wind (in Quechua, *Wayra*) used him to reveal the riches of the Cerro Rico to the world. Fortunately, we have an account that seems to be from Gualpa himself, or as close to him as we may get (see appendix). In 1572, on orders of just-arrived viceroy Francisco de Toledo, a Spanish priest interviewed the nearly 70-year-old Andean man as he lay dying in his home in Potosí.[2]

The discoverer was by this time known as *don* Diego Gualpa, the title "don" signifying noble ancestry. He claimed to have been from the Cuzco-area province of Chumbivilcas, a retainer for the ill-fated Inca Huascar, a keeper of sacred feathers. Gualpa was also at Cajamarca, he said, when Francisco Pizarro and his followers ambushed and captured the Inca Atahualpa in 1532. Young Gualpa attached himself to a Portuguese soldier who used him as a personal servant or yanacona but who also protected him from Spaniards who had treated him poorly. Diego Gualpa ended up in Porco mining silver a few years later.[3] He claimed that he and other yanaconas routinely passed the hill or mountain of Potosí (he does not call it Potoc'chi in the testimony, but we must keep in mind that this was filtered through a priest in 1572) on their way back and forth between Porco and La Plata, or Chuquisaca, the budding regional capital on the eastern slope of the Andes.

Gonzalo Pizarro, younger brother of Francisco, had even ordered test diggings low on the mountain's flanks, but they yielded nothing. The occasion Diego Gualpa gave for his discovery of the great mines of the Cerro Rico was that he and a friend had been sent to the mountain's summit to search for a shrine dedicated to the resident spirit, or *huaca*. The pair found an offering, he claimed, which they removed and took down the hill to deliver to their masters. Presumably it included gold and silver objects, but the testimony offers no details.

On the way downhill the two men were separated, according to don Diego Gualpa, who said he was hit by a gust of wind so powerful it flattened him and nearly knocked him out. As he lifted himself, he saw that his hands were marked by a substance he immediately recognized as pay dirt. Gualpa wrapped several pounds of this material in his blanket and took it to Porco to refine. He found it rich, but his current master and other conquistadors were not convinced that the ore had come from the hill already called, apparently, Potosí.

Finally, one Spaniard accompanied Gualpa back to the red mountain, but again the wind kicked up, and was soon so fierce that it dashed the man to the ground and blew off his hat, angering him so much that he began to beat and curse Gualpa. The two soon returned to Porco, where word of Gualpa's discovery reached the man called Villaroel, a Spaniard who moved quickly to stake claims aided by his indigenous retainer, the yanacona Chalco.

No llamas or deer or upturned roots appear in Gualpa's story, as in many other accounts of Potosí's fateful discovery, but wind figures prominently. Wayra (or *guaira* in Spanish phonetics), the Quechua word for wind, would continue to be providential in Potosí for several decades. Yet even this seemingly native account of Potosí's discovery smacks of Catholic legend, of the innocent yokel who witnesses an apparition, only to struggle desperately with supposedly learned authorities to prove its truth. Was Gualpa's discovery real?

## ANDEAN METALLURGY AND GEOLOGY

By the time Europeans and Africans reached South America in the early sixteenth century, Andeans had spent thousands of years extracting and working gold, silver, copper, tin, mercury, salt, lapis lazuli, emeralds, turquoise, nephrite, obsidian, and many other minerals. Andean stone masonry was among the most advanced in the Americas, giving lie to the notion of "Stone Age" primitivism. One need only visit the former Inca capital of Cuzco or the ruins of Machu Picchu to see this matchless artistry firsthand.

In Central and South America as well as parts of the Caribbean, gold-silver-copper alloys were commonly used in jewelry and grave goods, and in coastal Ecuador and Colombia even the difficult metal platinum was worked, ingeniously soldered with gold dust and burnished. Metalworkers in Bolivia and Peru developed arsenical bronze, yielding durable tools and weapons, and at the great temple complex of Tiwanaku near Lake Titicaca, bronze ties held massive, hand-carved building stones in place.

Andean metallurgy was so ancient that few rich metallic mineral deposits remained unknown by the time the Spanish arrived. The conquistadors and their successors suspected this right away, and when native Andeans failed to lead them to gold or silver mines, the Spanish claimed they hid them out of malice. Some native peoples certainly did so out of self-protection, but mineral wealth could work both ways; even oppressed Andeans could get rich or gain status in mining, as hinted by Cieza de León above. Ultimately, keeping "bullion-starved" Europeans away from American treasure was all but impossible.

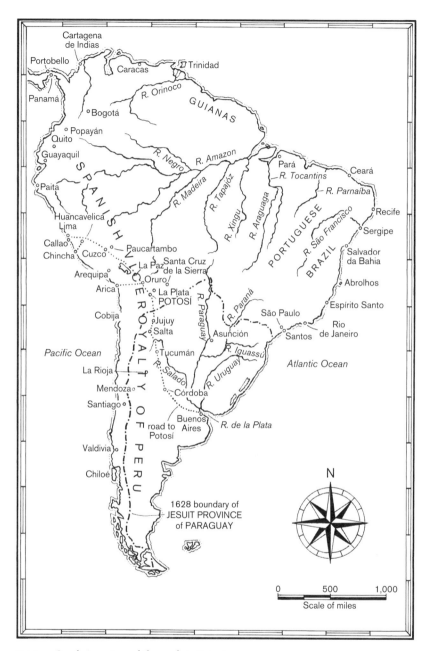

MAP 2. South America and the roads to Potosí.

The Incas who survived conquest were notably fickle about revealing precious metals mines, and it thus seems highly improbable that the Rich Hill of Potosí was truly discovered in 1545, more than a decade after Cajamarca. The Cerro Rico's red color alone would have signaled heavy mineralization to pre-Columbian prospectors, and the mines of Porco were close by. Perhaps religious veneration limited mining activity. We do not know for certain, but there is evidence that Aymara lords inhabiting the Potosí region "gave" the Incas the Porco silver mines as a ritual of submission, and this has led some scholars to argue that the Cerro Rico was in turn an offering made by exiled Incas to the Spanish king amid the rebellion of Gonzalo Pizarro.[4] What we do know is that Potosí's history changed radically after 1545.

The Cerro Rico lies in the heavily mineralized Eastern Cordillera of the Bolivian Andes, one of a chain of rocky mountains rising to the east of the great Altiplano, or South American high plain, located in the southern tropics and interspersed with vast lakes and salt flats. The bulk of Bolivia's highlands consists of massive sediment beds, thrust up, twisted, and occasionally punctured by ancient igneous swellings and volcanoes. The terrain has changed. Now high and dry, Potosí was at one time, perhaps as late as 14 million years ago, wet and low. Volcanic ash or tuff layers discovered in a mine on the Cerro Rico contained a variety of fossil leaves of middle Tertiary to Pliocene ages, collected and catalogued by geologists in the 1920s but first encountered in colonial times.[5]

Bolivia's active volcanoes are found in the Western Cordillera, bordering Chile. Volcanism here is so recent that it often covers older mineralized zones, some of which were discovered by prospectors setting out from Potosí. Faults, uplifts, and wet-season moisture feed numerous hot springs all over the highlands, including the famous Ojo del Inca, or Inca Baths, just down the hill from Potosí on the road to Oruro. The stream of warm and mineral-rich water flowing from this spring at Tarapaya was used in colonial times to power dozens of ore-crushing mills. Salt springs are abundant throughout highland Bolivia, and they provided reagents to Potosí's early silver refiners. Massive salt beds such as those of Uyuni lay to the southwest at several days' hard walk, but most of the salt used in colonial times came from the nearby town and springs of Yocalla.

Ancient volcanic and hydrothermal activity most likely dissolved and redeposited the great silver and tin veins of Bolivia's Eastern Cordillera, the

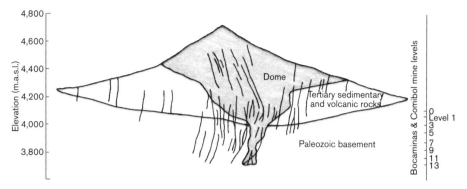

Geological Cross-section of the Cerro Rico de Potosí.

richest in both metals of any in the world. Only Nevada's Comstock Lode might have vied with Potosí's Cerro Rico for silver concentration in a single spot, but Comstock played out after only a few decades. As of this writing the red mountain of Potosí is still producing silver, tin, zinc, lead, and other metals, and it never seems to have stopped doing so despite many cycles since its discovery in 1545. Current estimates range from 30,000 to 60,000 tons of silver produced to date, and geologists estimate that the Cerro Rico, easily the world's richest silver deposit, contains an equivalent amount dispersed in low-grade, refractory ores that would require sophisticated processing.

Most geologists today agree that the nearly 4,800-meter-high Cerro Rico is an approximately 14 million–year-old silica-rich volcanic dome that was fractured internally in subsequent millennia. The fractures became ore veins, mineralized by rich hydrothermal fluids and magmatic steam rising up from below. Some veins extend into older sediments below the dome, including the fossil-bearing Caracoles tuff.[6] Metallic veins of this kind often contain quartz, and the high silica content of the Cerro Rico's host rock has been the bane of indigenous miners since colonial times. Silicosis, a lung disease caused by inhalation of sharp, tiny bits of glass-like rock, remains the primary killer of mineworkers. The corrugated, maroon-colored crest of the Cerro Rico is mostly silica in the form of weathered, iron-stained quartz.

The silver-rich veins of the Cerro Rico are about a meter wide on average, but several larger veins were exploited in colonial times. Bodies of rock containing numerous small veins have also been blasted out, leaving behind large and dangerous galleries. Most of the veins dive steeply into the mountain from the surface, striking northeastward. Upper-zone ores were richest thanks to what is called supergene oxidation, and some hunks of native (i.e., pure) silver were found. Ores at depth tended to be of lower grade, or more difficult to refine. Within a few decades of discovery, colonial miners reached the water table and with it unoxidized or sulfide ores below about 400 or more meters' depth. The deepest level mined in modern times, Level 16, reaches 1,150 meters below the summit.

The Cerro Rico's distinctive red hue comes from surface oxidation of iron and other metallic compounds, and it was rich, reddish ores that drove Potosí's initial boom. As miners got deeper into the hill in the 1560s they encountered dark gray sulfide ores. These could be quite rich but they were difficult to smelt using then-available technologies. As will be seen in chapter 3, mercury amalgamation, introduced in 1572 from Mexico and adapted to Potosí's high-altitude conditions and peculiar ore chemistry, solved the problem.

Although miners wanted to believe that Potosí's great silver veins got wider and richer as they descended, the reverse was nearly always true. Beyond an enriched zone near the water table, silver ores declined in quality or became more refractory, and sometimes veins disappeared altogether. Yet these challenges were offset by Potosí's unusual geological configuration. First, it was crisscrossed by numerous, very large polymetallic vein systems, and second, even poorer ore bodies were laced with native silver, spurring further excavation. That the Cerro Rico still stands today is a minor miracle. In most countries such an ore-rich mountain would have been leveled and turned into a pit long ago.[7] The hollowed mountain's current supporters recently filled a giant hole near the crest with a concrete plug and then with mill waste, but it continues to sink. A small stone tower maintains the Cerro Rico's official altitude.

Did pre-Inca peoples mine silver at Potosí? Scientists Colin Cooke, Mark Abbott, and Alexander Wolfe have argued that lake sediments from near Potosí prove that the Cerro Rico was exploited, not just in Inca times but long before: by at least 1000 CE, well over 500 years before the Spanish arrived.[8] Given the centuries of exploitation of the mountain itself it is hard to verify this claim by surface archaeology, yet it seems unlikely that Andean miners would have missed such a major deposit. All we know for certain is that the mountain could not have been mined too *extensively* before 1545, when Diego Gualpa was knocked down by a providential wind.

Although the Incas controlled the vast highland region around Potosí when the Spanish arrived in the 1530s, they had only held it for about a century, and local pre-Incaic cultures persisted. First, the population of the larger province consisted of both Quechua and Aymara speakers, with Aymara nobles dominant. The region surrounding and to the north of the Cerro Rico was home to the Qaraqara lords, joined to the east by the Charkas, for whom the greater Potosí region was named after the Spanish established their district capital in 1539 at Chuquisaca, today's Sucre. The Spanish called the district Los Charcas, the name of its dominant indigenous group, but thanks to Porco and Potosí it was also known as La Plata.

The Qaraqaras were farmers and pastoralists, growing potatoes and other tubers along with quinoa at high elevations, supplementing these staples with maize, capsicum peppers, coca, and other items grown or collected in distant, warmer valleys. Surviving in the Bolivian Andes was complicated by extreme altitudes and uncertain rainfall, so vertical control of ecological "islands" was essential. The Charkas occupied generally lower-altitude zones to the east of Potosí. Their settlements abutted the hotter Chaco region that stretched all the way to Paraguay, home of semi-sedentary Guaraní speakers known collectively as Chiriguanaes or Chiriwana.[9] Under Inca rule, Charkas marked the southeastern frontier of Tawantinsuyu, the Inca Empire. Three semi-sedentary Charka ethnic groups, the Chuy, Yampara, and Chicha, served as buffers against the lowland Chiriwana.

The confederated Qaraqaras and Charkas shared certain religious beliefs with the Incas and other highland agriculturalists to the north. For example, features in the landscape were usually sacred, often regarded as sentient and capable of reanimation. Sentience was assumed of material objects in general, including the human corpse. Mummies and bones of ancestors were carefully housed, consulted through divination, and carried to ceremonies. Agricultural and animal fertility were central concerns, as in most premodern societies, and Andean shamans prescribed appropriate rituals to ensure seasonal regeneration. Shamans were also healers and some, including women, were herbalists.

Little is known of Qaraqara and Charka religious practices, but early colonial documents suggest periodic veneration of sacred mountains, some of which, like Potosí's Cerro Rico, contained silver. The mountains of Porco, which under Inca rule served as the empire's primary source of silver, were especially significant. *Huacas,* or sacred sites and shrines, almost always included mountain summits, and sometimes other prominent features, such as caves, boulders, or outcrops. The huacas inside mountains might include bodies of exceptionally rich ore reached by tunneling from a sacred outcrop, usually signaled by a clustering of three stones. Mines, in other words, were not simply holes in the ground from which one extracted wealth; they were sacred spaces or portals to the underworld.

Such was the case at Porco, reached by the Pizarro brothers Hernando and Gonzalo in 1538.[10] Indigenous mineworkers included not only Qaraqaras and Charkas but also Andeans brought by the Spaniards from highland Peru. When the Spanish attempted to suppress religious veneration of Porco's huacas, Andean miners shifted their rituals to another, more distant site. Even in Potosí, indigenous beliefs and practices persisted despite persecution. In 1588, a priest working near Potosí reported Andean wind furnace refiners making offerings of coca leaves and conversing with their ovens in hopes of better yields.[11] Similar conversations, and offerings, were said to occur underground, precursors of the modern cult of El Tío, a trickster deity.

The Cerro Rico and Huayna Potosí—the hill in front of it facing the town—continued to be venerated openly in non-Catholic ways until 1599, when the Jesuit iconoclast José de Arriaga spoke of final "extirpation," part of a larger campaign against so-called idolatry throughout the Andes. Native beliefs persisted, but the two mountains were solemnly rededicated to St. Bartholomew, exorcist of demons.[12] St. Bartholomew, still Potosí's patron, is venerated with a major festival each August, marking his triumphant "defeat of the devil." Although disputed, the meaning of the name Potosí may also have religious significance.[13]

For all its stony eminence, Potosí was more than rocks and huacas. The Cerro Rico was part of a larger ecosystem that was home to many types of native animals, wild and tame. In the desolate puna above the potato and quinoa zones roamed herds of domesticated llamas and alpacas, and above them, wild vicuñas. These fleet camelids, prized by the Incas for their exquisitely soft fur, were periodically hunted and sheared. Also popular was the meat of the vizcacha, a high-mountain dweller something like a cross between a marmot and a hare. Even harder to catch were rheas, flightless but speedy birds of considerable girth. More stunning at these altitudes were huge flocks of pink flamingos, drawn to the shallow intermontane lakes by brine shrimp.

Long before the Spanish arrived, teams of llamas transported baskets of coca leaves, salt, textiles, and many other commodities over snowy passes and through narrow canyons—sometimes across hanging bridges of woven grass—to distant outposts on the Inca frontier. One important Inca fortress or *pucara* was located southeast of Potosí at Oroncota, an imposing rampart overlooking the Pilcomayo River, a tributary of the Río de la Plata.[14]

When the Incas conquered southern Bolivia in the early fifteenth century, they tapped into preexisting trade circuits and expanded their extensive road network. In reaching Porco and Potosí, the Spanish simply followed in the footsteps of the Incas. Although still vulnerable to attacks from the Chiriwana or Chiriguanaes of the eastern lowlands, the Spanish quickly planted vineyards along the Pilcomayo River below Oroncota and set out on periodic expeditions to attempt conquest and to search out new mines. The native peoples of Potosí's vast hinterland were never fully conquered and they remained the majority. European and African colonizers were in most places a thin veneer.

## FROM PERU TO POTOSÍ

Apparently uninterested in exploiting Potosí, the Incas relied on the silver mines of Porco and the gold mines of Carabaya. There were many other mines, but these two sites were especially prized. Gold and silver jewelry, ornaments, and utensils were produced in substantial quantities under Inca rule, often by artisans selected from among conquered subjects such as the Chimú of north coastal Peru. Gold and silver objects accumulated in the royal city of Cuzco, the beating heart of Tawantinsuyu, but they were also scattered among palaces and shrines as far away as Quito and even highland Argentina. Young sacrificial victims buried atop some of the highest mountains in the Americas were accompanied by Inca silver and gold statuettes and cloak pins, along with salmon-colored *Spondylus* shell and fine textiles and feathers.

This characteristic of Inca life and ceremony was well known by the empire's neighbors and enemies, and when the Spanish reached the outskirts of Tawantinsuyu both from the northwest and from the southeast, during a brief penetration of the Río de la Plata, they heard rumors of a golden kingdom in the mountainous interior. By 1529, after years of punishing reconnaissance along what is today the Pacific coast of Colombia and Ecuador, Francisco Pizarro won an exclusive grant to conquer and subjugate this still mysterious golden kingdom that had come to be called "Pirú," or "Perú." Setting out from Panama, Pizarro and a few hundred men, most of them lacking formal military training but hardened by tropical sorties, put ashore near the present-day border between Ecuador and Peru and began moving inland.

After founding the town of Piura, the de rigueur act of a conquistador in a new land, Pizarro marched on toward the south and up into the Andes. He had 168 men and 60 horses. The men carried bucklers and wore armor and steel helmets, and some carried harquebuses, crude predecessors of the musket. More important were steel swords and steel-tipped lances. By chance the party was invited to Cajamarca, a hot springs town in Peru's north highlands. The Inca Atahualpa, fresh from victory over his half-brother Waskar, wished to see the Spanish visitors' weapons and animals in an enclosed space. Francisco Pizarro used the opportunity on 10 November 1532 to ambush the Inca, capture him, and hold him for ransom.[15]

Over the next eight months, the captive Inca's subjects gathered gold and silver and brought it to Cajamarca, where it was said that a sizeable stone building was filled to the rafters with glimmering treasure. Despite the promise to free him, Pizarro ordered Atahualpa executed by garrote after a drumhead trial in July 1533. Without a sacred leader, Tawantinsuyu began to unravel. Yet a legend was also born, twisting the facts of the Inca's death but maintaining pre-Columbian symbolism. Many native Andeans came to believe that the Inca Atahualpa's severed head would someday serve as the seed of a revitalized empire, one capable of driving out the Spanish once and for all.

Atahualpa's ransom, soon followed by a massive hoard of Cuzco treasure, signaled to the world that Peru was synonymous with unfathomable wealth. When it was all melted down, the Inca's ransom amounted to over a million pesos' worth of fine gold, and about the same amount in silver. The Cuzco hoard more than doubled these amounts.[16] It was enough precious metal to upset European and Mediterranean money markets when it arrived in Seville in 1534. Charles I of Spain, also Holy Roman Emperor Charles V, became a world monarch, a new Caesar.[17] He used Inca treasure to conquer Tunis and finance construction of St. Peter's Basilica. Would-be Pizarros flooded into the Andes from all over the Iberian Peninsula and beyond, each in search of his own Tawantinsuyu or Eldorado. Amid this flood of gold- and silver-hungry Europeans, the discovery of Potosí was almost fated.

## BONANZA MEETS BLACK LEGEND

However providential, Potosí's discovery occurred in a time of troubles. The first Spanish conquistadors in the Andes, including the brothers Gonzalo and Hernando Pizarro, had been led to the Porco mines soon after the fall of the Inca Empire, and in 1545, when Diego Gualpa found silver ore on the slopes of Potoc'chi, civil war raged among the Spanish. In 1542, Charles V restricted access to conquered subjects, which sparked rebellion. Rebellion drew royal reprisal. We learn from several testimonies that Potosí's early miners were despoiled by both rebels and royalists, and as seen in the introduction, the Cerro Rico was itself a prize. For rebels like Gonzalo Pizarro, who relied on the silver of Porco to sustain troops, Potosí constituted a symbol of the possibility of American independence.

Secession was not out of the question, driven home by Gonzalo Pizarro's defeat of the colony's first viceroy, Blasco Núñez Vela, near Quito in 1546. The viceroy's head was treated as a trophy, much like the one stuck on a pike in Cieza de León's 1553 woodcut of Potosí. Gonzalo Pizarro's uprising ended in 1548 when he, too, was captured, throttled, and beheaded. Royal forces under Pedro de la Gasca won out, and Spanish householders of Potosí and Porco henceforth scrambled to proclaim their loyalty to the Spanish crown. One of the Rich Hill's five major veins, as illustrated by Cieza, was named for royalist captain Diego Centeno, killer of several Pizarro partisans.[18]

Cieza de León's iconic woodcut image of the mountain and town prefigured Spanish feuds. The square and adjacent streets, later known as "the little cobbled square" (*el empedradillo*), would serve throughout colonial times as a public theater of violence, particularly for footloose Spanish men anxious to defend their honor. Such men were known euphemistically in the Andes as *soldados,* or "soldiers," and Potosí became fixed in the Spanish imagination as a hotbed of quick-draw murders.

Yet the more widely disseminated image of Potosí outside Spain and its colonies—of hellish toil inside the bowels of a giant mountain—was at least partly derived from the writings of Dominican friar Domingo de Santo Tomás. Santo Tomás was the first among a chorus of critics writing of Potosí's abusive labor situation in 1550, well before the era of Viceroy Toledo, who is blamed for setting up the *mita* labor draft. Here is Santo Tomás's most quoted passage:

> It must have been about four years during which this land was about to be lost [i.e., during the Gonzalo Pizarro rebellion] that there was discovered a *mouth of hell*, into which have entered, as I say within that time, a great quantity of people, which by the greed of the Spaniards they sacrifice to their god, and these are some silver mines that they call Potosí.[19]

Stressing that the New Laws of 1542–43 were being broken, Santo Tomás went on to emphasize the hardships of travel to the mines, which he considered almost as punishing as mine work. He challenged those who claimed that native Andeans thrived in Potosí's silver mines. If this were true, he claimed, it was only for some lucky yanaconas. What Santo Tomás described vividly if briefly for Charles V and his Indies Council was a fast-emerging world of forced labor by *encomienda* or neo-feudal allotment, punishing forced migration to what amounted to a frozen desert, and terribly inflated prices for basic subsistence foods and fuels. Early notary records paint a less dire picture, but they do back Santo Tomás's claims about high food prices and forced resettlement of indigenous workers.[20]

In these first years after the end of the Peruvian Civil War, mine labor at Potosí was arranged variously, from African slavery to the kind of personal retainer-ship experienced by the yanacona Diego Gualpa. The encomienda, a tributary system dating to the conquest, was central, and it drew the ire of Santo Tomás. Notary records from the 1540s describe dozens of troops of workers held in encomienda trekking to Potosí from Cuzco, La Paz, Arequipa, La Plata, and other regions. As Marie Helmer and Peter Bakewell have shown, a 1549 inquest found some 5,000 Andeans held in encomienda working on the Cerro Rico, often arriving in turns.[21] Several headmen or *kurakas* testified that the work was hard and some encomienda subjects were mistreated, but most claimed surprise at the abundance of food in Potosí's growing marketplace. The mines brought hardship, to be sure, but things were tough all over the high Andes in the aftermath of conquest and civil war. Bonanza at least offered pay dirt.

Draft labor had not yet been formalized, but Santo Tomás, much influenced by his fellow Dominican Bartolomé de las Casas, gave words to future proponents of the Black Legend to match Las Casas's *Brief Account of the Destruction of the Indies*. The stark terms used by Santo Tomás and Las Casas fueled the imaginations of Theodor de Bry and other illustrators and promoters of the so-called Black Legend of extreme Spanish cruelty and greed. This

Interior mine scene, Theodor de Bry, *America, Part IX,* 1601. Courtesy of the John Carter Brown Library at Brown University.

hellish image of the Cerro Rico was recycled in England well past the age of Cromwell. Was Potosí a gift of heaven or a man-made "mouth of hell"? Before answering, it may be worth looking at what early Potosí mining entailed.

## MINING THE RED MOUNTAIN

Once indigenous prospectors identified outcroppings of rich silver ore on the surface of the Cerro Rico, mine owners—most of them Europeans, but including some native Americans and free people of African descent—staked claims and followed them underground. Mine magistrates roamed the mountain accompanied by scribes, mapping and recording each claim. Discoverers got double claims, and smaller claims were set aside at each "discovery" or vein system for the king. The king's mines were worked by private persons who paid a higher tax rate, a third instead of a fifth of total output. In theory, the king owned all subsurface wealth. He was simply kind enough to allow his subjects to excavate his treasures in exchange for a modest "royalty."

At first, workers dug open pits high on the slopes of the Cerro Rico, some quite large, but chasing rich veins meant sinking shafts into the hillside at a precipitous angle. Before long, these primitive shafts got deep enough that mineworkers had to climb in and out on notched logs and hanging ladders made from twisted rawhide. A double ladder of this type soon appeared in the deepest mines, allowing workers to climb up one side and down the other, as illustrated by de Bry. Gravity was unforgiving, and danger from falls, loose boulders, and cave-ins increased with depth.

Work inside the mountain also grew hot as the mines dove deeper, whereas temperatures outside were cold year-round. It was partly for this reason that many native miners stayed underground for multiple shifts. Notary records mention tools such as hammers, chisels, and crowbars, all made from imported Basque iron. Documents also mention enslaved African blacksmiths as early as 1549, the sort of men who forged and repaired these vital tools. Some mine workforces were mixed: a contract from the same year placed three enslaved Africans in a mine in the Estaño Vein alongside native Andean yanaconas.[22]

Mine work was soon divided between *barreteros,* or men picking away at a vein's ore face deep underground with steel-tipped iron bars, and *apiris,* those charged with shouldering heavy leather or cloth ore sacks for the climb out. At the mouth of the mine, ore was dumped from the sacks and sorted on a terrace or *cancha,* sometimes by women and children, and the best ore repacked for transport by llama teams to indigenous millers using stone rocker mills (*quimbaletes*). European-style crushing mills powered by waterwheels or large animals (and in a few cases, human beings) appeared in the early 1570s.[23]

Llamas carried lighter loads than Spanish-bred mules but the camelids were well adapted to Potosí's rigorous altitude and coarse pasturage. They tended not to overgraze, and they reproduced quickly, making them relatively cheap. Llamas, or "sheep of the land," as the Spanish called them, could also be slaughtered and eaten, their flesh preserved in the open air as *charqui* (hence "jerky"). Periodic llama sacrifices were expected in native Andean culture, and greedy Spanish officials tried in vain to forbid slaughter. A whole class of native herders and handlers, the *llameros,* tended these all-important animals, but they were not unknown to recently arrived Africans. A rare document from 1549 notes the sale of 111 llamas along with an enslaved African driver, 23-year-old Andrés Terranova. Llamas were highly valued in these early years at 10–13 pesos a head; they sold for half as much by 1559.[24]

Potosí relied on llamas for cargo transport throughout the colonial period. Only in the first quarter of the seventeenth century did mules offer serious competition. Mules had the advantage of bearing heavier loads, but they sometimes suffered at extreme altitudes and had to be bred and broken in

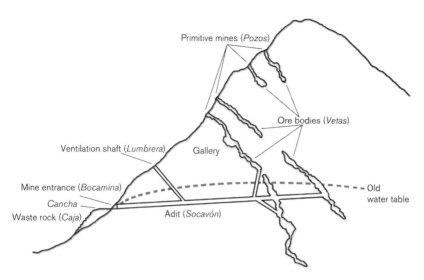

Cerro Rico with idealized mines and drainage adit (after Bakewell).

Argentina and driven north at considerable expense. Horses, or at least those brought by the Spaniards, did not adapt well to Potosí's extreme altitudes and harsh vegetation, nor were they as sure-footed as mules on rugged mountain tracks. Burros, another Spanish import, were a hardy and adaptable alternative, but they tended to be more stubborn than either mules or llamas, and their growth was stunted if bred at high altitude. Teams of woolly burros were used primarily for short-haul trips to and from neighboring valleys, frequently carrying maize, corn meal, wheat, and flour to the Imperial Villa.

As the Cerro Rico's mines got deeper some reached the water table. Such mines had to be bailed or abandoned. Potosí's mine owners, despite flashes of ingenuity and education, as in the case of the Florentine Nicolao del Benino, seem not to have resorted to the complex windlasses developed in Mexico about this time, preferring instead to hand bail or perforate the hillside with adits—horizontal tunnels known in Spanish as *socavones*. Benino was a pioneer developer of these tunnels beginning in the 1550s.[25] To be fair, there were few animals capable of powering windlasses at 15,000 feet or more above sea level. Horses and mules were known to expire just climbing the mountain when pushed too hard.[26]

In the absence of black powder or other explosives, introduced only in the 1670s, tunnels like the one pursued by Benino were hugely expensive and time consuming. Investors paid workers to chisel through worthless bedrock for hundreds of yards. Only when they reached interior vein systems and drained off water did the great adits pay off. When they did, it was bonanza all over again, at least until the water table was reached a second time. Drilling socavones was risky: aiming for ore bodies deep within the mountain was a crapshoot, and failing to maintain the proper grade could lead to defeat by flooding. In his own 1572 account to Philip II of Spain, Benino reported at length on the promise and difficulties of such projects. His own adit took nearly thirty years to complete, with some breaks when money ran out, and its final length was not quite 750 feet (250 *varas,* or Spanish yards).[27]

Mine work was terribly onerous, a fact that not even Potosí's strongest promoters denied. Luis Capoche's 1585 account may be compared with that of Hieronymite priest Diego de Ocaña, writing about fifteen years later. Both observers speak of workers chipping away at hard rock in near-total darkness, not knowing day from night. Apiris struggled to shoulder sacks of ore weighing seventy-five pounds, which they then had to carry even as they climbed ladders or squeezed through narrow, snaking passages. The work got more dusty and dangerous and the climb out more difficult as the mines went deeper.

ORE THEFT OR WORKERS' COMPENSATION?

Miners traded shifts in order to keep extracting ore twenty-four hours a day, leaving many tunnels and shafts reeking of urine and human feces. It may not have been the hellish scene depicted by Theodor de Bry or described by Domingo de Santo Tomás, but mine labor inside the Cerro Rico in the sixteenth and seventeenth centuries was more punishing than almost any other job at the time, perhaps exceeded only by work in the mercury mines of Huancavelica, located at a similarly punishing altitude in Peru.

What kept the workers at it, besides force? An early and enduring custom among Potosí mineworkers was to "high grade," or to take a piece or two of superior ore, basically as a gift to oneself for a hard day's work—a personal bonus. Early Spanish mine owners, desperate to retain workers in a highly competitive labor market, permitted the custom as long as it did not exceed certain informally agreed-upon limits. High grading was customary, and the practice became so entrenched in Potosí's mining culture that it persists to this day.[28]

Called *corpa* by the miners (and later *kaj'cha* or *kapcha*), chunks of high-grade ore spawned a gray market. Indigenous women who sold chicha, coca, hot foods, and other commodities and services outside the mines and in town accepted corpa as payment.[29] Since Andean men and women both knew a given rock's value in a city full of miners and refiners, corpa could serve as cash. Indigenous market women then periodically sold the ore they collected to refiners, either indigenous wind smelters or *guayradores* or later to Spanish mill owners. Although it traveled an informal and essentially indigenous route from mine to town, corpa or high-grade ore reentered the great silver stream, transformed into ingots, bars, and coins, and shipped off to the king of Spain or into the global market. The Imperial Villa thus became a site of multiple exchanges of ore and raw silver for a thousand other commodities.

## BUILDING THE IMPERIAL VILLA

Like most mining towns, Potosí was an accidental city, a haphazard city, at first a tent camp in the Roman military tradition, a *real de minas*. Despite a rough start, however, Potosí was at birth invested with intense civic pride. Not long after the formal founding of the town, Potosí boasted a coat of arms and a motto. It was the undisputed "Treasury of the World...Envy of Kings." As we have seen, one of the Cerro Rico's first and richest veins was named for the royalist conquistador Diego Centeno, a beacon of loyalty to Emperor Charles V.

The city won further recognition. After helping Spain emerge from a 1557 bankruptcy, Philip II decreed Potosí an Imperial Villa in 1561, formalized by Peru's Viceroy Conde de Nieva on November 7 of that year.[30] By this time, according to the Spanish magistrate Juan de Matienzo, nearly 20,000 native Andean men lived in the city. Matienzo counted only men because he was interested in formalizing a labor draft to increase silver production. In 1577, once that draft system had been put in place by Viceroy Toledo, the subject of chapter 3, Matienzo estimated a total of some 40,000 native Andean inhabitants, now counting women and children, and 2,000 Spanish heads of household, plus a large number of uncounted Spanish women and children. The city's total population was thus apparently above 50,000 by the time of Viceroy Toledo's early 1570s reforms. Within a few years the Imperial Villa had more inhabitants than all but a few European cities.

The city of Potosí was divided into Spanish and indigenous sectors by a main gulch or channel. The waters of this gulch, La Ribera, flowed down from the snow-capped Kari-Kari mountains to the east of the Cerro. On the more or less flat slope north of the gulch lay the Spanish town, centered on the main plaza, or Plaza del Regocijo. On the hillier south or Cerro side of the Ribera there spread Potosí's vast indigenous sector, complete with its ethnically divided parishes—fourteen of them by 1585. Here amid the township-like *rancherías* lived the bulk of Potosí's huge and often transient indigenous population: the Pacajes, Lupacas, Quillacas, Chichas, Carangas, Yamparaes, and other groups.

In 1565 the Potosí town council passed an ordinance to keep non-Indians out of the rancherías. It reads like classic township segregation:

> In view of the inconveniences and vexations that follow from allowing Spaniards, mestizos, and mulattos to enter the Indian townships, the law just passed must be observed and enforced by the bailiffs . . . such that no black man or woman may live or go among the Indian townships, nor trade with the Indians, due to the harm they do them . . . that no bread be sold among the townships . . . and as there exist among the Indian men and women of the townships mestizo orphans who acquire the customs of the Indians, any Spaniard may remove them for their service, notifying town justices, or to do whatever is necessary for their benefit.[31]

Clearly the point here was to divide and dominate various subaltern groups, not to protect native Andeans.

As for Potosí's stately Spanish grid, some suggest it was only laid out when Viceroy Toledo arrived in 1572.[32] This seems unlikely, as house plots on blocks appear to have centered on a plaza in Cieza de León's time. As has been noted, just above the plaza was a cobblestone-paved space, or *empedradillo,* which became infamous. Only slightly more peaceful, if we are to believe Potosí's chroniclers, were the many houses constructed for wealthy townsfolk within a few hundred yards of the main plaza. A notary record from 1549 describes an early house in the center: "a large single-floor structure with two storefronts and their back rooms, and a kitchen with a portion of patio, and two pairs of doors with their locks and keys." This house, next to one belonging to Hernando Pizarro, sold for 1,300 pesos.[33]

Potosí was somewhat unusual in that adjacent to the central plaza was a huge indigenous marketplace, the rectangular *qhatu,* dominated from an early date by native Andean women trading food, chicha, coca, and other items for ingots or raw silver ore (corpa, as described above). Other plazas, some of them pocket-sized, fronted or abutted a dozen churches, all of them crude, tamped-earth affairs roofed with ichu grass, but soon becoming more imposing, built of dressed stone and lavishly adorned within. These smaller plazas sometimes specialized in foods or drinks, like chicken or (by the early seventeenth century) yerba mate. Most important, perhaps, was the "Calle de la Coca."[34]

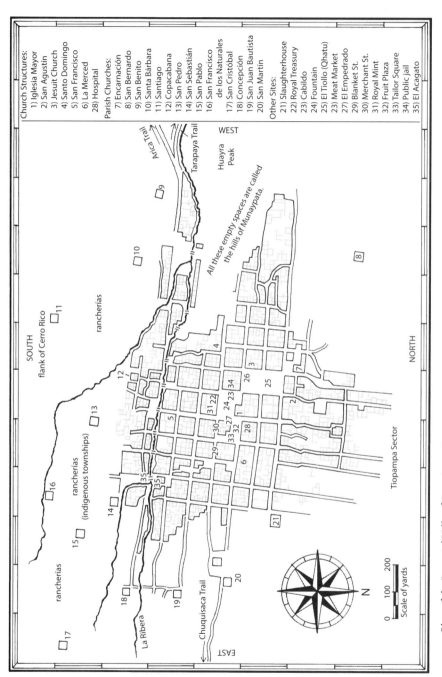

**Church Structures:**
1) Iglesia Mayor
2) San Agustín
3) Jesuit Church
4) Santo Domingo
5) San Francisco
6) La Merced
28) Hospital

**Parish Churches:**
7) Encarnación
8) San Bernardo
9) San Benito
10) Santa Bárbara
11) Santiago
12) Copacabana
13) San Pedro
14) San Sebastián
15) San Pablo
16) San Francisco
   de los Naturales
17) San Cristóbal
18) Concepción
19) San Juan Bautista
20) San Martín

**Other Sites:**
21) Slaughterhouse
22) Royal Treasury
23) Cabildo
24) Fountain
25) El Tiollo (Qhatu)
23) Meat Market
27) El Empedrado
29) Blanket St.
30) Merchant St.
31) Royal Mint
32) Fruit Plaza
33) Tailor Square
34) Public Jail
35) El Acagato

SOUTH
flank of Cerro Rico

rancherías

rancherías
(indigenous townships)

rancherías

La Ribera

Chuquisaca Trail

EAST

Arica Trail

Tarapaya Trail

WEST

Huayra
Peak

All these empty spaces are called
the hills of Munaypata.

NORTH

Tiopampa Sector

N

0   100   200
Scale of yards

MAP 3. Plan of the Imperial Villa of Potosí, ca. 1603.

The Imperial Villa's churches absorbed considerable capital from the start. Spanish, indigenous, and African artisans used fine woods brought from the lowlands to construct Moorish-style latticework ceilings in La Merced, Santo Domingo, San Francisco, and other convents and chapels. Indigenous parish churches were not far behind. Smiths of various ethnicities also used abundant silver to fabricate altars, lamps, censers, candlesticks, and other religious paraphernalia, most famously for the city's main church or Iglesia Mayor. Potosí's waves of church building reflected the ups and downs of mine production, and of individual fortunes.

It was almost ironic given its rocky surroundings, but Potosí lacked quality building stone. Most of what was readily available was friable sandstone and limestone, along with hard-to-dress river boulders, mostly of volcanic origin. All these types of stone may be seen today in the foundations and façades of the Franciscan, Mercedarian, Augustinian, and other monastic compounds, as well as the church of St. Bernard and the convent of St. Theresa.

It was only in the seventeenth century that private persons seem to have begun building lavish houses with stone portals and large patios. Most personal dwellings in Potosí remained cramped and low, in part to conserve precious heat. Residential properties in the late sixteenth-century notary books were often referred to as simply "a thatch-roofed hut with its patio" (*un bohío con su cancha*). Wood balconies with shutters eventually appeared, serving as elevated and largely female viewing posts for the city's many religious and civic processions.

### WHERE THE MONEY WENT

Just from the year 1548 to that of 1551 the royal fifths have been worth more than three million ducats, which is more than what the Spaniards found with Atahualpa, or what they found in Cuzco when they discovered it.[35]

One of the first official buildings in Potosí was the royal treasury office, known as the *cajas reales*. A thick-walled and gated structure, the royal treasury was located on the main square opposite the Imperial Villa's main church. Here, according to mandate, a magistrate and assayer recorded and taxed all silver produced in all the mines within Potosí's jurisdiction, most notably the Cerro Rico.

Each silver ingot or bar was assayed, weighed, and assessed a tax of 20 percent, the so-called *quinto real,* or royal fifth, derived from Islamic practice. The fifth was paid in cash or raw silver, and once a bar or ingot was taxed it received a stamp and official assay marks to show that it was now legal tender. Scribes recorded taxation and assay grades in smeltery books and other official ledgers, which have served historians as the main record for estimating total silver production.

The king's fifth went to fund wars, which is to say it went to pay interest on debts to Charles V's and Philip II's foreign creditors in southern Germany, northern Italy, and Flanders. It also paid the salaries of the colonies' royal officials, although the assayer received his pay as a small fraction of all silver processed, a fee tacked onto the *quinto real.* Other royal monies paid for coastal defense and ship construction in the event of pirate attacks or to outfit militias sent to put down indigenous uprisings.

Once taxed, most private silver went to rich merchants who had advanced funds to Potosí's mine owners. They then settled their accounts with distant factors, moving massive mule-loads and shiploads of silver across mountains, plains, and oceans. Global commerce was the wholesale merchants' forte, and most such merchants were junior factors linked to larger wholesalers in Lima, Seville, Lisbon, and elsewhere. Some had ties to Mexico City and later to Manila, Macao, and Goa; still others were tied to major European trading hubs such as Antwerp, Genoa, and Lyons.

Although their benefit was considerable, the Spanish king and rich merchants did not monopolize Potosí silver. Much was consigned and sent to relatives or to religious foundations back in Spain. When visiting Potosí around the year 1600, the Hieronymite priest Diego de Ocaña earned two pesos cash for every mass said. Ocaña also set up payment plans for wealthy Potosí residents to send money to the shrine of the Virgin of Guadalupe in Extremadura, not far from the Pizarros' hometown of Trujillo.

Private cash remissions recorded in notary books resemble those sent home by modern immigrants. Migrants' letters that proved undeliverable survive. Many are similar to the following, sent by Juan Sánchez to his wife, Eulalia García, in the town of Mirandilla, Extremadura:

Potosí, 8 March 1557. "Milady: Three years ago I wrote you [and sent the letter] with Juan Díez Palomo, and I sent you 110 pesos of good money. I surely hope you received it, as I am frightened at not having seen a letter from you, nor do I know if you all are alive or dead. I beseech you to write me always. I don't even have a single letter from my father or any sibling."[36]

In this case it appears the silver sent home to Europe had been taxed, but much more silver escaped Potosí in the form of untaxed ingots, bars, and disks. Our only clues regarding the volume of this illicit traffic come from periodic denunciations and criminal prosecutions, along with the descriptions of non-Spanish merchants who received contraband silver as payment for untaxed goods and enslaved Africans. Rare material evidence comes from shipwrecks, which often carried more silver than their manifests declared. Put simply, silver was an uncontrollable substance. Even so, in the sixteenth and early seventeenth centuries it tended to flow into a fairly small number of global streams matching supply to demand.

### SILVER AND STATUS AMONG NATIVE ANDEANS

The sudden wealth of Potosí had local consequences, too, among them the reordering of native Andean social hierarchies. For example, bonanza enabled social climbing for indigenous commoners, some of them women. El Inca Garcilaso de la Vega, in his *Royal Commentaries of the Incas,* offers the following anecdote:

> In Potosí, in 1554 and 1555, there was a parrot that spoke so well that when the Indian men and women passed by in the street it would call them by their respective tribes, saying "Colla," "Yunca," "Huairu," "Quechua," and so on, without any mistakes, as if it realized the meaning of the different headgear they used to wear in Inca times to distinguish themselves. One day a beautiful Indian woman passed down the street where the parrot was. She was attended by three or four servants, who treated her as a lady *palla,* or member of the royal blood. When the parrot saw her, it shrieked and laughed: "Huairu, Huairu, Huairu!" the name of a tribe that is looked down upon by all the rest. The woman was very much humbled in front of the bystanders, for there was always a crowd of Indians listening to the bird. When she was opposite it, she spat at the bird and called it *supay,* "devil." The Indians said the same, for it recognized the woman though she was disguised as a *palla.*[37]

El Inca Garcilaso's tale of the parrot and the poseur may not be true, but it fits well with a broader social trend accelerated by Potosí silver in the sixteenth and seventeenth centuries. Namely, indigenous nobles from the preconquest era were often taken down a peg by upstarts who found space and money to reinvent themselves in vibrant new cities such as Potosí. Only a mangy parrot might be able to "out" a pretender in a world of instant opulence.

Widely scattered after the conquest, noble Inca lineages in cities other than Cuzco tended to die out. Even the prominent Atahualpa family in Quito lost its conquest-era titles and properties. Potosí's Inca descendants fared a little better. They included forgotten men and women like Antón de Miranda Inca of Cuzco and his wife, María Alcapuco of Andahuaylas. Married twenty-seven years, the childless couple filed a will in Potosí in 1590, leaving most of their estate, including 500 pesos in silver cash, to the city's Mercedarian monastery.[38]

The Inca couple asked to be buried beneath the altar of the Mercedarian church and that the priests of the order say numerous masses for their souls. Their will also reveals that many caciques or native headmen owed the couple money, and the document makes clear that Antón and María were chicha vendors with a store on the "Flour Plaza." They also owned a house in the Imperial Villa and a farm in a distant valley where hired indigenous workers took care of their livestock and presumably grew maize. The maize was brought to Potosí by a train of seventy llamas "with their gunnysacks and ties." The couple left an Andean man and a boy 20 pesos each for their service on the farm, and two Andean girls in the household got 10 pesos each for their drudgery. The noble couple left 50 pesos to their head servant, María Apanama, suggesting that she was in charge of chicha production. In this case, Inca nobility was parlayed into commercial success, but not succession.

Diego de Ocaña, who begged for alms in Potosí in the year 1600, describes a visit to the house of "a very rich Indian," Pedro de Mondragón, who advanced silver coins to mine owners in exchange for raw ingots. Mondragón was a typical bullion merchant except that he lived in the indigenous way, according to Ocaña. The merchant's house was cramped and he sat and ate on the floor. "And he has all of his capital in his house at all times," Ocaña claims, "before his eyes. He has a room filled with silver, in one part the bars, in another the ingots ['pinecones'], and in another, in some jugs, the coins [reals]. I was quite stunned to see so much silver in one place and I asked him how much was there, that I was seeing, and he replied to me: 'There are 300,000 pesos of assayed silver.'"[39] Mondragón was in fact a mestizo, son of a Spaniard and an indigenous noblewoman. He dressed in the Spanish fashion yet he preferred to live "like an Indian." This social and economic hybridity left Diego de Ocaña perplexed, but it was pure Potosí.

Indeed, indigenous entrepreneurship was key to the overall success of Potosí, city and mines. Women were central, many of them hiring out to Spanish householders seeking to bring in rents. Cieza de León had this to say: "And [the demand] is such that many Spaniards enriched themselves in this site of Potosí having nothing more than two or three Indian women working by contract for them in this marketplace."[40] As Jane Mangan has shown, indigenous women looked out for themselves as well, and many accumulated substantial capital in the early years, including real estate.[41] Potosí was thus a space for self-realization as well as cutthroat capitalism. The two went together. What may surprise us is how a range of indigenous economic actors, women and men, persisted long after discovery, defining the city and its environs in the "age of wind."

In the generation following discovery in 1545, the Rich Hill and Imperial Villa of Potosí developed in tandem. The mountain was denuded and honeycombed as the adjacent city—indigenous and Spanish—spread out and sprouted monuments to neighborhood piety: parish churches, monasteries, even a pair of hospitals. Potosí had arisen from near-wilderness to fuse mountain, mines, and city. There had been a shrine or huaca on the Cerro Rico before the Spanish arrived, but no pre-Columbian settlement on the site of the Imperial Villa. Potosí was thus a new and modern phenomenon, underpinned by racial subjugation and resource extraction, but already seeking to get beyond both.

Potosí was also born in violence and controversy, first as a means to finance the rebel conquistadors, then as a destination for native workers held in various types of serfdom, joined by enslaved Africans. Whereas no Spanish commentator denounced African slavery outright in these years, many, beginning with Fray Domingo de Santo Tomás, used the African condition as a baseline to criticize mistreatment of native Andeans. Already by 1550, Potosí was a notorious "mouth of hell," a theme elaborated by Las Casas and spun by Protestant enemies into the Black Legend of innate Spanish greed and cruelty. Yet the Imperial Villa was clearly also a place of Andean entrepreneurship, both male and female, from processing ores to retailing coca. Such were the paradoxes of bonanza.

As if struck by a magician's wand, a vibrant and populous city appeared at 4,000 meters (13,200 feet) above sea level in the barren Andes Mountains at the southeast edge of the old Inca Empire. A veritable gusher of silver made this improbable city possible, but how long could it last? How many times could Potosí's mines be revived? Could the city reinvent itself without them? Mining towns have always faced such challenges, but Potosí's ability to keep rising from its own ashes would be determined not only by a sustained Spanish willingness to make native Andeans suffer underground and in the ore crushing mills, and by the whims of weather, demography, and disease, but also by the limits of human ingenuity and the increasing depths of the Cerro Rico's mines.

# TWO

# Age of Wind, Age of Iron

As they have no use of bellows to carry out their smeltings, these
Peruvian Indians used some copper tubes three palms long to
blow with their mouths with effort. And for the smeltings that
required greater force, they made use of the same wind, building
some little furnaces of loose stones in the countryside, in the
higher parts, each stone placed on top of the other without mortar, hollow like little towers, about two palms high. And into
these they placed the manure of their animals and a bit of firewood, not having charcoal; and with the wind rushing through
the openings between the stones they smelted the ore.

—LUIS CAPOCHE, 1585[1]

SUCH, ACCORDING TO SEVILLE-BORN Potosí mine and refinery owner
Luis Capoche, were the first Andean wind furnaces, simple constructions
placed on exposed hillsides or ridges. Capoche goes on to describe how a
Spaniard altered the native design to make it more reliable and productive.
He credits Juan de Marroquí, apparently a native of Seville like himself, for
developing a clay version of the same device called a *guayrachina* [Quechua
for "wind-powered"] or simply *guaira* ["wind"], from which he profited
greatly. It is an interesting story, but likely apocryphal.

Based on his 1549 visit to Potosí, chronicler Pedro de Cieza de León
offered another origin story for the clay guaira. He credits the Incas rather
than a Spanish tinkerer:

In earlier times, the Incas being so ingenious, when they discovered silver
ores in some parts that could not be refined with bellows, like those here in
Potosí, in order to profit from the ore they made certain clay vessels of the
size and type of a large flower pot in Spain, having all over it certain slits or
ventilation holes. In these things they placed charcoal, and the ore on top,
and arranged upon the mountains or upon their sides where the wind was
strongest, they extracted silver, the same which they purified and refined later
with their little bellows or pipes through which they blow. In this way they
extracted all this great quantity of silver that has come out of this mountain.

"Estos yndios estan guayrando," ca. 1603. Courtesy of the Hispanic Society of America, New York.

> And the Indians went off with the ore to the heights all around it to extract silver. They call these vessels Guayras.[2]

What seems clear from both writers is that the Castilian bellows furnace proved useless for smelting most Potosí ores, and thus the indigenous guaira in its several forms became the standard technology for silver beneficiation up to the 1570s.

Luis Capoche goes on to describe the Andean method of cupellation, in which lead, or lead sulfide, was used as a flux to ease silver smelting. Lead cupellation was a refining process well known to European smelters and silversmiths in the sixteenth century, but it remains unclear if there was an Andean precursor or body of knowledge on the use of lead flux; it was likely necessary to make the guaira furnaces work.[3] Capoche provides a detailed description of the guaira of his day: "[It is a] clay structure about as high as a common yard, with four angles, or corners, elongated, almost square, hollow, and open at the top; it has made for its four surfaces, or sides, openings or little windows so that through these the wind has more effect."[4] Guairas were placed on pedestals to capture more wind, according to Capoche, and the combination of elements rendered it a perfect marvel, "doing a favor for mankind." The product was a "leaden paste" that was then further refined by native Andeans in their homes, producing silver of roughly 93 percent purity.

According to Capoche, the modified Andean wind furnace was capable of yielding fine silver after a series of controlled steps. It was an ingenious technology that required relatively little fuel and hardly any capital investment. The only serious concern for a modern observer, leaving aside the eventual need for charcoal, would be the lead fumes released by cupellation, especially if the alloy described by Capoche was refined *inside* native Andean homes.[5] But for Capoche, the guairas of Potosí were not a danger or even a source of competition for the water-driven mills of his own time. They were a kind of comforting spectacle in danger of disappearing:

> The *guairas* are placed upon the summits and flanks of the mountains and hills within view and walking distance of this city, which makes a pleasant sight in the darkness of the night, with so many fires in the countryside, some placed in line along the points and pinnacles of the mountain in the manner of luminaries, and others haphazardly situated along the creek banks and ravines, and all of them together render a festive and agreeable view. In past years the number of *guairas* reached 6,497. Right now almost all remain, although a great part of them are in ruins, as they do not use the *guaira* as before.[6]

Potosí's age of wind was also an age of global imports, many of them brought to the shores of Peru by the "bonanza" winds that filled Spanish sails. Thanks to what economists might call its comparative advantage and the enormous efforts of Andean mineworkers and refiners of both sexes and all ages, Potosí produced enough silver to fuel a tremendous boom in commerce, much of it interoceanic. The Imperial Villa was barren aside from its bounty in silver, and thus everything necessary for life and work and much that was superfluous had to come from afar.

This chapter traces Potosí's first three decades of production, emphasizing indigenous control of mines and refineries, typified by native wind furnaces or guairas. The chapter then discusses imported technologies such as the bellows furnace, adopted in Porco, and imported legal traditions, mostly for staking mining claims and trading them in the marketplace. The era represents a technological tug-of-war but there was also a quick influx of commodities and luxuries from around the world, all bought with raw silver. Iron and steel produced in northern Spain were essential to mining as well, and even indigenous inhabitants took up European and Asian fashions and consumption habits. As some French linen producers said in this era, textile factories—in Europe, Asia, and the Americas—became proverbial gold and silver mines in their own right. As it "consumed the world," Potosí paid for its opulence by harnessing native Andean labor, entrepreneurship, and technology. But what did it mean for Potosí to be a largely "Indian" enterprise in its first decades after discovery, and what caused this to change?

The Holy Roman Emperor Charles V—King Charles I of Spain—retired to a small monastery at the foot of the rugged Sierra de Gredos southwest of Madrid in 1556. His son, crowned Philip II, inherited many of his father's military, fiscal, and political burdens, but the emperor's title passed to an Austrian cousin. Charles had struggled mightily against the Ottomans, the French, and other foes, and Philip would continue these struggles and incite others. The failed invasion of England known as the Armada disaster of 1588 was only the most dramatic.

What made Habsburg Spain Europe's most formidable war machine was money, or more accurately, credit: the ability to borrow huge sums to field armies and assemble navies. What gave Spain credit was in large part an early flood of silver from Potosí, the bonanza that came close on the heels of Atahualpa's treasure. The Cerro Rico became iconic for this reason as much as any other, and this is why Potosí interested the Ottoman sultan and other European and Asian princes.

Despite our knowledge of the European side of this story of silver used to finance global wars, a number of myths about how Potosí functioned in the era of Charles V and Philip II have persisted. Historians for many years assumed that upon discovery in 1545 Potosí was simply taken over by con- quistadors and other greedy Europeans, and that these men forced indige- nous workers held in *encomienda* or kept as *yanaconas* (or even as slaves) to work the Cerro Rico's mines for them. In exchange, these nameless "Indians" got nothing but abuse, injuries, and silicosis. To read early polemicists such as Fray Domingo de Santo Tomás, this would seem about right. Other histo- rians assumed that the infamous labor draft known as the *mita* had been in place from the start as well, picked up directly from the Incas by the wily and greedy Spanish and turned to their gain.

The historical record includes vivid descriptions of abusive behavior but it also challenges the simplicity of our assumptions, forcing us to reconsider the old, stock narrative of silver mining as blunt force trauma in the service of the evil conquistadors and the Machiavellian kings of Spain—images from the Black Legend. In a nutshell, records show that from discovery in 1545 until 1572, when Peru's Viceroy Toledo arrived to revolutionize Potosí's mining and refining sectors, the subject of the next chapter, it was largely independ- ent native Andeans who extracted and refined most silver from the Cerro Rico. It is true that indigenous mineworkers were most often tributaries of

Spanish overlords, and it was Spanish merchants who handled the lion's share of outgoing silver, but the crucial refining sector was almost entirely in native Andean hands during Potosí's first boom. Some indigenous traders, like the "Inca" couple mentioned in the previous chapter, also grew wealthy from the first bonanza. This is certainly not the story one is told when visiting Potosí today.

WAGES AND WIND

Indigenous entrepreneurship in early Potosí owed much to the guaira. Ingenious but simple, as we have seen, the guaira used llama dung, *yareta* moss, or charcoal plus oxygen from daily downdraft winds to smelt rich, oxidized ores found in the upper reaches of the Cerro Rico. Some modifications appeared—first using clay to seal the formerly stone-slatted furnaces and second to add lead as flux—but Potosí's hundreds of guaira operators, or *guairadores,* were indigenous. Some were apparently women, like Isabel, "yndia huayra," who appears in notary records donating 630 pesos' worth of silver bars to her son, Francisco, in 1559.[7]

Mining remained under indigenous control as well, evidenced in part by deals struck with Spanish claimants. Spaniards who owned mines often chose to live far away and to subsist on rents provided them by indigenous dependents or hired hands. Examples of Spanish-indigenous partnerships are not unusual in early records. In one 1559 case a native Andean woman named Beatriz inherited a mine near Porco from a conquistador and then leased half of it to another Spaniard who promised to buy tools and advance coca to attract workers. In another case, a Spanish mine owner ceded a portion of his claim in the Estaño Vein on the Cerro Rico to his yanacona, Martín Huanca, in exchange for a portion of its yields.[8]

Reading these documents literally one may get the impression of equal power sharing between Andeans and Europeans, but it is clear in many cases such as the two above that Spanish entrepreneurs were "gaming" native claimants and workers, binding them legally and exploiting their inheritance or lack of capital. It was in part for this reason that the Spanish crown mandated free legal counsel for native subjects all over the Americas. The documents above were drawn up with the aid of court-appointed interpreters as well, another crown-mandated practice. The Spanish-American legal system was not fair, but neither was it entirely ineffective or corrupt. Although their struggles were legion, native claimants gained more leverage with the creation of the Audiencia of Charcas, a powerful royal circuit court, in 1561.

For the historian sifting through the mountains of colonial records relating to early Potosí, it soon becomes clear that both native Andeans and Spaniards made use of the legal system to their advantage, and native claimants and contractors learned how to defend their interests. Yet indigenous claimants were "protected" only inasmuch as local magistrates and courts agreed to enforce and uphold the law. Some Catholic priests like Fray Domingo de Santo Tomás spoke out against abusive practices and aided in native defense, others did not. Sometimes emotional or homiletic rhetoric was used to draw attention to abuses that were already unsustainable as everyday practice. Put another way, native Andeans and Europeans began a long process of negotiation and struggle that would last beyond the end of the colonial era. Potosí's mineral treasure served as a fulcrum.

Most of what we find in notary records by the 1550s are sales and leases of mines among European claimants and hired administrators, many also European. Administrators or majordomos were expected to assemble work crews of indigenous yanaconas or anyone else available. In 1559, for example, a Genoese mine owner named Jácome Dondo contracted with a fellow Genoese, the master carpenter "Benito," to administer his mines, "placing in them the necessary Indians and *yanaconas* and overseers."[9] How native workers were assembled in this case, we do not know. As for these early workers' identities, non-Christian yanacona names are sparse, but examples from a 1549 contract include Ñaupa-cusi, Huancasa, Yupa, Paucar, Gualpa, and Condori.[10] Adding to the mix, enslaved Africans were listed among Potosí mineworkers in a few cases from 1559.[11]

Detailed descriptions of mine work from the early years after discovery are rare, but contracts contain fragments. A mine discoverer in 1549 traded ten "statures" (of 5.5 ft., or 1.67 m, each) of his sixty-yard claim for access to ten Andean workers. The discoverer would provide the following tools: "picks, hoes, crowbars, and sledgehammers." One contract from 1550 set up by absentee owners and administered by their sons and nephews described an open-air mine in the Veta Rica on the Cerro Rico. The mine would employ seventy native Andeans, apparently all yanaconas sent from Cuzco, in excavating fifteen yards of mine. According to the contract: "they must work these fifteen yards all year without missing a day, and one day a week they must work to clean out the fifteen yards of mine, opening it up." Should it cave in, the workers were to spend forty days repairing and reopening the mine before removing new ore. The partners were each to share half the mine's yield but nothing is said about compensating, feeding, clothing, or housing native workers, or even providing them with tools. A document from 1560 suggests that such yanacona work teams had native overseers as well, and these men likely handed over silver to mine owners by quota.[12]

Writing in the early 1580s, Luis Capoche described mining at Potosí during its first boom-and-bust cycle, up to the 1560s, as follows:

> At first it was like this: many freelance Indians chose to sign on with [Spanish] mine owners who left them to develop and work so many yards of mine, from which they took the name "Indians-by-the-yard" [*indios varas*]. And the mine owner gave them iron bars which they then tempered and sharpened at their own cost and supplied their own candles.[13]

Capoche then describes how native miners selected ores according to their richness, bargaining with Spanish mine owners for the products of their own labor. As Peter Bakewell and others have shown, Capoche is not the only source to identify freelance native workers called *indios varas* and *indios ventureros*.[14] Many indigenous mineworkers kept high-grade ores to smelt for themselves as a kind of wage supplement, the *corpa* described in the previous chapter. Some ores were rich enough to be smelted in the wind furnaces or guairas, but others were not.

Such sharecropping-type arrangements could not last forever, but for a time it was native Andeans who essentially ran Potosí's mining industry. As Capoche says: "And all the mines enjoyed this kind of profitability in the time when they found rich ores, and the Indians possessed all the wealth of the kingdom, because everything depended on this trade, nor was there any other salvation than the silver the Indians produced in their wind furnaces."[15] Even in good times, according to Capoche, there was a hierarchy of producers. Some mine owners left rich deposits to indigenous workers who seem to have organized almost everything, and others sought more control, blending hired and drafted work forces and personally overseeing ore selection.

By 1585, when Capoche was writing, these ore-sharing arrangements had become rare, but for some workers and mine owners—and more especially, renters of mines owned by others—they remained convenient well after the radical changes of the 1570s discussed in the next chapter. Essentially, native workers provided their own tools and candles and selected the best ores in a given mine, leaving behind large amounts of ore to be picked up for amalgamation.

What emerged was a partial shift to wage labor in the early decades, and with it the appearance of a class of workers called *mingas* or *mingados*. Although paid by the day, the work of the mingados was no less dangerous than that of draft laborers. Capoche describes paid or "rented" work in the Cerro Rico as follows:

> The general means by which they work these days is by the day wage [*jornal*], giving each officially allotted Indian three-and-a-half reals [just under half a peso], and to those *mingados*, which is to say those who are rented, four reals; and between the two they work the mines, some chiseling out the ore and others removing it and carrying it up via a hanging ladder of three strands.[16]

Capoche describes the difficulties faced by these workers, and also the mistreatment many draftees received from Spanish mine owners. In short, early practices of ore sharing and wage labor did not represent a golden age of free market social harmony, but rather pragmatic solutions to the problems of early silver production.

A 1568 review of mine works in nearby Porco for the previous two years included salaries for hired Andean workers who labored alongside African slaves and yanaconas. The workers were supplied with maize, along with fifty jugs of lard "to illuminate the mines and adits of His Majesty's mine which is worked day and night." Investors also paid 30 pesos to a barber-surgeon "for his work in the year 1567 curing the injured and sick blacks and Indians who work in the mines." In 1569, the Potosí town council called for a review of mineworker wages.[17]

Whether forced or free, the work of silver mining in Potosí was desperately hard, and Spanish mine owners and renters sought every means to transfer risk onto the shoulders of native workers and refiners. Capoche describes the extreme efforts and hardships suffered by workers not even able to afford leather ore sacks, which wealthier mine owners supplied:

> The Indians take out the ore, [each load] amounting to some two *arrobas* [approx. 50 lbs.] in blankets belonging to them, tied around the chest and the ore [borne] across their shoulders, and they climb up three by three, and the one in front carries a candle in one hand by which they see where they are climbing and descending, as the mines are dark and without any visibility.[18]

Capoche goes on to describe how one Andean mineworker fell to his death after being beaten by his Spanish overseer. The description is remarkably similar to the one later published by Jesuit naturalist and visitor to Potosí José de Acosta, which was then illustrated by Theodor de Bry (see image on page 33). Making workers carry ore down the mountain in their blankets had been outlawed in 1572.[19]

Capoche does offer some contrasts, however, in describing sharecropping-type minga workers: "The minga Indians have some advantages and are better treated, since they are contracted with some freedom and they have the right to take away some *corpa* of ore, which is to say a large piece, as their daily wage, and if this were in some way limited they would not return to the mines."[20] By the time Capoche was writing, many mingas or mingados were mita workers who had stayed on after their draft was up.

Social change at the top of the mining food chain also became evident as Potosí matured. Widows began to inherit mines on the Cerro Rico in the 1550s, and female ownership of mines soon became common. Widows and other female owners usually hired a male administrator, but some women took more direct control, needing men only for filing legal papers. Doña Juana de los Ríos pursued a case against an administrator from 1562–68 related to her mines in the Veta Rica and the Estaño Vein.[21] Seeking royal promises of justice, she made use of the Audiencia of La Plata.

Churchmen were also fighting for power and space in these early decades. In 1565, the Potosí town council demanded that indigenous headmen or caciques periodically round up mineworkers to build the city's main church. Priests were in turn ordered to serve the fast-growing indigenous parishes at the edges of the Imperial Villa, which led to more church building. Later in 1565, the council ordered physicians to care for native Andeans in these parishes suffering from what may have been influenza.[22] Clerics also owned mines. Potosí "priest and vicar" Cristóbal Díaz de los Santos purchased a house, mines, and 800 llamas for 9,360 pesos in 1572, just as Viceroy Toledo arrived to transform the Imperial Villa.[23]

### IRON AND INDUSTRY

One type of metallurgy unknown to native Andeans prior to the arrival of Europeans was iron making. As can be imagined, iron and steel tools proved critical to the success of Potosí. As it happened, the Spanish possessed some of Europe's richest iron deposits, and Basque ironmongers were accomplished and well connected to the silver mining districts of the Americas. Basques were prominent in Potosí, where their dominance of mining, refining, commerce, and local government provoked resentment from other Spanish ethnic factions.

In an early attempt at mercantilist-style trade and manufacturing restrictions, the Spanish crown favored Basque ironmongers and Spanish merchants by forbidding colonial iron mining and manufacturing. In part to maintain a balance of trade between the metropolis and the colonies, it was decreed that Spain was to produce iron and the Indies were to produce silver and gold. Thus all iron and steel ingots, bars, rods, and sheets, along with manufactured items such as nails, horseshoes, hammerheads, knives, machetes, pickaxes, hinges, locks, and other hardware, had to be imported from Spain. Colonial blacksmiths were free to fashion or alter whatever items they wished, but raw iron and steel *had* to be imported through Spanish intermediaries, a fact that many later writers blamed for Spanish America's lack of industrial development.[24]

Despite restrictions on local production, iron and steel tools revolutionized Andean mining, enabling workers to chip away at hard rock more effectively, and giving refiners the means to crush ores with percussive water-driven stamp mills, whose numbers grew tremendously after the arrival of Viceroy Toledo, as described in the next chapter. Pulverized iron was even used as a reagent in some Potosí silver refineries. Overall, iron and steel proved to be the most widely consumed of European imports, and certainly among the heaviest and most difficult to transport.

Some early blacksmiths were aided by enslaved Africans, a persistent practice that may have extended to silver smelteries as well. In 1559, a bellows furnace located along Potosí's Ribera, perhaps for reducing ingots to bars, was sold along with its main worker, 40-year-old Antón de Terranova. Smelteries and forges demanded considerable charcoal, which had to be produced far from Potosí. Two Potosí assayers signed a contract in 1559 with a charcoal producer named García Michel; they demanded fifty llama loads per month for a year.[25]

Copper items were also imported from Spain and other parts of Europe, notably Sweden, but there was no monopoly on this metal in the colonies, and local deposits were worked throughout the colonial period. Copper was mostly used in the manufacture of kitchenware, but some was consumed by the sugar industry, as well as in cannon and bell manufacture. Copper eventually figured in the amalgamation process as well. The same was true of tin, which is abundant in Bolivia in the form of cassiterite. A small amount of copper was also alloyed with silver to produce coin metal, religious objects, and silver table service.

After being broken up with iron and steel tools, ores had to be transported in sturdy sacks to the guairas and mills. Animal hides mostly came from cattle introduced by the Spanish, and tanneries were built outside many towns in the valleys below Potosí—by law downriver to protect the municipal water supply. Animal fat was also rendered to make tallow candles, increasingly necessary as mines dove deep underground. Raw fat, sometimes from llamas, was also burned in lamps.

Mineworkers tore through their clothing quickly as well, and pre-sewn breeches, shirts, and jackets were sent from textile-producing cities such as Cuzco. Thousands of indigenous women all over the high Andes toiled daily in the manufacture of these outfits, from spinning to weaving to sewing. Sometimes produced in foul sweatshops, indigenous clothing items were often treated as tribute and thus their makers were left uncompensated.

Sturdy woolens came from as far away as highland Ecuador as well, and native-produced Quito broadcloth soon became the standard fabric for artisan outfits in Potosí.[26] Cheaper baize and cotton fabrics, along with hemp sandals, rope, cordage, and basketry, came from many other parts of the colonies, from Tucumán to Mexico.[27] In short, Potosí demanded a wide range of artisan manufactures from Europe and Asia, but also from Spain's other American colonies. Everyone wanted a piece of the bonanza, and cities such as Quito and Cuzco became virtual dependencies. Had their cloth producers not been handicapped by wholesale importers of luxury fabrics based in Seville and Lima, these regional centers might have developed more sophisticated industries. Global demand for Potosí silver was simply insatiable, and the Cerro Rico and the adjacent Imperial Villa were immediately recognized as the motors of an emerging intercolonial and global economy.

### AN ANDEAN EMPORIUM

Also huge is the trade in this villa of European cloth, and it is so great that each year it amounts to more than 1,200,000 pesos that is consumed and enters by sea from the port of Arica as well as that which comes from Cuzco, not counting some 500,000 pesos' worth of woolen stuff, baize, and grogram from Quito, from Huánuco, and La Paz, and 100,000 pesos' worth of local cloth, and 25,000 in cloth from Tucumán, which is a lot of cotton linen, carpets and ornamental cloths, honey, wax, and Indian cloth.[28]

Life at 4,000 meters (13,200 feet) above sea level was not without hardship, especially at the height of the Little Ice Age. Cloth was in high demand in perpetually frigid Potosí, the thicker and more windproof the better. Notary records reveal a steady stream of imports from Europe along with numerous indigenous fabrics from all over greater Peru, many of high quality if their cost is any indication. Fine woolens arrived each season in Potosí from England, Flanders, Holland, France, Italy, and Spain itself, often described in terms of thread count, and in often fanciful colors.

Important as woolens were for warmth in Potosí, people of all social classes consumed considerable silk and linen as well. Silk fabric came from Granada and from parts of Italy, but soon European silk was undersold by a vast array of textiles, along with raw silk, from China. Chinese fabrics arrived in huge quantities after 1571, when the Manila galleon trade officially began.[29] Chinese textiles, plus cotton print fabrics from India, continued to arrive in the high Andes through the seventeenth century despite repeated crown trade restrictions pushed by Seville's powerful merchant guild, or Consulado. Linen typically came from Rouen, a major cloth-manufacturing center in France, and also from Holland and Ireland.

In her 1588 will, María Pomachumbo, native of Cuzco and widow of Spaniard Salvador de Talavera, listed a wide range of luxury fabrics and other goods in her Potosí inventory. She had an "old-style *cumbe* cloth outfit from the time of the Inca" plus "sleeves of a white silver fabric that go with the same outfit." Pomachumbo also possessed "a shawl from Trujillo that looks Chinese," some cork-soled *alpargatas,* or espadrilles, along with fine gold Andean shawl pins and gold and emerald jewelry in the Spanish style.[30] Pomachumbo apparently did not own Venetian glassware, but it was available. A sale record from 1589 notes thirty "glass cups from Venice" selling for 100 pesos.[31]

How did all these exotic luxury items reach the high Andes? Mule drivers, known as *arrieros,* were the long-haul truckers of their day, and their capital consisted of these carefully bred and trained animals. A revealing document from Potosí's notary books records the 1587 sale of an eleven-mule team by one Mosco ("Fly") Sánchez to Alvaro Díaz. The mules, branded on the right leg with an "A" topped by a small circle, were named "La Morisca" (chestnut color), "Leona" (brown), "La Doctora" (chestnut), "Chapetona" (brown), "El Tirano" (black, male), "Contramaestre" (light chestnut, male), "La Criolla" (brown), "Colomote" (chestnut, male), plus three females whose color is not given, called "Buscarruydo," "La Vizcayna," and "La Mulata." The team sold for only 750 pesos, suggesting that some of these colorfully named mules were getting old.[32] Enslaved individuals were sometimes sold along with mules, as in the case of Juan, a 20-year-old man born in the colonies and described as mulatto. He was sold in Potosí along with "a roan-colored mule, long tail" for a combined 1,000 pesos. The mule's brand is not listed, but Juan was branded on the face, a common punishment for runaways.[33]

## CHICHA AND WINE

They are accustomed to drinking in public, many people gathering together, men as well as women, and the same hold great dances in which they make use of ancient rites and ceremonies, bringing back to memory in their songs their past paganism.[34]

From the start of mining operations at Potosí in 1545, Spaniards regarded chicha, or maize beer, as both a necessity and a dangerous vice. Spanish priests and civil authorities railed against native Andean drinkers and their mostly female suppliers throughout the colonial period, yet the business could not be suppressed, nor even effectively taxed. As with coca, Spaniards horned in on the maize trade early, recognizing the profitability of chicha as a basic stimulant and source of calories. Already in 1549, Potosí's first recorded silversmith purchased 100 bushels of maize, then worth over 700 pesos. At such a price it could only be used to make chicha.

In 1559 two Potosí mine owners sold "a storehouse for selling maize" located on "the old *plazuela del maíz.*" Also sold were "an old tent and two half-*pochas* to measure maize" and some scales and weights.[35] Worried about a shortage of maize, the Potosí town council accepted an offer of 4,000 pesos from two rich Spaniards to fill a granary. Things may have gone too well, since by 1567 the town council outlawed "Indian" drinking parties in Spanish households, even on feast days. Even so, Spanish mine owners imported maize, some of it already milled into flour, by the ton.[36]

Jane Mangan has shown how lucrative the chicha market was in Potosí's first century and a half, and how some indigenous and mixed-heritage women, the *chicheras,* grew modestly wealthy from it. In times when maize flour ran short, chicheras brewed beer from wheat flour, producing the first known *Hefeweizen* in Bolivia. City officials, not to mention Potosí's many bread bakers, who relied on steady imports of wheat flour for their livelihood, were not amused.[37]

Wheat and maize flour often came from towns in or near the Pilcomayo River basin such as Yotala, on the road to Chuquisaca. The Pilcomayo's braided streams in turn powered gristmills.[38] Fresh and savory, wheat bread became the staple carbohydrate of *potosinos* of all social stripes, its price set by the town council. When a bread shortage ended in January 1564 the council set prices at twenty 12-ounce loaves for a peso, or twenty-two "Indian loaves" for the same price. "Indian" bread was made from coarser and possibly healthier flour.[39]

Spaniards demanded their own fermented beverage, wine, essential to the Mediterranean diet and to the Catholic faith. Although some Spaniards drank to excess, Castilians, like most southern Europeans, prided themselves on moderation. The prohibitive cost of Spanish wine in the early colonies, and particularly in remote mining towns like Potosí, helped promote abstemiousness, especially in the first decades after discovery. A 1559 contract suggests even wholesale wine prices remained high in Potosí. Two silversmiths imported 400 jugs at 20 pesos each, a major investment. In 1567 the Potosí town council forbade sale of wine to "blacks and Indians," saying that "in addition to the damage that results, this commodity has gotten more expensive."[40] The only way to bring costs down was to produce wine locally.

By the 1570s, the era of Viceroy Toledo, locally produced wines were reaching the Imperial Villa in prodigious quantities. Imports of Spanish wine had also increased enough for their prices to drop somewhat by this time, but Peruvian vintages sold for half as much or less. Most wine was sold in gallon-sized earthenware jugs or *botijas,* usually sealed with tar or resin. Spanish wine remained on the market to please more distinguishing palates, and also to reinforce status. Cheaper local plonk found popularity among artisans and other working as well as idle folk of all types.

Wine came from Arequipa, the Moquegua Valley, and also coastal Peru via the port of Arica, where mercury from Huancavelica and Spain was shipped to the highlands.[41] Ica, Pisco, Nasca, and eventually Tacna benefited from their sea links to Potosí's "mercury port." On the other side of the Andes, the Spanish found warm valleys where grapevines survived and occasionally flourished despite high altitudes. Vineyards were planted around Mizque and near the old Inca fortress at Oroncota, on the Pilcomayo, and in the Cinti and other valleys farther south, near Tarija. The vineyards of Pilaya and Paspaya eventually predominated, and they persist today. With these relatively proximate sources, plus the premium wines of Spain, it appears not to have been cost-effective to ship wine to Potosí from the early vineyards of central Argentina and Chile, although they were already well established. Spanish wine held onto market share in the early years. A 1589 notary recorded "vino de Castilla" selling for 25 pesos a jug, about the cost of a decent horse.[42]

Brandy, or *aguardiente de uva,* was developed in Peru for widespread sale only around 1640. Considerable amounts of this liquor, now called *pisco* in Peru and Chile and *singani* in Bolivia, were shipped to Potosí from the vineyards of Peru as well as the lower valleys to the east and south of the Imperial Villa mentioned above. Sugar cane brandy or *aguardiente de caña* was also known, sometimes used for medicinal purposes. Today miners guzzle it from small plastic bottles after offering a splash to El Tío.

### COCA AND OTHER STIMULANTS

Some say that it is money. . . . It is true, true that with coca they do business in the old way, they do not forget their tradition of exchanging some things for other things; and thus it is that everywhere coca is sold in bulk, so that for a fistful of coca they give a fistful of corn or of dried meat, which they call *charqui,* or of any other thing. And because of this kind of commerce they say that coca is money.[43]

Like chicha, the coca leaf (*Erythroxylon coca*) was both a necessity and a vice for native Andeans. Since unlike alcohol coca chewing did not interfere with motor function, but rather enhanced it while also suppressing hunger, the Spanish soon discovered that they could become rich by supplying the leaf to Potosí's many thousands of indigenous mine and mill workers.

An early champion of coca was crown official Juan de Matienzo, who headed the regional circuit court at La Plata in the 1560s, prior to the arrival of Viceroy Toledo.[44] Matienzo went so far as to argue that the best way for Spaniards to tap independent indigenous silver production was by introducing more coca. According to Matienzo, Potosí's economy was controlled by native Andean mineworkers, refiners, and traders of all sorts: "In the end it is a great confusion that few understand; it is only certain that the best thing for that place is not to try something new other than adding Indians, which never harms and is always beneficial."[45] Matienzo did not bother to note that native Andean coca carriers received a paltry 10 pesos for a journey that took 130 days.[46]

As with chicha, most coca was retailed by indigenous women in outdoor market squares such as the Potosí *qhatu,* catercorner to the main plaza, but their suppliers were most often Spanish wholesale merchants with ties to Cuzco. Until the later colonial period, when coca plantings were greatly expanded in the hot valleys east of La Paz and Cochabamba, most coca came from the old Inca plantations east and north of Cuzco, including a concentrated zone that fed into the trading post at Paucartambo. The fields of Los Andes, as the Spanish called Inca "Antisuyu," were in hot-country valleys, such as the Tono and Toaima, several days march northeast from Paucartambo. An early shipment record from 1549 shows that coca from this region was already prized in Potosí. Ninety-six bags sold for 19–1 / 2 assayed pesos each. Coca from "Chuquiabo," the lowlands east of La Paz, sold for 14 pesos per basket in the same year, so it is difficult to know if these units were commensurable. A 1550 order for 2,000 *cestos* of Cuzco coca referred to plantings controlled by Hernando Pizarro.[47] The cesto, a large basket of coca weighing 25 lbs., became the standard unit.

Paulina Numhauser has traced links between Spanish owners of coca fields east of Cuzco and indigenous women who acted as retailers but also occasionally as wholesalers in the Imperial Villa. Numhauser found that by the late sixteenth century Cuzco's coca link to Potosí had not only created a new Spanish elite class of "coca lords," but also an elite female indigenous class.[48] Like the Potosí mita, forced indigenous labor in Cuzco's coca sector generated its own polemics, in part because work in the hot lowlands of the upper Amazon basin exposed highland natives to a variety of diseases, including leishmaniasis, a disfiguring and sometimes fatal parasitic infection.

In the Imperial Villa, indigenous women typically sold coca on consignment for Cuzco or Potosí wholesalers. Consignment contracts with factors go back to the late 1550s, but detailed inventories only appear later. An example of a successful coca dealer in Potosí in its heyday was Francisca Carva [possibly Carhua], whose 1588 will lists over 100 baskets of the green leaf along with a wide range of indigenous textiles, outfits, and jewels.[49] Carva possessed considerable silver as well, a portion of which she donated to the cult of Our Lady of Copacabana and other religious confraternities. She also gave generously to clothe the city's poor, mandating distribution by ranking Franciscans and Jesuits. Jane Mangan traced the business of another, more modest retailer, Isabel Cotaqui, who agreed to sell coca on consignment for a Spanish woman in 1590.[50]

Coca was the habit-forming drug of choice in Potosí, closely followed by chicha, wine, and other alcoholic beverages. But as one might expect given its

Coca vendor, Felipe Guaman Poma de Ayala, ca. 1615. Courtesy of the Danish Royal Library, Copenhagen.

native American associations, tobacco was also consumed by potosinos of varying status, and like coca it had to be imported from distant hot lowlands including coastal Ecuador. Some came from as far away as Nicaragua.[51] Tobacco was smoked in clay pipes in the sixteenth century. Cigars came later, and snuff became the rage in the mid-seventeenth century, crossing gender lines and alarming moral gatekeepers.

Drugs used in a strictly medicinal way included sarsaparilla, *cañafístula* (American senna, a purgative), *quina quina,* and eventually quinine bark (*cascarilla*), discovered in the Ecuadorian Andes in the early seventeenth century. Quinine remains the drug of last resort for chronic malaria. Quina quina was a febrifuge and sarsaparilla, a type of "root beer" ingredient found near Guayaquil, also in Ecuador, was believed to calm the symptoms of syphilis, which the Spanish called the "French disease" or *mal francés*.[52] *Solimán,* a mercury-based ointment, also appears in colonial merchant and apothecary inventories. It served as an antiseptic, but its toxicity made it a popular poison as well. Dozens of herbal plasters and mineral creams were used, as was a local mineral called *piedra lipe,* or the "stone of Los Lípes," named for the remote district southwest of Potosí. It was used as an astringent among other things.

The Jesuit Bernabé Cobo wrote extensively on all things Andean, from Inca history to the properties of minerals. Among Peru's most famous minerals were bezoar stones, some of which were found in the guts of vicuñas and guanacos. These mineral accretions might strike us as gross or simply useless, but in early modern times they were believed to have great healing power. While visiting Potosí Cobo saw an exceptional bezoar stone that had formed around an arrowhead and part of a shaft. He concluded that the animal from which the accretion had been taken had eaten medicinal herbs after being wounded and these had become concentrated around the projectile, in effect sealing it off.[53] A small dose of such a precious accretion ought to go a long way toward restoring health.

### SLAVES AND SLAVERY IN EARLY POTOSÍ

Spanish invaders killed many indigenous Americans in wars and skirmishes, forced marches into jungles and deserts, slave-like labor regimes, and many other abusive practices. Far more native Americans were felled by diseases unwittingly introduced by Europeans and Africans. Not until 1650 or so did most native populations bottom out, beginning a slow climb that continues today. The Spanish crown outlawed enslavement and sale of native Americans soon after Columbus's voyages, with the exception of resistant groups such as the Caribs and the Mapuche of Chile. Draft labor and serfdom could be extremely onerous and even deadly, but most native Andeans were legally exempt from chattel slavery, a status almost entirely reserved for sub-Saharan Africans. Potosí's notary books record the 1587 sale of an enslaved indigenous woman from Bolivia's eastern lowlands. She was baptized Margarita, said to be 32 years old. She was sold by a Potosí resident to a man from Cochabamba for 300 pesos.[54] Margarita was not unique, as evidenced by a freedom note from 1550, in which Inés, an enslaved woman from the Caribbean pearl island of Cubagua, was freed by a Spaniard who had bought her in Panama. Inés was branded on the chin with the enigmatic letters "m. m."[55]

Labor systems such as the mita and *yanaconaje,* along with demands made by *encomenderos* and priests, put intense pressure on native American men in Potosí, although many women were also taken from their homes and made to serve Spanish masters or supplement their menfolk's tribute obligations. All of this meant that Spanish settlers were never satisfied by indigenous labor, yet only those in charge of cash crops or with access to precious metals could afford to buy slaves.

Sub-Saharan Africans were brought to the Americas soon after 1500, and the first to arrive in the Andes came with the conquistadors. Some Africans mined gold at the old Inca diggings of Carabaya, in the upper Amazon, and in northern Peru.[56] But it was only with the expansion of Potosí's silver mining economy that African slavery became a key component of Andean economy and society. In Potosí itself, enslaved Africans appear to have served much as they did in administrative capitals such as Lima, Bogotá, and Quito.

Many slaves were women forced to perform domestic service and wet-nursing, whereas men mostly served as grooms, artisans, or estate managers. In Potosí, only a few African men appear to have worked underground. Most were spared these tasks and expected to either gain skills in silver refining or in some other craft, such as blacksmithing or shoemaking, or to drive mule and llama trains. Only the Potosí mint seems to have been a major site of long-term slave employment in the city proper, but several slaves worked in bakeries as well. A 1578 contract describes a "black master confectioner" working with two boy apprentices.[57]

Rich potosinos from an early date treated household slaves as both status symbols and necessities. According to notary records, famous Potosí writers such as Luis Capoche and Alvaro Alonso Barba both owned slaves, male and female.[58] For wealthy women, slaves were typically included in dowries, treated as mobile capital along with clothes, furnishings, and jewelry. The only rich potosinos known to have owned significant numbers of enslaved Africans were those who possessed large estates in distant fertile valleys, especially the southern vineyards. Some such estates counted well over a hundred enslaved African workers by the mid-seventeenth century. Other enslaved Africans produced sugar around Mizque, southeast of Cochabamba.[59]

The thousands of enslaved Africans who reached Potosí in the early colonial period came mostly from West Central Africa once Buenos Aires was opened for traffic in the late 1580s, but before this time slaves from Senegambia and other parts of Upper Guinea were most common. One thing we know for certain is that slave prices were always high in Potosí, and slave traders and merchants could expect to trade captives directly for silver rather than for other commodities they would have to resell. To pick an example, 20-year-old Pedro Zape sold for 570 pesos in January 1578 despite being called an "infamous gamester." Thirty-five-year-old Antón Bioho sold for 625 silver pesos cash in 1587 despite chronic stomach trouble and a serious tobacco habit. Similarly, Luisa Jolofa, 30, sold for 600 pesos in 1588 despite a stab wound.[60] All three names suggest origins in Upper Guinea. People of African descent, enslaved and free, played key roles in the regional economy and their cultural presence and contributions to society were frequently noted by locals and visitors alike. Nearly all of Potosí's town criers were enslaved Africans.

Contract labor or indenture was also important. Potosí's notary records contain many hiring agreements known as *asientos* and *conciertos*. In 1570 a free mulatto blacksmith named Juan de Mendoza signed on with a Potosí householder for general labor.[61] The agreements were binding, and the most common ones tied native Andean *forasteros,* or those not attached to villages or kin groups, to Spanish overlords. Some agreements suggest that male labor in particular was highly prized. An indigenous migrant worker, Antonio Guamani of Cuzco, signed up for two years' general labor for 60 pesos per year plus food on 3 January 1577.

Female indentures may have been less expensive. María Chunca was assigned to work for carpenter Miguel Moreno for a year on 3 January 1577, making only 10 pesos for what was likely full-time domestic service. Another indigenous woman signed on to work in the household of a Spanish woman for six months, earning 8 pesos, the cost of a jug of Arequipa wine. Other contracts from 1577 suggest that women in household service got about

10 pesos per year, whereas men earned at least twice this amount. By 1587, male indigenous work contracts averaged 20 pesos per year. By contrast, a Spanish tutor earned 140 pesos in 1578, and enslaved African adults sold for approximately 500 pesos. At this time coins were rare, so prices were typically given in *pesos ensayados,* an accounting unit similar to the Castilian ducat.[62]

Like many mining districts the world over, Potosí faced crisis soon after its discovery. The easily smelted ores found near the surface of the Cerro Rico played out and the age of wind furnaces or guairas flickered. Indigenous-run mines and refineries had been the rule at Potosí since the first claims were staked, and this had given rise to a peculiarly shared production model, and to a vibrant, polyglot urban marketplace.

Indigenous teamsters, traders, and merchants adapted quickly to bonanza life, and many managed to profit by it even as they made their Spanish over-lords and sponsors rich as well by handing over generous quotas or selling stimulants on consignment. Violent conflicts arose as in the days of conquest, but in general the first decades of silver production at Potosí appear to have been generous enough to advance many fortunes, both European and indigenous. Wealthy people of all sorts purchased enslaved Africans, some of whom may have found ways to earn cash and purchase freedom.

When the easy ores played out, however, crisis loomed and tensions rose. The Cerro Rico was littered with piles of unsmelted ore and seemingly useless tailings. The fabled guairas that lit up the night skies had reached their limits. Without some radical innovation, some new plan of action, the Imperial Villa and its mines faced stagnation if not total abandonment. To some, it already appeared that the much-touted "treasury of the world" had been a mirage.

# THREE

## *The Viceroy's Great Machine*

The Imperial Villa Rica of Potocchi. Thanks to its mines, Castile is Castile, Rome is Rome, the pope is the pope, and the king is monarch of the world. And the Holy Mother Church is defended and our Holy Faith protected by the four kings of the Indies and by the Inca emperor. Today it empowers the pope in Rome and our lord the king, don Philip III.

—FELIPE GUAMAN POMA DE AYALA (CA. 1615)[1]

IN 1568, SPAIN'S PRUDENT KING, PHILIP II, selected an educated blueblood, don Francisco de Toledo, as fifth viceroy of Peru. It was a fateful choice with global implications. Arriving in Lima in 1569, Viceroy Toledo soon left for the high Andes to assemble a great silver machine for his monarch. If all went as planned, this mechanism would pump the fabled riches of Potosí into royal coffers in unheard-of quantities, and it would make the whole colony, Guaman Poma's neo-Inca kingdom, the envy of the world once again. By the time Toledo left Peru for Spain in 1580, the age of wind was over in Potosí. A new machine age had begun, and this age demanded workers. Toledo vastly expanded the *mita* labor draft, disrupting tens of thousands of native Andean lives and vexing the conscience of Spain's kings for centuries to come.

Viceroy Toledo did exactly what was expected of him. A model late-Renaissance bureaucrat, he brought an unsentimental and unforgiving sense of urgency, efficiency, and reason of state to a vast and rugged colonial region marred by chaos and division since the conquest. A representative of the new lettered class of men who "reconquered" Spanish Peru in the years around 1570, Toledo aimed to subordinate private ambitions to the interests of the royal fisc. Anyone who stood between him and his project was a potential traitor.[2]

Toledo sought to bring all of greater Peru's resources to bear on the problem of increasing precious metals extraction in order to advance the global project of the Spanish monarchy: the defense and spread of the Roman

"La Villa Rica Enperial de Potocchi," Felipe Guaman Poma de Ayala, ca. 1615. Courtesy of the Danish Royal Library, Copenhagen.

Catholic faith. "Reform" meant applying new technologies to mining and refining, improving supply lines and building infrastructure, drafting new laws and naming magistrates, and most importantly, forcing concentrated village life, the market economy, and rotational labor service upon tens of thousands of native Andeans. Toledo also believed that taming Peru required rewriting Inca history and murdering its surviving royalty. In 1570, he personally oversaw the execution of Túpac Amaru I, the youthful Inca heir brought to Cuzco from the jungle hideaway of Vilcabamba. Túpac's sacrifice heralded the beginning of a new era of colonial subordination. As suggested by Guaman Poma and other indigenous commentators, it also spurred Inca revitalization from the shadows.

This chapter treats Viceroy Toledo's 1572–75 tenure in Potosí, during which he consolidated the mita labor draft, forced construction of reservoirs to power refineries, introduced the mercury amalgamation method of refining, and founded the royal mint. The chapter then examines how the "machine" Toledo set up functioned, with its mix of imported technologies and local innovations. Potosí silver production spiked in 1592 thanks to Toledo's efforts, but the mita drew a swarm of critics. This chapter also ties Potosí to Asia with the opening of the Manila galleon traffic after 1571. The human and environmental costs were huge, but for the first time the globe was linked together from sea to sea with a "chain" of silver.

## THE MITA

Until recently, mining demanded armies of workers. Viceroy Toledo saw immediately that resuscitating Peru's silver industry would require mustering such an army. Slaves were an option, but the Spanish crown refused mine owners' pleas to subsidize importation of African captives. Toledo supported slave labor in Greater Peru's mines, but he did not see this solution developing in time to save his indebted and embattled king, Philip II. Instead, he turned—like the Inca rulers he was so anxious to discredit as tyrants—to native Andean peasants. He would revive and modify the mita labor draft.

Nearest at hand were the widely scattered Quechua- and Aymara-speaking farmers and pastoralists of the highlands, their villages and outlying plots and pastures stretching from northernmost Argentina all the way

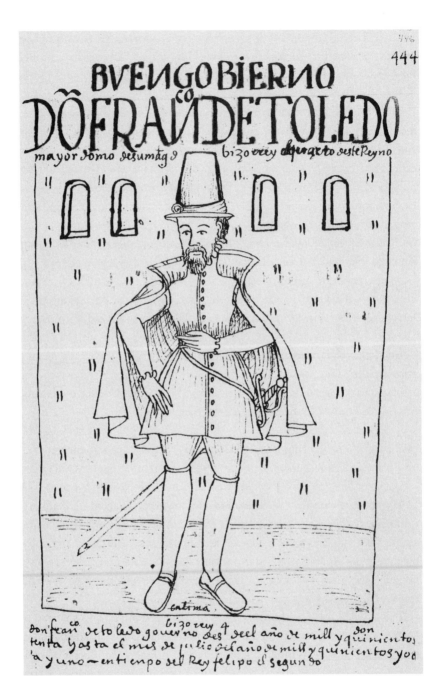

# BVENGOBIERNO
## DÕFRANDETOLEDO
mayordomo desumag y           bizorrey dfuzexto deste Reyno

*entima*

don fran co de toledo gouerno des q deel año de mill y quinientos
ten ta ha sta el mes de julio octaño de mill y quinientos y oo
a y uno — en tiempo del Rey felipo el segundo

Viceroy Francisco de Toledo, Felipe Guaman Poma de Ayala, ca. 1615. Courtesy of the
Danish Royal Library, Copenhagen.

to Cuzco, over 1,000 km from Potosí. This vast and lofty area would serve for several centuries as Potosí's core mita net. Here and there it spilled into lower and greener terrain, as around Mizque, Cochabamba, and Tarija (see map 5 on page 144).

Divided into seventeen districts, the hundreds of villages and kin units falling within the Potosí mita catchment zone were each to provide the mines and mills with 16 percent of their able-bodied men each year (one was to serve every seven years), a total of 13,500 men at any one time based on Toledo's 1572 census. Of this number, 4,500 men worked underground in the Cerro Rico in rotation. Remaining men worked in the refining mills or at tasks arranged by royal magistrates and private businessmen. Mine work after 1572 was continuous: day and night. Work-sharing contracts in Potosí's notary books bear this out.[3]

A parallel but smaller mita supplied the mercury mines of Huancavelica in Peru's highlands east of Lima. Thanks to Viceroy Toledo, Huancavelica's Santa Bárbara mines, opened in 1564, had 3,280 mita workers in rotation by 1577. This was even deadlier work than that at Potosí, and the main Huancavelica diggings came to be known as "la mina de la muerte."[4] Other mita rotations were established at mines throughout the Andes, including gold and silver camps in greater Quito and New Granada, but none came close to the scale of Potosí or even Huancavelica.[5]

Spaniards alone could not manage such a vast system, and most lacked the basic language skills. Thus caciques and *kurakas* served as middlemen, rounding up and counting workers, making certain each district's quotas were filled and turned over to Spanish magistrates. Toledo named five such *capitanes de la mita*. After Toledo left for Lima in 1575, Juan de Matienzo, president of the Audiencia of Charcas, raised the mita quota to just over 14,000 workers per annum. Although native captains proved unable to sustain this number for long, Spanish expectations had been made clear. The king, even if he would not admit it in writing, had forced his most vulnerable subjects to mine his treasure at great risk to their lives.

The mita was never uncontroversial in Toledo's own day; his solution to Potosí's labor problem was perceived as both brilliantly hardheaded and terribly cruel. Theologians in Lima approved of the mita only to reject it on their deathbeds as mortally sinful. Yet despite early and lasting criticism, the Potosí mita proved durable.[6] The draft was only outlawed in 1812 when a liberal parliament ruled Spain and its colonies from Cádiz during the Napoleonic occupation. Even so, it sputtered on until Simón Bolívar declared it over in 1825. No king of Spain was willing to kill what Toledo had created.

Yet neither was Toledo's mita sustainable at its original scale. The mines of the Cerro Rico literally ate men, and long-term displacement and high mortality upset the underlying subsistence base that Toledo took advantage of and attempted to reorder. What most diminished the mita was a combination of indigenous death by disease and indigenous willpower, by way of flight but also self-hire to mine owners willing to pay a premium to secure increasingly valuable workers.

Already by 1600, Potosí's mita workers numbered about 10,000, and over half the mineworkers in town were receiving wages. Known as *mingas,* as described in the previous chapter, these free workers were usually more skilled than the drafted *mitayos.* Some were old hands.[7] Even so, powerful mine and mill owners in Potosí were loath to let go of their allotments of draftees, whom they could always underpay, swap to other owners, or otherwise exploit. A growing guild of mining capitalists, the *gremio de azogueros,* fought bitterly to keep the mita until the very end of the colonial period.

Mita work was not unpaid. It was not permanent. It was not slavery. Yet it was coerced and vastly undercompensated, and it severely disrupted native Andean subsistence patterns. Just to give an idea, in 1596 the Jesuit Antonio de Ayáns estimated that a Potosí mitayo's subsistence costs totaled at least 26 pesos per month. Wages were scarcely 10 pesos a month, assuming they were paid as promised. Potosí's isolation and high consumer demand drove up the price of essential commodities. Ayáns broke down basic costs in 1596 Potosí as follows: a half-bushel of *chuño,* 10 pesos; one alpaca, 4 pesos; fish, chilis, and salt, 2 pesos; firewood and straw, 4 pesos; coca, 5 pesos; chicha, 1 peso; total, 26 pesos.[8]

If Ayáns was correct in his estimates, the mandated wage for mitayos would have barely covered the cost of half a bushel of freeze-dried potatoes or chuño. There would be nothing left over for cooking fuel, much less animal protein or stimulants such as coca and chicha. As a result of this discrepancy between wages and living costs, most mitayos arrived in Potosí with as much food as they could herd or carry, along with whatever they could sell. A stockpile of chuño was especially important, as was jerked llama meat. Coca, chicha, chilies, and fish had to be purchased in town.

## ACCIDENTS

And of the sad things that have happened to these people, of which memory is fresh, I shall relay several to Your Excellency so that you will understand the labors they suffer and how much this ore costs them, such that we could say it was rather blood than ore. And such was the case in the mine they call La Muñiza, in the Veta Rica, where a Spaniard, working in company with another, brought fifty-six Indians; with twenty-eight he worked by day, and with the rest, by night. The mine was dangerous, especially in a gallery they had expanded to a large degree, such that when Francisco de Oruño entered to inspect it, he being the [royal] inspector at the time, knowing the risk the Indians faced, he ordered the work suspended until certain repairs necessary for security were done, even issuing a formal decree to this effect. And the owner of the mine alleged in writing that these repairs were not necessary, and that the decree had been animated by a passion against him, that the mine was quite secure, appealing and filing certain proceedings. With this these sad people came to perish, as only two days later this the mine collapsed, catching all twenty-eight Indians underground, the ones sent to work at night. And the next day in the morning all the judges went up the mountain, accompanied by a large number of Indians and their wives, children, and relatives who rent the air with their cries and wails. And so much earth and rock fell upon them [the buried miners] that they were unable to pull them out straightaway, but rather with the passing of time, as they cleared it away, they located them. The Spaniard was jailed, and after much trial and detention, he was condemned by the Royal Audiencia to a fine of 8,000 assayed pesos, part for the royal chamber and the rest to be distributed among the widows according to the number of children they had.

—LUIS CAPOCHE, 1585[9]

Thus did Luis Capoche describe one of many mine disasters that occurred in Potosí's Cerro Rico in the first years after Viceroy Toledo formalized the mita. In this case all the legal protections that mineworkers had, including the intervention of an inspector capable of suspending operations until safety measures were taken, proved useless. The viceroy's own mining laws were ignored and twenty-eight miners died in a cave-in that they and others had seen coming. The tragedy was unusual only in the high number of men killed in one fell swoop, and in the fact that the mine owner was jailed and fined.[10]

Capoche goes on to tell a second story of trapped miners, in some ways sadder than the first despite the smaller number of victims. In this case, seven indigenous mineworkers and their Portuguese overseer survived a massive cave-in, but they died after several days spent trying to clear the rubble (see appendix). One can hardly imagine a worse fate than being trapped underground, able to speak with loved ones through a hole in the rubble but not to escape, left to die of hunger and exposure. It was stories like these that burdened the conscience of the king of Spain as well as his viceroys and other officials, and that made it seem as though the mita had been nothing more than a deal with the Devil. Almost casually, Capoche added: "And only a few days ago seven or eight Indians died in the mountain, and if one had to write about this at length, one would expend much paper."[11]

For Capoche, a direct beneficiary of the mita, what Toledo had created was not a "great machine" but rather a "fierce beast," thirsty for Indian blood:

> And it is common that they bring down dead [workers], and others with cracked skulls and broken legs, and each day in the mills they are wounded. And the simple facts of working at night, and in such a cold country, and tending the ore crushers, which is the hardest work due to the dust they get in the eyes and mouth, all this is enough to do them great harm. And thus the hospital is full of wounded Indians, and more than fifty of them die each year, and *this fierce beast* swallows them alive. And at this moment, between the tribunals of the judge of native affairs and the mine magistrate, they are pursuing more than seventy criminal cases related to Indian deaths.[12]

If these sorts of routine horrors were reported by an eyewitness observer sympathetic to the king and to fellow Spanish silver mine and mill owners, what of those who found real fault with the viceroy's great machine? Who were they and what impact did they have?

### THE MITA'S EARLY CRITICS

Even before the mita was formalized in the early 1570s, Spanish critics railed against mineworker abuse at Potosí. The first and loudest critic was the Dominican friar and friend of Bartolomé de las Casas, Domingo de Santo Tomás. It was Santo Tomás who first declared the Cerro Rico a "mouth of hell."

Viceroy Toledo arrived in Potosí fully aware of the Cerro Rico's reputation. In part for this reason he repeatedly asked King Philip II to approve of the expanded mita he had devised for Potosí. The king remained silent.[13] Toledo consulted theologians including the archbishop of Lima, ultimately winning their blessing, as they believed the checks and controls he had put in place would serve to protect native peoples. Some historians have suggested that Philip II was torn by the decision to uproot thousands of native subjects in the name of mineral treasure, but in the end he did not stop Toledo.

The king's silence may be contrasted with a string of critics of Viceroy Toledo's mita, many of them Jesuit priests in the late sixteenth and early seventeenth centuries, when the labor draft—and Potosí's silver production— were at their highest. Despite these critiques, often echoed by later viceroys and high court judges, the mita was not abolished. Like the enslavement of millions of Africans and their descendants, once put in motion the mita labor subsidy became a conscience-killing addiction.

One of the broadest critiques of the Potosí mita was penned by the Jesuit Antonio de Ayáns in 1596. We have seen how he calculated the cost of a mita worker's subsistence in Potosí, contrasted with the paltry wage paid by mine and mill owners. Ayáns took pains to describe harsh work conditions and other hardships suffered by mitayos in Potosí, but he focused mostly on the disruptive trek to the mines that his parishioners had to make from the outskirts of Cuzco.

Ayáns describes how regional governors routinely forced mitayos and their family members to serve in their households or in their fields, to purchase goods they did not want or need, to overcharge them for head taxes or tribute, and even to serve them sexually in way stations or *tambos*. Ayáns did not propose abolition of the mita, calling instead for law enforcement to curb its excesses. If these abuses were not remedied, according to Ayáns, the Andean Altiplano would soon be depopulated.

In 1603, Padre Alonso Mesía Venegas echoed Ayáns in a letter to Viceroy Luis de Velasco, arguing for the *empadronamiento* or census-like registry of some 50,000 Andeans said to be living in and around Potosí. Once registered, these Andeans would prove sufficient to staff the mines and refineries, he claimed, leaving residents of the more distant provinces to subsist and pay tributes much like native inhabitants of Quito and other "kingdoms" where mine mitas were rare or highly localized. Mesía Venegas admitted that supplying enough food for the locally based workers would be a problem, but he offered various fixes, proposing construction of a granary in Potosí specifically for Andean mineworkers. The priest's suggestions were ignored.

Of the hardships suffered by caciques whose provinces had become depopulated but their mita quotas remained high, Mesía Venegas offered the following statement made by one such cacique to a Jesuit (perhaps himself) from 1601:

> Father, I am obliged to bring in thirty-one Indians and for the last six months I have been short sixteen, and each week I have had to pay 126 pesos to hire replacements, and in order to do this I have sold a mule I had, plus my llamas and my clothes, and I have searched for a loan, even begging among my own Indians, and having no solution to this shortage of Indians last week I pawned my daughter to a Spaniard for the sixty-four pesos I was short, and this week I do not know what to do except to hang myself.[14]

Mesía Venegas may have lacked a practical solution for the mita's horrors, but he was an eyewitness who had spent considerable time in Potosí. He argued for better mine inspectors, not mere "gentlemen" or even "good Christians," but rather "unattached men, workers who understand the mountain and go about like snakes all day." He added:

> The work the Indians do in the mines is tremendous, mostly due to incorrect allotment, and when the mines hit water they make them work in the midst of it, and because the ladders do not have their proper scaffolding, which we call rest platforms—an absolutely necessary thing when an Indian has climbed twenty statures [33.5 m or 110 ft.], clinging to a rope with no place to stop and catch his breath, and with nowhere for those going up to make way for those going down.[15]

As sympathetic as he was to the plight of native Andean mitayos, Mesía Venegas remained a priest. On chicha, he had this to say: "In Potosí, I being there one feast day, passing through the necessary streets to reach the college, just before dark, I saw three public drinking parties, two in corrals and one on the street itself, with their dances and drumming and chicha-filled gourds in their hands, such that in their former idolatry they could not have occupied themselves in this exercise with greater security and devotion."[16] Mesía Venegas advised the crown to order the city's constables to dump all chicha vessels and place any responsible caciques in jail for six days on the first offense and twelve days on the second. Otherwise there would be "no remedy for this vice, so pernicious and noxious to their souls and bodies."[17]

Not all critics of the mita were Jesuits. One outlier was the Hieronymite friar Diego de Ocaña, who lived in Potosí for nearly fifteen months around the year 1600. Ocaña did not write a formal appeal, but rather offered chilling visions of mine labor in his memoir, echoing the Dominican Fray Santo Tomás:

> God sustains this machine of this mountain miraculously, because all of it from below to above and all around, in all parts it is full of mouths, and in the part inside it is all hollow, such that one cannot know upon what it stands or what sustains it. *It is a portrait of hell to enter inside,* because seeing so many caves, and so deep, and so many lights in diverse parts, and to hear so many blows of those striking with the iron bar, it is a din that causes a man to lose his judgment and even his senses. There are some great adits through which the veins are connected and worked; and inside, in the crossings, there are some open spaces so wide and later some parts so narrow, sometimes straight and other times heading below, that should the Indian's candle be snuffed out, he will fall headlong.[18]

Ocaña was a Spaniard who visited Potosí to beg for alms to serve the cult of the Virgin of Guadalupe back in Extremadura, but he could not help but notice the price indigenous workers paid to yield the silver he and others so desperately coveted.

In 1610, several Jesuits at the Potosí *colegio* or high school, along with several mine and mill owners, offered an opinion for mita reform. It is a notable document in that the Jesuits relate that it was well known how Toledo's religious advisers changed their minds once they realized what the mita really entailed. What these priests offered in place of the Toledo mita, however, was the same plan put forth by Mesía Venegas, namely "populating" the city and neighboring valleys around Potosí with "free-floating Indians" who would then be controlled by a census and assigned to new parish priests. Forced labor for the mine and mill owners would not disappear, it would simply be more concentrated.[19]

### DEATH AND THE MITA: INDIGENOUS VIEWS

Catholic priests and royal magistrates frequently denounced the Potosí mita in writing, whereas only a few native Andean opinions have survived. Even so, memory of the mita lives on among Bolivian villagers. Tristan Platt discovered evidence of a colonial ritual in the village of Pocoata in which workers were sent off as in a funeral, and Thomas Abercrombie reported that even in the late 1970s villagers in K'ulta, northwest of Potosí and like Pocoata well within the old draft zone, offered ritual libations marking the departure of mita workers to the mines. The Cerro Rico was "Blood Mountain," its meaning equated with cash money.[20]

As N. D. Cook has shown, the relatively populous province of Chucuito, on the southwest shores of Lake Titicaca, was critical to the Potosí mita. About 2,200 workers were sent to the Cerro Rico yearly around 1600, and they made the 500-kilometer (300-mile) trek with their wives and children. It took them nearly two months. A contemporary report described the journey as follows:

> I have twice seen them and can report that there must be 7,000 souls. Each Indian takes at least eight or ten llamas and a few alpacas to eat. On these they transport their food, maize, and chuño, sleeping rugs and straw pallets to protect them from the cold, which is severe, for they always sleep on the ground. All this livestock normally exceeds 30,000 head.[21]

The same commentator said that only 2,000 of the total number of migrants returned: "of the other five thousand some die and others stay in Potosí or the nearby valleys because they have no cattle for the return journey."[22] In 1617 a Chucuito headman charged with rounding up mitayos complained that he could only muster 1,194 of the 1,854 workers demanded of him in 1613. The Potosí mita was slowly killing off one of the highlands' most fecund provinces. The indigenous population of Potosí's indigenous parishes, meanwhile, swelled, going from about 50,000 at the time of Toledo's arrival in 1572 to some 76,000 by 1611.[23]

A flipside of these horrors of forced migration and deadly work was the rise of regional lords, the above-mentioned "mita captains." Charged with rounding up workers from their home districts and mediating between them and Spanish magistrates and mine owners, some indigenous mita captains became powerful and rich. Notary records show that several such native lords purchased enslaved Africans to serve as personal pages and cooks. Others dressed in the latest European fashions, bore arms, and rode fine horses. Known as *mallku* under Inca rule, these were mostly Aymara regional lords.

An early example of the successful mita captain was Juan Colque Guarache, whose 1576 petition to the crown blended fulfilling Potosí's mita obligations with ancient links to Inca nobility.[24] Colque Guarache was in charge of sending workers, llamas, and supplies from the Killaka and Asanaqi districts northwest of Potosí in the hills and mountains around Lake Poopó.

In the Imperial Villa itself, the Killaka and Asanaqi mita workers and their families occupied the parish of San Bernardo, whose church was built in part under Colque Guarache's patronage. Aside from his own "subjects," Colque Guarache was charged with sending workers from two other neighboring ethnic districts, Awllaka-Urukilla and Siwaruyu-Arakapi. In Potosí these groups lived in the parish of San Pablo. When mita musters took place at the base of the Cerro Rico each Monday, Colque Guarache was there to make certain his charges were ready to serve their turn.

Another mita captain who amassed a fortune was Diego Chambilla.[25] Chambilla, paramount chief of the Pomata district, was a highly educated native noble who used his position and literacy to expand business ties all over the southern Andes. He signed contracts with dozens of subordinate headmen as well as Spanish merchants and officials. One set of connections linked him to Potosí's female indigenous vendors, mostly in the sale of capsicum peppers or *ají*.

### THE MILLS

> Working one night at a water-powered refinery along the river-bank here four Indians were killed in the ore crusher (*mortero*) when a wall collapsed and smashed them. And in another mill, an Indian climbing up from the ore crusher was struck in the head by a cam, which smashed him to pieces.[26]

As we have seen, underground mine work at Potosí was punishing and sometimes deadly. Mill work, which Luis Capoche knew well since he was a mill owner, was only slightly less so. Daily exposure to clouds of silica dust and toxic substances like mercury, lead, and zinc, as well as bone-crushing machinery, was known to be nearly as hazardous as working in a mine. Due to dust inhalation alone, some considered mill work worse than mining.

Spaniards had been building hydraulic and horse-powered ore crushing mills since they arrived in the Indies, sometimes influenced by German, French, Italian, and other non-Iberian millwrights. Several such foreigners were in Potosí in the early 1570s, some listed as builders or designers of water-driven stamp mills.[27] The mills were complex and expensive, in part because

Cerro Rico and silver refinery, ca. 1603. Courtesy of the Hispanic Society of America, New York.

large, durable timbers were needed for camshafts and other moving parts. A typical mill cost 5,000 assayed pesos, which one may compare with the cost of hiring a free Andean worker: as little as 20 pesos a year. A 3,500-peso order for dressed timber from 1588 gives an idea of the expense involved in setting up a mill; building a church would have been cheaper.[28]

Viceroy Toledo believed that multiple hydraulic mills, or *ingenios de agua,* were essential to Potosí's revival, and the records show a boom in their construction after 1572. Potosi's royal magistrate or *corregidor* displaced a number of indigenous inhabitants when assigning mill plots, prompting the town council to intervene, promising compensatory lots. An October 1572 contract described a mill wheel 18 feet in diameter and a foot wide, connected to a cammed axle to lift and drop six stamp hammers. Builders Bartolomé Ramón and Juan Fernández would be aided by an enslaved African man named Juan, sent from La Plata, along with a number of hired Andeans. Several unnamed mulattos worked the forge at another amalgamation mill in 1573. As Peter Bakewell notes, by 1577 a standard design was implemented, with a 24-foot mill wheel and either eight or twelve stamps.[29]

Mining continued apace but on Toledo's arrival there were huge mounds of discarded ores and tailings on hand, waiting to be processed. After 1572, re-milled ores and tailings were mixed with salt and mercury in vast amounts among Potosí's hundred-plus refineries, causing a spike in silver production and with it a spike in mercury emissions, discussed below.[30] The notary records are filled with sales of tailings and muds that might profitably be run through the mills more than once. Toledo's restructuring was hugely profitable, but it had unintended consequences. With new technologies came a proliferation of lawsuits and patch-like decrees. A frustrated Toledo banned lawyers from Potosí and all mining camps in April of 1573 for "driving lawsuits," but the order died.[31]

When it came to the vital question of water, Potosí was both cursed and blessed. Located in the high southern Andes not far from the Atacama Desert, the Cerro Rico was blessed with a high water table thanks to a short rainy season. This plus the prominence of the peak meant its mines were less prone to flooding than those in other districts, such as Porco. When it came to powering mill stamps, however, Potosí was cursed with an average annual rainfall of only about 63 centimeters or 25 inches. Even in good years the rains were unpredictable, and the stream that ran through town, La Ribera, was a nasty dribble by July or August. On the plus side, Potosí boasted a hot springs farther downstream, at Tarapaya, and this steady source of water was sufficient to power a few dozen mills—as long as one could afford to transport heavy ores on the backs of llamas.

The great hope for the milling industry lay in the modest Kari-Kari mountain range to the east of town. The Kari-Kari mountains were not high by Andean standards, but at just over 5,000 meters (16,000 feet) above sea level they could capture a bit of snow and substantial rain from time to time. A cluster of old glacial cirques formed small seasonal lakes or marshes in the rainy season, and Toledo and his advisors decided to turn a dozen or more of these natural depressions into full-scale reservoirs. The reservoirs were in turn linked up to the Ribera, or main creek, via a series of canals and aqueducts. Thus, the Imperial Villa could be supplied with water to power crushing mills year-round if the reservoirs were properly managed. The Kari-Kari endeavor was a huge public works project, the only one of its kind in the Spanish colonies with the exception of the drainage of Lake Texcoco to protect Mexico City from seasonal flooding.[32] Both projects relied on the labor of thousands of indigenous draftees. The difference in this case is that the Potosí project actually worked, although thanks to poor maintenance it occasionally proved deadly.

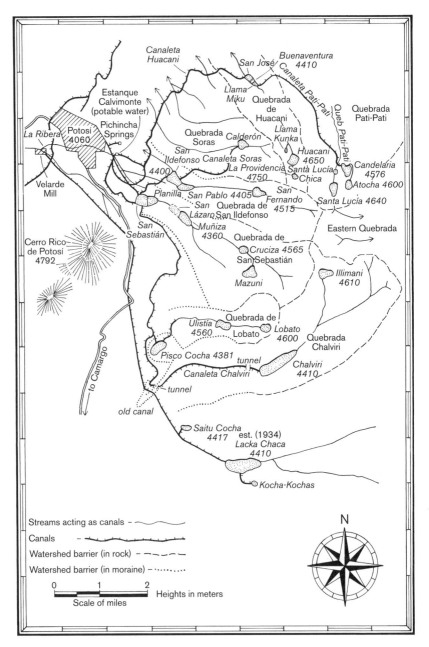

MAP 4. The reservoirs and aqueducts of Potosí's Kari Kari Range (after Rudolph).

Toledo eased credit for those willing to invest in ore crushing mills, but they were of little use by themselves. They simply pulverized ore that had to be refined by some method other than smelting. The method favored by Viceroy Toledo was mercury amalgamation, known since ancient times but only practiced on a near-industrial scale in the mid-sixteenth century. In the 1550s a merchant from Seville named Bartolomé de Medina developed a process, apparently with help from German acquaintances, to refine the silver ores of Pachuca, Mexico. Medina's method used salt along with mercury to extract fine grains of silver from worthless host rock. The resulting amalgam was washed and heated to drive off the mercury, which was partly recollected in a still-like device called a retort, leaving behind a pinecone-shaped ingot of pure silver known as a *piña*.

Where did the steady supply of mercury come from? Miraculously, according to some observers, Spain had possession of two of the world's most productive mercury deposits: Almadén, in La Mancha, and Huancavelica, in Peru. There were even mercury mines in Habsburg Slovenia, at Idria, and these proved crucial in the 1620s and later when production at Almadén and Huancavelica dropped.

In 1572, Medina's amalgamation method was modified by technicians employed by Viceroy Toledo, and soon it became apparent that Potosí's future would be closely tied to its supply of mercury, then known as *azogue* (from the Arabic *az-zuq*). Contracts and decrees referring to the "new mercury refining method" (*beneficio nuevo de asogue*) appear frequently after February 1572.[33] Only a modest portion of the liquid metal used in the Medina process could be recovered by using retorts, and certain types of ore seemed to "consume" more mercury than others. Substantial mercury ended up in the atmosphere, waterways, and soils, but a large part was rendered inert in a muddy residue called calomel.[34]

Subcontractors who bid for the exclusive privilege ran the mercury mines and refineries at Almadén and Huancavelica, but the Spanish crown set prices and routed supply, in part to gain steady revenue, but also to keep tabs on usage in hopes of checking tax evasion among silver miners and refiners.[35] It was not long before the crown advanced mercury on credit to Potosí's many silver refiners, a group known as *azogueros* or "mercury men," in hopes of stimulating the industry. This practice created a lasting dependency and deep debts, further tying Potosí's private citizens to the crown.

Mercury was extracted from cinnabar, a sulfide ore used since ancient times as a pigment (vermillion).[36] Mining cinnabar was among the deadliest tasks imaginable, rivaled only by refining it to extract mercury vapor using earthenware condensers. As had been done in the mercury mines of Almadén in Spain, the heavy, liquid metal of Huancavelica was packaged in sheepskins. It was then carried down to the Pacific coast at Chincha on mules or llamas, where it was taken by ship to Arica. Here it was warehoused and periodically sent, again on llamas or mules, to Potosí. Mercury was sold by the hundredweight to mill owners from the offices of the royal treasury, located next door to yet another Toledo innovation: the royal mint.

## THE POTOSÍ MINT

Viceroy Toledo's Andean interventions were many, and nearly all were controversial. This was true of the mita and the amalgamation mills, but also of the royal mint, established at Potosí in 1574 and fully operational the following year. There had been a mint at Lima, the viceregal capital, and it had been moved briefly to La Plata, a few days' walk to the east of Potosí. But Toledo was not a trusting man. He believed that silver processing and taxing ought to be concentrated in the Imperial Villa itself, in the shadow of the Cerro Rico. Otherwise, he felt, there would be too many routes for silver to escape the king's taxmen.

The royal mint was not meant to convert all of Potosí's silver into coins, but rather to render a portion of it—Toledo suggested a third—into money to smooth transactions within the colonies themselves, in this case within the very large Viceroyalty of Peru, which stretched from Panama to Buenos Aires. Outside the everyday marketplace, two such transactions that demanded cash were paying native laborers and paying tribute: the wage / head-tax nexus. Toledo hoped to see the king recoup this coinage given out in payroll and recollected as tribute. The mint was also valuable in collecting seigniorage, a coining fee charged by the king.

The Potosí mint, like many early modern institutions, mixed state and private interests. Its employee roster reflected this blend. Crown officials appointed a treasurer, assayer, smelter, master of weights and measures, and a bailiff. These men in turn hired lower-status individuals, usually Spanish-born men, to serve as coiners, porters, and assistants. All mint officers and employees were made to sign oaths promising honest behavior. They were also bonded by prominent Potosí householders. There was some physical labor involved in these jobs, particularly assaying and coining, but the hardest work performed in the mint consisted of two things: smelting coin metal and cutting and preparing coin blanks for stamping. These jobs were done by indigenous draftees and enslaved Africans.[37]

Much like the mints of Europe in the sixteenth century, the early Potosí *casa de la moneda* was more artisan shop than factory. Nothing was mechanized, not even the bellows for the furnaces. Coins were made by hand. Rich merchants and mill owners brought silver bars to the mint from the royal treasury office next door, where they paid their most important tax, the *quinto real* or royal fifth. They then contracted with the mint's blank-cutting overseers, of which there were initially four, for a quantity of coins, usually to be produced within a couple of weeks.

Profits were drawn off in the form of fractional fees according to a royally mandated schedule. The king in the end got a small percentage of all coins created or their equivalent in bullion, as did the treasurer, cutting-house overseer, bailiff, and so on. These officers were critical since they guaranteed the proper weight and quality of coins with the king's name on them. The assayer, whose initial was also stamped on the coins alongside the "P" of Potosí, faced the death penalty should his products not meet the royal standard. Since coin metal was just under 7 percent copper by law, the merchant or mill owner came away with a slight cash profit, too. For him, high production volume was key.

Since *potosinos* at all social levels had long been accustomed to trading ingots, bars, and bits of silver—and even hunks of high-graded ore, or *corpa*—the royal mint struggled at first. This surprised Viceroy Toledo, who assumed that a mint in the heart of the Imperial Villa would be embraced. Many people had complained loudly, after all, of the absence of trustworthy currency. Yet silver merchants and mill owners were wary of the highly regulated environment of the mint, which kept careful records and thus might be used to pressure or even prosecute someone who fell from favor.

Even so, within a decade of its 1574 launch, Potosí's richest merchants began to see how the royal mint could open new avenues of profit making, essentially lubricating the regional credit market. Before long a vibrant futures trade in silver, paid for with advances of coin, was in place. Like several of Toledo's other innovations, this one would turn out to be cursed, a

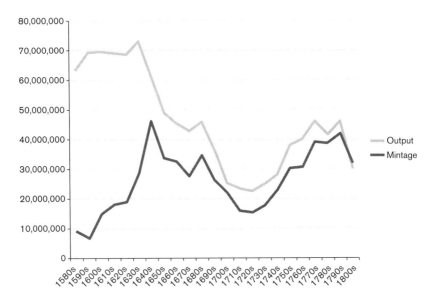

Potosí's registered silver output vs. coin mintage in pesos, ca. 1570–1810.

new avenue for creative accounting and ultimately large-scale malfeasance. It would later become clear that Potosí lacked the stable institutions needed even to watch over a rule-bound royal mint, much less to regulate high finance.

### RESULTS

> Without surpassing or exceeding the limits of truth I can affirm that this Imperial Villa of Potosí ... is the richest, most opulent, and most renowned of any known on the entire planet, and the one to yield the most rents to its king, and more silver has gone out from it alone than from all the others in the world put together, and one could even say that it enriches all of Europe, Asia, and Africa.
>
> —MARTÍN DE MURÚA, 1616[38]

Viceroy Toledo's great machine yielded the results desired by Philip II. Potosí went from bust to boom almost overnight, and by 1592 the Cerro Rico was producing more silver than anyone could have imagined. In that year alone the mines and mills yielded 444,000 lbs. or 200,000 kg of pure silver, or rather, that was how much Potosí's mine and mill owners *reported*. How much more escaped the books is unknown. Potosí would never again register so much silver, but official annual output remained above 300,000 lbs. or 136,000 kg through the early 1640s, when a lasting crisis hit.

Toledo had been given a nearly free hand and he had used it to revitalize Potosí by introducing mercury amalgamation and water-powered stamp mills and their necessary infrastructure. Just as importantly, Toledo formalized and expanded the mita to supply a steady flow of workers to the Cerro Rico and to the mercury mines of Huancavelica. In addition, Toledo moved the royal mint to Potosí in hopes of priming a genuine money economy. Other "reforms" included the vast native resettlement program known as the *reducciones* that went far beyond the mita zone, plus punishment of native enemies, from the rebel Incas of Vilcabamba to the Chiriguanaes of the La Plata frontier. Toledo even sought to diminish the fame of the Incas in print by encouraging historians to paint them as intolerable tyrants.

Toledo failed to kill the memory of the Incas, and the Chiriguanaes chased the viceroy out of their territory. Maroons threatened the silver pipeline in Panama in the last years of Toledo's tenure, and, thanks largely to Francis Drake, "pirate heretics" menaced the Pacific for the first time. Soon after the viceroy's departure for Spain in 1580, the forced resettlement program of the *reducciones* lost force, and even the Potosí mita diminished in scope and intensity, replaced by squads of free workers and eventually systematic buyouts. For all this, no one doubted the significance of Toledo's work throughout the Viceroyalty of Peru. He was the great lawgiver, the incorruptible "majordomo of the king," the model viceroy.

## ALL THE KING'S HORSES

What we call the Spanish Empire was known in Viceroy Toledo's day as the Hispanic Monarchy, a scattered conglomeration of kingdoms, principalities, duchies, protectorates, and military outposts. The "Western Indies," as the Spanish Americas were called, fell under the jurisdiction of the Kingdom of Castile, and the Habsburg kings of Spain relied mostly on income gathered from these domains to prosecute their wars. Beginning with Charles V, the Habsburgs were especially reliant on American silver, which in this era came mostly from Potosí.

A "composite empire" was not easily governed, and the Spanish Habsburgs spent vast amounts of American silver just trying to hold onto their inheritance. The Netherlands were in open rebellion beginning in the 1560s, and various Italian subjects resisted Habsburg claims, often with France (or the pope) as spoiler. War with the Ottomans put a huge strain on Spain's naval capacity, and corsairs of all nations preyed on Spanish treasure vessels and other shipping. Potosí silver was the sinews of early modern war but it was also the target of many newly armed predators.

Historians do not dispute the importance of Potosí silver in funding Habsburg Spain's seemingly endless wars on all fronts, but they have disagreed on the nature of royal finances, specifically the king's creditworthiness. For many years, it was assumed that Philip II made mostly bad choices when it came to borrowing money from European bankers, most of them Genoese or German. Despite a flood of American treasure, Philip II was forced to suspend payments in 1557, 1575, and 1596. These repeated "bankruptcies" have been touted as evidence of chronic fiscal mismanagement.

Scholars have revisited Philip II's accounts only to discover that he was far more fiscally conservative than once believed.[39] Although he did spend beyond his means, and pet projects such as the massive Escorial Palace led critics to say he had discovered a magic formula for turning silver into stone, the king suspended payments only on short-term loans and when cash ceased to flow, for example when a treasure fleet was delayed. Backed by the promise of Potosí silver, royal bonds remained sound. Indeed, Spanish *juros* were among the best investments available.

Although economic historians have rightly stressed that Castilians were taxed far more heavily than Spanish Americans, there remains no doubt that the king's credit relied on one type of commodity future: Potosí silver. And just as Potosí silver was the sinews of war and the sap of the tree of state, it was also the blood of trade. The trick for ambitious Spanish kings such as Philip II was to tax his millions of subjects' production and commerce just enough but not too much, so as not to strangle either. Introduction of a modest sales tax in 1592 was enough to provoke armed rebellion in Quito. Long-distance commercial agents were also touchy, limiting Philip II's mercantilist aspirations. Trade was officially routed through merchant consortia, or *consulados,* and these merchants handed a portion of profits to the king in exchange for exclusive control of various products and routes. There was never any question about who held the reins of power when push came to shove. Ultimately, however, the king for whom "the world was not enough" was always negotiating with the consulados and with his mostly foreign bankers over access to American silver.

Fiscal responsibility may be an obsession of our time, but for Philip II and his successors, treasure was a means to a millenarian end: hastening the second coming of Jesus Christ by the spread and defense of Roman Catholicism. Viceroy Toledo's attempts to harness the subsidiary kingdom of Peru's resources toward maximum production of Potosí silver were thus central to a global hegemonic project, not one of wealth generation for its own sake or even a European "Grand Strategy." Yet for subjects of the king's many and diverse domains, royal tax demands could seem less than righteous, prompting evasion, contraband trade, and even outright revolt. The mercantilist ideal of a closed imperial system would be more fully developed by other European monarchs in the seventeenth century, but Philip II's incessant search for new revenue streams enabled by access to massive amounts of Potosí silver set the stage for modern state finance.

### POTOSÍ GOES TRANSPACIFIC

It was precisely when Viceroy Toledo began building his great silver machine in Upper Peru that the Spanish opened regular transpacific trade with China from Mexico via the Philippines. Named for Philip II when he was still a prince, and partially conquered in the 1560s, the Philippines and especially the port of Manila on the northern island of Luzon gave Spain a foothold in Asia from which to compete with the Portuguese, at the time the only other Europeans active in the region.

The East and Southeast Asian trade circuit was ancient and rich in exotic commodities, yet like Europe and the Mediterranean, it was starved for hard cash, particularly silver. Japan produced silver, but not enough to fill the void. Spanish America, and especially Potosí in the decades after Toledo, was poised to meet transpacific demand. Despite some fairly solid estimates, we remain uncertain as to how much Potosí silver reached Asia via this route. In the late sixteenth century, annual shipments of several million pesos' worth were common.[40]

At first a military outpost in the Portuguese style, Manila became the seat of a circuit court and home to Spanish royal officials, along with merchants and missionaries, most of them connected to their bases in Mexico, whose viceroy technically ruled the archipelago. In 1571, regular sailings of the

Manila galleon or *nao de la China* began, departing from and putting in at Acapulco each year. Right away, Lima's merchants began sending feeder ships to supply the transpacific galleons with Potosí silver in exchange for silk and other fine Asian goods. Potosi's notary records list Chinese fabrics in detail, along with lacquerware, porcelain, fans, carved ivory, spices, and other East Asian imports.[41]

It was a heady moment in the history of global commerce. For the first time since the days of Columbus, colonial traders could bypass Spain altogether, sending hard cash to Asia directly from the Americas in exchange for cheap, high-quality luxury goods. There was even a trade in East and South Asian slaves, whose numbers were significant in Mexico. Asian slaves were quite rare in Potosí, but several arrived from Lima in the early seventeenth century.[42]

The Pacific rim was connected, but what was good for the colonists, and even for Lima's consulado, was not good for Spain's peninsular merchants. Representatives of the powerful merchant guild of Seville howled in protest, pressuring Philip II and his successor, Philip III, to close the Potosí feeder line from Lima to Acapulco and to limit overall shipments of silver to Manila.

Indebted to the Seville merchants, the king complied. But there was no stopping the transpacific flow once it began. The China trade via Manila was simply too lucrative even for the most loyal Spanish bureaucrat or military officer to ignore. Priests and other Church officials were also involved. One individual to benefit from the new system, if only by accident, was Isabel de Barreto. Wife of the explorer Alvaro de Mendaña, Barreto left her native Lima in 1594 as co-leader of the ill-starred Solomon Islands expedition. Mendaña died soon after landing along with most of the expedition's crew, but Barreto reached Manila, sold her remaining ship, purchased a load of Chinese silk, and returned to Peru via Acapulco, making a killing in the exchange.[43] This was the new world of transoceanic trade that Potosí silver had helped to create.

Francisco de Toledo was the only viceroy to visit Potosí in its heyday. A firebrand, he chastised residents for disorderly mining practices and for felling every tree and bush within 25 leagues of town. Laying down his laws in 1574, he told potosinos that with proper management, the Cerro Rico alone would provide enough silver to last 300 years.[44] It was an extravagant claim, but it was taken to heart by Spain's kings and other world monarchs.

For certain European observers, the mita-driven and mercury-soaked "machine" Toledo created and set in motion was a marvelous automaton. It might need fuel, grease, or repairs, but as long as "Indians" could be found to staff it, it would not cease to pump treasure into the world. Toledo's decrees were disputed, and native workers resisted, yet in the end the silver-making machine, now also a cash machine with the addition of the mint, took on a life of its own. The viceroy's great apparatus was a modern marvel, yet observers also noted that it was a noisy, crushing, twenty-four-hour polluting killer, a monster that ate men and poisoned women and children. Was this trade-off simply the price of modernity, or perhaps better said: the price of Spain's claim to be the defender of the Universal Faith?

After Toledo, the steady beat of Potosí's mills and the clink of its newly minted coins hammered away at the Spanish conscience. Priests, headmen, and villagers, even some local elites denounced the mita as immoral. As one priest put it, even if the king's demand for treasure was righteous, Toledo's Potosí and Huancavelica mitas were effectively killing New World converts in the name of financing the struggle against Old World heresy. God's imagination could not possibly be so limited.

Yet Potosí silver had long since become addictive, and more so with Toledo's promise of a limitless stream. Even as Toledo consolidated the machine of the Cerro Rico and the mills of Potosí, prospectors fanned out into the countryside in search of new strikes, some of them promising. Potosí's incessant demand for workers, mercury, fuel, timber, and all manner of food and merchandise kept most peoples' attention focused on the Imperial Villa, but it had also become a base, effectively a regional capital once the corregidor moved here from La Plata on Toledo's orders. The restored Imperial Villa became newly legendary for its opulence and decadence, its piety and violence. Thanks to Toledo, it was one of the most populous urban conglomerations on the planet, possibly the first great factory town of the modern world.

# FOUR

# An Improbable Global City

Chat and conversation among the Indian prostitutes, sitting in a circle.

They say: "Sister, dear, let's go to Cuzco, to Potosí, to Huamanga, to the mines, to Lima . . . The Spaniards and the blacks will give us money. Perhaps we'll die with the adulterers, with the Spaniards."

They say: "Sister, friend, let's go to the cities, to Lima. Sister, let's not die. There, even if we die with the Spaniards, it won't be with the Indian *mitayos*."

—FELIPE GUAMAN POMA DE AYALA, CA. 1615[1]

IN 1592, THE YEAR OF POTOSÍ's highest registered silver production, a foreign resident merchant known as Cornelis Lamberto sought legal help. Lamberto, who had left his wife, Inés de Pavia, in Seville some years before, had been ordered to return to her. By royal decree, foreigners were not to stay in the colonies if unmarried or if separated from wives in Spain or elsewhere. Rootless outsiders could not be trusted. Lamberto protested that he could not travel due to an advanced medical condition, the symptoms of which are described in excruciating detail in his written petition by a series of doctors he called upon as witnesses. Unless he was paying the doctors to perjure themselves, Lamberto was most likely suffering from late-stage syphilis.[2]

One Potosí surgeon testified that five years earlier he had opened a pustule that had appeared midway between Lamberto's anus and testicles. It had never properly healed. The ailing merchant had been urinating out of this new orifice ever since, and other openings had lately appeared nearby, including one on a buttock. Some had been closed by the application of "buttons of fire," a reference to a therapy known as cautery.

Given these problems, which had cost Lamberto many thousands of silver pesos to treat, mostly without success, five of Potosí's top physicians argued against forced travel. Lamberto could not even ride a horse or mule on a woman's sidesaddle without great pain and danger of infection, and besides, one doctor noted, he could not possibly sustain "carnal access" with his wife since the inflammation caused by an erection would do irreparable harm. More significantly, no semen could pass through his member, as that "artery," too, had been severed. La Plata's regional circuit court agreed with the surgeons' warning and recommended that Cornelis Lamberto travel only after being cured. He had written proof of sending cash remittances and bar silver to his wife in Spain as well. Inés de Pavia was being cared for properly, not abandoned.

Potosí was known for its nightlife. An anonymous visitor in 1603 reported: "There are 700 or 800 men, more rather than less, who are idle, and whose occupation is ambling and gambling, and there are 120 women, [respectably dressed] in shawls and petticoats, who are openly known to occupy themselves in the amorous profession, and there are a great many Indian women who occupy themselves in the same business."[3] As suggested by the opening quote from around 1615, penned by the native Andean writer Felipe Guaman Poma de Ayala, prostitution was understood to be common in mining towns such as Potosí.

It is tempting to emphasize, as many colonial observers did, the debauchery that seemed to follow from Potosí's silver bonanza, certainly not an outcome desired by Viceroy Toledo. Yet we must balance this image of the lawless boomtown with what appears to be a functional marketplace and a burgeoning administrative and religious center. The Imperial Villa was large enough and permanent enough to sustain a wide range of behaviors, yet it was also fragile enough and its population transient enough to be plagued by social as well as economic uncertainty. Men like Cornelis Lamberto came from afar and met their fates, yet Potosí, improbable city and inexhaustible mine, survived, regenerated by the blood, sweat, and brains of each new migrant.

This chapter treats the rise of the Imperial Villa of Potosí as a city that was home to tens of thousands of consumers of everything from Cuzco coca to Chinese silk. It looks to women's lives as well as men's, and spans the social hierarchy. By focusing on consumption, this chapter ties Potosí more closely to the rest of the world. We saw in the last chapter how Potosí silver fueled Habsburg pretentions in Europe and the Mediterranean even as it linked up to East Asian markets via the transpacific trade after 1571. But another important new link appeared around 1590: to West Central Africa via Buenos Aires, a disputed trade route that allowed Portuguese slave traders direct access to Potosí silver. Some luxury trade goods reached the Andes from this direction, but far more important was an influx of West Central Africans who brought new cultural influences to Potosí, and their labor contributed to the complexity of the urban and regional economy. In the end we are faced with a paradox: was Potosí an eternal boomtown in cosmopolitan flux or just a "normal" Spanish colonial city suffering from its own peculiar growing pains?

## THE IMPERIAL VILLA OF POTOSÍ
### IN 1603: A SKETCH

There also used to be on this mountain much hunting of vicuñas, guanacos, and vizcachas . . . There were also deer with antlers, and now not even grass is found on the mountain, not even where you could find the roots of trees, which is what is most alarming, since all of it is a rocky mass with very little or no earth on it, spread over with the tailings from the veins, which are of live rock.

—ANON. 1603[4]

In 1603, an anonymous Potosí visitor composed a detailed description of the city, mountain, and mines, outlining the major transformations that had occurred in just under sixty years. The account includes the watercolor image of the Cerro Rico with a refining mill in the foreground that we saw in the last chapter (see image on page 80), plus a detailed city plan (basis for Map 3) and the miniature watercolor depicting native Andeans operating wind furnaces or *guairas* that opened chapter 2 (see image on page 47).[5] The 1603 report was evidently commissioned by Peru's Viceroy Luis de Velasco the Younger. He had been promoted to Lima from Mexico City in 1596, and reforming the Potosí *mita* was one of his aims. A string of future viceroys would make the same righteous claim to fame, but to little avail.

Despite its start as a rough-and-tumble mining camp, Potosí as painted and described in 1603 was laid out like most Spanish American cities: on a cardinally arranged grid centered on a main plaza. For a mining town in rolling terrain, this was somewhat unusual, but it was in accordance with Philip II's instructions. In 1603, the Imperial Villa was said to be permanent home to at least 60,000 native Andeans living in thirteen parishes arranged like townships or encampments against the north flank of the Cerro Rico. Another parish would soon be added. Known as *rancherías,* Potosí's native barrios did not follow the Spanish grid. The painter of the 1603 map rendered them as nothing but a field of boulders dotted with churches.

Spaniards, concentrated in the city center, were said to number at least 6,000, two-thirds of them men. The number presumably included other Europeans. Africans, most of them enslaved, numbered some 5,000. About 250 enslaved Africans arrived annually via Buenos Aires and Brazil each year. People of mixed heritage were not numbered, and the author of the description despaired at estimating the city's total population. He guessed that native Andeans alone might number as many as 120,000, adding, dismissively: "and it is quite certain that there are at least another 120,000 dogs, and they consume more food than even the Indians."

The Imperial Villa was governed by a *corregidor,* a lieutenant, and two *alcaldes* or municipal magistrates. There were also nineteen town councilmen—soon to number twenty-four, as in major Spanish cities such as Seville. A bailiff and fourteen lieutenants were charged with maintaining order in the city, its municipal police force. Two other magistrates kept order and hunted fugitives in the countryside. One scribe worked for the town council, and four others officially served the public in a range of capacities, recording loans, sales, consignments, dowries, wills and testaments, and other transactions. Forty notaries were said to operate independently.

Potosí was home to a sizeable bureaucracy thanks to Viceroy Toledo, who moved the corregidor here from La Plata and gave him power over the mita, the Cerro Rico, the mills, and the reservoirs. Deputies patrolled Porco and other surrounding districts. A royally appointed scribe served the mines, where disputes over claims and labor allotments were frequent. A dozen or more other officers staffed the royal mint and adjacent royal treasury. Three safety inspectors checked mines and refineries as mandated by the king. There were also several tax collectors and minor magistrates, along with dozens of lawyers and clerks (the lawyers having prevailed despite Toledo's attempt to ban them from the city). Serving Potosí's sick, like the unfortunate Cornelis Lamberto who opened this chapter, were three registered physicians, six surgeons, and ten phlebotomists.

The city's principal church sat on the main square facing the Cerro Rico. Its austere early nineteenth-century successor occupies the same space today. The original church was not yet an ashlar masonry structure, but its interior was lavishly decorated. The author of the 1603 account says that the *iglesia mayor's* fine silver lamps included one weighing over 200 lbs. (100 kg), fabricated at a cost of 12,000 pesos. The priest Martín de Murúa described

Potosí's main church a few years later, confirming the existence of a huge silver lamp:

> The main church is of medium size, although it ought to be larger given the people who surround the villa, but it is most rich in costly ornaments. The lamp that burns before the most holy sacrament contains 420 marks [210 lbs.] of silver, and two others, one of Our Lady of the Conception and the other of the sacrament contain 100 marks, and the chapel of St. Ann they adorn with three lamps of 80 marks a piece, and that of All Souls and St. Crispin at another 80 marks a piece. And this church is continually served by more than thirty priests, not counting deacons, sextons, and its vicar, all of whom enjoy very rich offerings and perquisites.[6]

Potosí's several monastic compounds housed Dominicans, Franciscans, Augustinians, Mercedarians, and Jesuits. The Imperial Villa lacked nunneries until after 1650, so women wishing to take the veil were sent to La Plata, Cuzco, Arequipa, or Lima. Several of Potosí's religious buildings were adorned with intricate *mudéjar* woodwork ceilings, fine *estofado* sculpture, elaborate canvases both imported and locally painted, and of course, handcrafted silver paraphernalia of all sorts. Many artisans were indigenous, including Francisco Tito Yupanqui, who sculpted the famous Virgin of Copacabana in 1582. A prayer to this Virgin was said to have saved a poor mitayo from death in a refining mill in 1603.[7] The Inquisition had no tribunal in the Imperial Villa, but it counted on a commissioner, plus three notaries and six *familiares* or common representatives (the Inquisition's "ears," more or less). Potosí also boasted an ecclesiastical court with its district attorneys and notaries.

The city counted eighty *pulperías* that doubled as grocery stores and taverns. Twenty-four shops specialized in European dry goods, which meant they also sold Chinese silk and Indian cotton fabrics. These imports show up routinely in merchant inventories. Twenty-five stores were said to be owned by Indians, devoted solely to selling hats, both European- and American-made. Another eight shops were devoted to selling hats to Spaniards. Hats were clearly needed in Potosí, as were shoes. Twenty-eight shoemakers provided footwear, mostly in goatskin, or "cordovan," but we know from notary records that artisans as far away as Quito were sending thousands of pairs of prefabricated shoes, including children's shoes, all the way to Potosí.[8]

American-made cloth from Tucumán, Quito, Huánuco, and central Mexico, plus simple jacket-and-breeches outfits sewn in the hinterland of Cuzco, sold all over town, clothing almost everyone of indigenous or African

debaxo al miferable Indio, y los otros que no alcançauan a o-
fenderle, moliã los metales, mouiendofe al cõpas de la rueda.

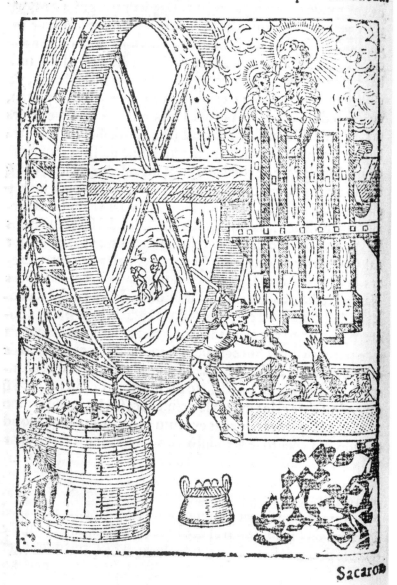

Sacaron

"Miracle of the Mill Stamps," ca. 1603, Alonso Ramos Gavilán, *Historia del Célebre Santuario de Nuestra Señora de Copacabana* (1621). Courtesy of the Hispanic Society of America, New York.

ancestry, especially men. Fine Andean *cumbe* cloth was sold mostly to indigenous women. It shows up frequently in their wills and inventories. According to the author of the 1603 account, coarser fabrics went to make 100,000 gunnysacks, used to carry ore from the Cerro Rico's dozens of mines. The city counted six master farriers and four candle makers. Chandlers fashioned candles for church use with imported wax, lumination being tied to the souls of purgatory. Tallow candles for the mines were often fabricated by native Andean women.

There were also six confectioneries and six pastry shops, plus twenty restaurants providing daily meals of meat or fish for 30 pesos a month. Some taverns doubled as inns. Fish were brought all the way from the Pacific Ocean via Cobija, but more came from the fresh but still distant waters of Lake Titicaca.[9] Potosí counted twenty-eight bakeries, said to consume 250 bushels of flour daily. Wine sales were estimated at 50,000 jugs a year, and chicha sales at 1.6 million jugs. Potosí's butchers slaughtered some 4,000 head of beef cattle each year, along with 50,000 sheep and 40,000 llamas. A salaried magistrate oversaw the municipal slaughterhouse.

Native Andeans and others consumed an estimated 60,000 baskets of coca a year, plus 14,000 baskets of chili peppers. Sugar consumption totaled some 24,000 lbs., and cane syrup about 2,000 jugs. Fruit conserves amounted to about 12,000 lbs. Lowland farms provided 20,000 cheeses and 25,000 jugs of lard, along with substantial ham, bacon, and salted pork loin and tongue. Several thousand jugs of olives and olive oil were consumed annually in Potosí, mostly imported from Spain at this time, although olive groves were beginning to mature in Peru. A sale of "dates, almonds, and fat olives" from 1587 no doubt originated in the Mediterranean.[10]

Eight thousand jugs of vinegar may also have been imported from the Iberian Peninsula according to the 1603 report, although Peruvian vineyards were already producing it. Jerked meat, made from various animals, totaled 120,000 lbs. Figs, produced by this time in Peru, came to nearly 100,000 lbs., and prior to the massive eruption of Huaynaputina Volcano near Arequipa in 1600, Potosí consumed 600,000 lbs. of raisins each year, probably including prunes and apricots.[11] Garden vegetables and fruits were brought to market daily from warm valleys to the east and north.

Native Andean staples included freeze-dried potatoes, or *chuño,* which came from the highlands, some 20,000 bushels a year. Indigenous women in the countryside spent considerable time preparing this food. To this was added 40,000 bushels of fresh potatoes and 40,000 bushels of oca, another tuber often used to thicken soups. Quinoa is not mentioned in the 1603 account, but it is noted elsewhere. It was typically consumed in soups and stews. Maize consumption totaled 50,000 bushels or more, most for brewing chicha.

The anonymous author also gives considerable attention to Potosí's mines and refineries, but there is a sense in this and in Diego de Ocaña's account from about the same time that the city itself, the Imperial Villa, had become a wonder or marvel in its own right. It is clear from both reports that women—Andean, African, European, and mixed—were at the heart of this transformation. Potosí, always cycling through thousands of migrants, was also reproducing itself thanks to a numerous and increasingly diverse female population.

## ENTERPRISING AND ADVENTUROUS WOMEN

There are more than 100 women's houses where they are occupied in laundering clothes, and it is a lucrative thing and they
have much to do, making their rounds, washing and starching a
flat lace collar at 4 reals, and any fancy one at 8 reals.

—ANON. 1603

Although often imagined as a man's world, the Cerro Rico and Imperial Villa of Potosí survived thanks to women.[12] Traces of their actions suffuse the documentary record, particularly in notary books and town council minutes, but also in court cases and ecclesiastical registers. Chroniclers such as Luis Capoche tell us how indigenous women provided labor power to mineworkers in the form of nourishment. Many such women, mostly peasants from highland villages, trekked to the flanks of the Cerro Rico with their husbands and male relatives loaded down with food and cookware. Some hiked up the mountain daily to deliver hot meals. Others set up stalls to sell stews, roast meat, and whatever else was available. Some indigenous women opened small restaurants and a few got rich, but most went home to life in the countryside when menfolk finished their "turn" in the mines and refineries.

Some women pursued lives independent of male relatives, temporary mates, or husbands. This required a degree of banding together and occasionally locating powerful allies who could serve as patrons or legal protectors. Male Spanish authorities tended to identify women only in terms of their relationships with men: as wives, widows, mothers, sisters, daughters, concubines, or prostitutes. One means for women to escape this trap was to participate as sisters in religious sodalities, although even here women were expected to listen to if not follow the orders of a male priest. Feminine power was by definition subversive.

Yet signs of female independence were everywhere in Potosí. Diego de Ocaña claimed that indigenous women in particular were remarkably free-willed and prone to leave their husbands when unsatisfied. Ocaña remarked on another kind of situation, emphasizing the reliance of certain footloose Spanish men on indigenous and African women—also pointing to self-destructive masculinity:

> The number of Spanish people in Potosí is many, almost as many as the Indians; and many "soldiers" who wander around without a trade of any kind. And these sustain themselves on gambling and by living in concubinage with rich black women and with rich Indian women, who supply them with food and clothing; and these [soldiers] have nothing more to do than to wander around all day on the cobbled part of the square, where none but the most valiant tread, and their quarrels are so numerous that hardly a day goes by in which there are not two or three deaths of men stabbed right through.[13]

Despite civil and religious strictures and limitations, a mining town as large as Potosí offered special opportunities for enterprising women. Potosí's hundreds of market women were mostly indigenous but also included women of mixed and sometimes Spanish heritage. By 1600 or so they were perceived as a threat to male shopkeepers and grocers. *Pulperías* were mostly the preserve of Spanish males. Whereas the owners of these shops, called *pulperos,* had to pay taxes and licensing fees to Potosí's city council, indigenous *chicheras,* as Andean market women were generically known, were exempted from these charges.[14] Throughout the seventeenth century, Potosí's pulperos sought help from the city council to suppress the great indigenous market or *qhatu.*

As more Spanish women arrived in Potosí, their economic roles began to vary. By the mid-seventeenth century as many as a fifth of all refining mills belonged to women, most of them widows. Many other women owned mines, farms, vineyards, and livestock ranches, along with urban real estate and shop fronts. One source of women's economic power derived from Spanish inheritance law. Partible inheritance automatically divided a dead husband's property between the widow and surviving children. The widow got half, the children, equal portions of the other half, regardless of sex.

Widows administered their children's inheritance until they reached legal adulthood at age 25. Combining this legal scenario with Potosí's vagrant and murderous men, actuaries favored the widow.

This is not to say that patriarchy was dead in Potosí, but its power was checked by willful women, Spanish inheritance law, local demographic patterns, and an abundance of economic opportunities made possible by silver. Powerful men pushed back, and women required male legal representation in nearly all court settings. Female literacy was rarely encouraged, and wealthy widows were sometimes exploited by unscrupulous renters or spendthrift sons. Despite all this, several Potosí widows did very well, consolidating family fortunes by choosing competent mine administrators and strategic marriage partners for their children. Like indigenous market women, some Spanish women excelled at the long game.[15]

Others were more impulsive. Indeed, one of the most interesting personages to visit Potosí in the seventeenth century was Catalina de Erauso, a Basque woman who escaped a convent to pursue a life of adventure in the colonies dressed as a man. Although her narrative does not provide dates, it appears that Erauso lived in and around Potosí between 1617 and 1619. She describes driving a pack of llamas to Chuquisaca for a Potosí mine owner before being recruited to help put down a rebel group led by a man she calls Alonso Ibáñez. The other clue she provides is the name of Potosí's corregidor, Rafael Ortiz de Sotomayor, under whom she served.[16]

Bartolomé Arzáns de Orsúa y Vela, a semi-reliable source for these years, does not mention Erauso but he describes Ortiz's campaign against a rebel group led by a "Castilian" called Alonso Fáñez (or Yáñez). He was captured and executed in 1617, as Erauso describes.[17] As one would expect from Erauso's heritage, she sided with the city's Basques, who backed the corregidor. Erauso says she served for two years under an unnamed sergeant major before being drafted into an Eldorado expedition led by a man called Bartolomé de Alba. I have found no mention of this expedition, although we know that one was sent out from Potosí about this time to fight Chiriguanaes along the southeast frontier of Tomina, east of La Plata.

Erauso goes on to say that she drove llamas from Cochabamba to Potosí, stopping along the Pilcomayo River on the way to mill flour, another plausible story. This bucolic interlude was sandwiched between picaresque adventures that included saving a woman from her cuckolded husband and narrowly escaping the noose after killing a man in a duel after a card game. Like a footloose *pícaro,* Erauso made her way back to Spain after a stop in Lima, where her gender subterfuge was exposed, yet she was granted a dispensation from the pope to go on wearing men's clothing until her death around 1650. She ended her adventures as a mule driver in Mexico.

If we may trust Arzáns, Erauso was not alone in her swashbuckling adventures dressed as a man. In the year 1653, according to Arzáns, there lived two "warrior maidens" in Potosí, doña Ana and doña Eustaquia. They were not sisters but they had been reared in the same household after one was orphaned, and they had grown up learning to fire weapons and handle swords with the older brother of one of the girls. Tired of enclosure, the two dressed as men and escaped to the streets of Potosí. They met a young man out to buy bread and he agreed to lead them around town.

By chance the teenage adventurers encountered members of the chief magistrate's night patrol, out to pick fights and rob the innocent, according to Arzáns, rather than to keep the peace or uphold morality. As one of the men approached with his sword drawn doña Eustaquia pulled out her pistol and shot him dead. The others fled. Aided by their companion, the girls made it back to their house, where an enslaved African woman who watched after them let them in. The townsfolk and magistrate remained puzzled by the incident.

Weeks later the "warrior maidens" hit the streets of Potosí again, accompanied by their young male friend, whom Arzáns claims to have met later in his life. The young women now brought along a guitar and dressed like gentlemen, sporting pistols, swords, and bucklers. While singing songs and playing the guitar outside a wealthy townsman's house the three were told to move on since it was assumed they were trying to seduce a woman inside. The girls responded to the challenge with a fight, one of them firing a pistol shot at a group of men that ended up lodged in a door. With this, out came everyone's swords and a melée ensued. As Arzáns describes it:

> They set upon each other from every direction, making such a din with their weapons that it seemed a hundred men were fighting; sparks of fire leaped from their swords, the fierce blows they were exchanging rang, and the voices of the men they were fighting resounded in the street. In the thick of the encounter one of the four said to doña Ana, "Ah, villain, you have wounded me," and rushing at her he administered a brutal thrust with such force that it pierced her shield and wounded her in the chest, tearing through her clothing, jacket, and mail shirt, and wounding her just under the left breast; the girl fell to the ground. When the valiant Eustaquia saw this, she leaped to place herself in front of her sister and, brandishing her cutlass in all directions and very conscious of the danger they were in, nudged doña Ana with her

feet, saying to her in great anguish, "Get up, sister, for our honor is at stake." The injured girl rose to her feet like a lioness and, recognizing the man who had wounded her, said, "Monster, now I will revenge myself for the wound you have given me"; rushing at him fiercely she gave him such a mighty blow with her cutlass that she broke his shield and wounded him in the hand. He, not daring to wait for another, again joined his three companions as doña Ana rejoined doña Eustaquia and the girls fought on like wild things.[18]

According to Arzáns, the "warrior maidens" were again helped by their young male companion (who by cowardice had avoided the fray) back to their home, where they spent two months recovering from their wounds. On a third escape attempt the girls were caught by Eustaquia's father, who locked them in a room and promised severe punishment. The girls managed to escape with the help of their female slave and her brother, who brought them mules and new suits of men's clothing.

Over the next four years the warrior maidens moved from Chuquisaca to Lima, then to Trujillo, returning to Potosí at age 20, when doña Eustaquia inherited her father's estate. He had allegedly died of grief. Arzáns says the girls lived together in La Plata for a few more years, but Ana died from old bullfighting wounds suffered in Lima. Eustaquia died soon after, "grieving for her beloved companion." Arzáns claimed to have seen portraits of the two women dressed as men on a visit to La Plata. "Their beauty," he says, "was beyond my powers of description."[19] Archival evidence of Potosí's "warrior maidens" has not yet surfaced, but other tales told by Bartolomé Arzáns de Orsúa y Vela have been corroborated.

### THE LONG ROAD FROM ANGOLA

Just as women have often been erased from the grand narrative of Potosí, enslaved Africans and their descendants have also been largely forgotten. Most of the enslaved inhabitants of seventeenth-century Potosí arrived from Angola and other parts of West Central Africa via Buenos Aires and Córdoba, an emerging trade hub in the center of Argentina. As we saw in chapter 2, the southern route was Potosí's logical Atlantic connection, yet it remained almost illegal thanks to the powerful merchant guilds of Lima and Seville. Once opened in the 1580s, however, the southern route via Buenos Aires could not be blocked. The anonymous visitor to Potosí in 1603 counted some 5,000 enslaved Africans, and by this time most new arrivals came from

Angola or Congo. Córdoba had a royal customs house by 1622, and its dependency on Potosí deepened. Even Buenos Aires was transformed into a slave society in the early seventeenth century due to this constant traffic.[20]

Around 1630, the governor of Rio de Janeiro, Salvador de Sá y Benavides, made the long overland trek to Potosí to scout commercial opportunities. He married in La Rioja, in northwest Argentina, and then went back to Brazil and eventually spent time at court in Portugal.[21] Despite ongoing struggles with the Dutch, who captured northeast Brazil in 1630 and the main Angolan slave port of Luanda in 1641, Sá did not give up on his dream of expanding the slave trade to Potosí, the South Atlantic's only reliable source of silver. Setting out from Rio de Janeiro, Sá led a successful expedition to retake Angola in 1648. The Dutch were driven from northeast Brazil soon after, in 1654. Through it all, Sá and other Luso-Brazilian officials and merchants supplied Potosí with West Central African slaves—this despite Portugal's own rebellion against Spain in 1640.[22] As will be seen in chapter 6, slaves continued to reach Potosí via Buenos Aires thanks to Dutch, French, and English slavers emulating Salvador de Sá.

The number of enslaved Africans and their descendants in Potosí grew steadily up to the mid-seventeenth century, although we have no proper census. Notary records amply demonstrate how enslaved women, children, and men were added to elite households, but many more were dispatched to the countryside to staff ranches, farms, and vineyards. Traffic in children appears to have been disturbingly common, and some Potosí householders sent special orders for specific types of slaves to Buenos Aires along with bags of silver cash.[23] Even some indigenous *potosinos* purchased enslaved Africans. In 1640, for example, María Ocllo purchased Cristina Angola, age 15, from a Buenos Aires slaver with ties to Salvador de Sá for 380 silver pesos.[24] Caciques and mita captains frequently owned Africans slaves, in part to enhance their status. In addition to domestic service and wet-nursing, some enslaved African women earned money for their owners by selling soups and stews on the streets of the Imperial Villa. Prices for enslaved women in Potosí typically exceeded those for men after 1640, reaching as high as 1,000 pesos.

Some enslaved African men were known for their willful independence, as in the strange case of "El Duende," or "The Hobgoblin." Writing in the early eighteenth century, the local historian Arzáns relates El Duende's tale, describing how he robbed, raped, and otherwise raised hell in the Imperial Villa in the early 1650s before being captured and executed. Astonishingly, El Duende, aka Juan Pérez, appears in the archival record, not as a hell-raiser but as a victim of a misunderstanding that blew up into a street fight. His case and other documents hint at a thriving black subculture, complete with rival armed factions as well as religious confraternities.[25]

In sum, although several enslaved Africans in seventeenth-century Potosí managed to carve out their own socio-religious spaces, and a few found the means to self-purchase or to purchase loved ones, they were still treated as commodities by people of means, much like bars of silver or "pieces of eight." Slaves, too, were described as *piezas,* or units of value, and like silver bars they were marked all over with brands, including the royal crown to prove taxation. The Imperial Villa may have offered some special opportunities for social advancement, but we should not overestimate this. The estate inventories of several Potosí elites suggest that the thousands of slaves they dispatched to tend their vineyards in the Pilcomayo basin lived in utter squalor and total isolation.[26]

CITY OF SPECTACLE

Like other major Spanish American cities, Potosí was renowned for its opulent festivals and processions, mostly religious but also celebrating secular milestones such as military victories, royal weddings, and prodigious occurrences. The line between sacred and profane was thin, however, and most religious festivities entailed carnal release and wildly inventive social inversion as ordinary elements. Only religious processions organized to end earthquakes, droughts, and plagues tended to remain solemn. Funerals could go both ways: mourning death before celebrating life.

Festivals and commemorations cost money, and in this Potosí was blessed. Some of the best descriptions of the city's colonial festival culture are found in the writings of Diego de Ocaña, alms collector for the Virgin of Guadalupe. Ocaña raised funds for his favorite virgin while cleverly doing his best to promote her cult among Potosí's vast and diverse population.[27] Ocaña describes an equestrian challenge that took place in the main plaza in late September 1601. Known as the "contest of the ring," it was part of the eight-day-long feast of Guadalupe.

If we can trust Ocaña, the contest was an opportunity to display wealth and status as well as piety. Elite men and women occupied adjoining grandstands, with an image of Guadalupe in a cabinet surrounded by 200,000 ducats' worth of silver bars and ingots. The elaborate fiesta included a showdown between a lance-bearing "knight of the Church" and Satan himself, or rather, a deft rider dressed as Lucifer. The lead characters in the coming battle between Good and Evil rode swiftly into the plaza, exchanging speeches and letters. When the Virgin's image was revealed by a dropped curtain, the master of ceremonies displayed a placard saying:

> In my lady, although brown,
> She encompasses so much beauty,
> That she holds up both heaven and earth.

Into the square rode the Prince of Darkness to deliver a letter that began in typical Baroque fashion:

> From the dark dungeon of these infernal caverns where I have my royal throne of torment, with those nobles of an angelic nature who descended with me, in the middle of the Stygian lake, burning with live flames of sulfur, incited by the great fire of envy . . . etc.

After this challenge to the Knight of the Church, the judges of the contest replied with their own letter, which began: "Your letter we receive, Prince of Darkness, in which we see demonstrated your ancient arrogance and how you and those of your kingdom are authors of falsehood." The rider dressed as the Devil snatched the letter and rode off in a flash, throwing broadsides that said:

> The Prince of Tartary, who of sulfur
> Sustains himself in the dark cavern,
> Will present himself at half past five,
> And he thanks those who shall suffer until then.[28]

Ocaña thus offers us a small taste of the rich culture of *comedias* or short plays that must have occupied so many idle residents of Potosí. A proper theater space or *coliseo de comedias* opened in 1616, but many plays continued to be performed outside. When word of Philip IV's coronation arrived in 1621, the city council planned celebrations that bankrupted the treasury. The canonization of Ignatius of Loyola the following year elicited even greater display.

Visiting in 1638, priest Pedro Ramírez del Águila found the Imperial Villa still addicted to display, both "pertaining to the divine service" and much "that may seem superfluous."[29] Sacred and profane were not easy to separate, as in the case of the fiestas described by Diego de Ocaña. Even as the city entered hard times, Ramírez del Águila called Potosí's celebrations "the greatest in the kingdom." He lauded the city for its astonishing liberality, another characteristic that attracted priests like bees to honey. As will be seen in chapter 6, alms seekers came from as far away as Baghdad.


## THE LITERATE CITY

Rare inventories hint at the books available in Potosí in its heyday.[30] Of special interest is the 1614 inventory of Portuguese bookseller Valentín de Acosta. Acosta, whose bookshop was on Potosí's main plaza, listed over 200 titles, about half of them religious. The remainder included books of chivalry, multivolume histories, songbooks, poetry collections, classical works, and technical manuals. Cervantes's *Don Quixote* does not appear on Acosta's list, but there is evidence from nearby La Plata that it was in circulation (part II had just been published in 1614).

Cervantes refers to Potosí in *Don Quixote* and other works, including the short story "The Jealous Extremaduran." These show up in local inventories a few years after Acosta. On Acosta's list was Mateo Alemán's prohibited 1599 novel, *The Life of the Pícaro Guzmán de Alfarache*. The second part was published in 1604, and it also appeared quickly in Potosí. Along with his many titles, Acosta kept a workshop full of bookbinding tools, but whether he published locally authored items, we do not know.

Acosta's shop also carried several copies of a multivolume *History of England,* another of "the Orient," plus a *General History of the World.* He also had fourteen copies of *The Great Tamurlane.* Acosta must have traded with Mexican dealers, as he listed fifteen copies of Fray Felipe Díez Lusitano's *Tratado de la Ciudad de la Puebla de los Ángeles y grandezas* (here "grandezas" may refer to Bernardo de Balbuena's acclaimed *Grandeza mexicana*).[31] Another Americas-based author was Juan de Castellanos of New Granada. Castellanos's massive history in verse, *Elegías de Varones Ilustres de Indias,* was also present. Classics included major works by Homer, Virgil, Ovid, Cicero, Lucan, and Caius Julius Caesar. A "modern classic" was a multivolume work on civil law by the Flemish neo-Stoic Justus Lipsius, translated from the Latin into Castilian Spanish. Lipsius was an author of signal importance in Habsburg Spain.[32]

Technical books included Bartolomé de Agüero's popular 1604 medical treatise, *Treasury of the True Surgery and Proper Way against the Common One,* along with classics such as Dioscorides's *De Materia Medica.* The

Portuguese book dealer also had copies of a 1587 title, *New Philosophy of Human Nature,* by the Spanish female physician and philosopher Oliva Sabuco de Nantes Barrera.[33] None of this was likely to help poor Cornelis Lamberto, the syphilitic who opened this chapter, but it appears Potosí's physicians were up to date with the literature. Various "books of secrets" are also noted, some presumably by Albertus Magnus. Other titles treated weights and measures, herbs, and drug preparations and prescriptions. Of special interest is Georgius Agricola's massive 1556 mining treatise, *De re metallica,* loaded with diagrams of ore-crushing mills, refining tubs, and draining apparatus.

Potosí produced literature in addition to consuming it, although most items circulated in manuscript. Typical were *comedias* or theatrical pieces to be performed during the city's innumerable festivals. A self-described "author of comedies" was Gabriel del Río, who in 1619 received a shipment of thirty-one Spanish comedies for his own collections. Another comedy author living in Potosí in 1621 was Juan Galindo de Esquivel; he was apparently a gambling addict. Curiously, gambling addicts unable to pay their fines were forced to sing and dance in comedies in Cuzco, although I have not found similar condemnations for Potosí. Comedy troupes and impresarios show up from time to time in Potosí's notary records as well.[34] Potosí's theater gave name to the "Calle de la Comedia," a point of reference both spatial and moral. Acting was a dubious profession. In 1647, a Potosí widow was sanctioned for carrying on affairs with several men. Her roommate was an unnamed actress: "una comedianta."[35]

### CITY OF VICE

Each day, all told, there are consumed in town 60 decks of cards a day, which in the course of the year makes 21,900, which at a peso and a half in current cash equals 32,850 pesos, and in assayed silver, 21,000.

—ANON. 1603

It should come as no surprise that the Spanish Empire's richest boomtown was also its most violent, vice-ridden, and otherwise criminally prolific. Perhaps only Seville and later Madrid vied for the title of Sin City, although one must not exclude Naples. Potosí's gambling dens predated its churches, and many were annexed to houses of prostitution. Sin could be profitable and even peaceful, but in Potosí excess silver and lax law enforcement encouraged violence. Claim jumping and ore theft prompted murder and reprisal, as did countless disputes over debts, boundaries, water rights, and sexual companions. Questioning a man's honor in Potosí could quickly end in death by duel or, less honorably, ambush.

Men in Potosí spent considerable time and money on gambling, often at much higher stakes than elsewhere. As will be seen in the next chapter, bets and losses reached obscene proportions during the great Potosí mint fraud of the 1640s. There were no bona fide casinos in the Imperial Villa, but private citizens and some government officials could buy rights to operate gaming tables for a few years at a time.

A modest casino appears in a notary record from 1590. This was a gaming company established by two men, Capt. Juan Balero and Francisco Díaz Guerrero. Each put in half the capital for a "gaming house and table," which not only entailed a building next to a private residence but also a "trading table, a chest of drawers, two chairs, and two benches." More important was the cash each man put up, totaling 10,000 pesos. The money would be lent to gamblers at cards and "tricks." Captain Balero was listed as cashier and bookkeeper. The company would pay out after one and a half years.[36]

Gambling was legal as long as it was registered and taxed. Card games were most popular, and the Spanish crown was quick to step in and mandate that all decks be produced and sold by a concessionaire who had paid for the royal monopoly. It appears that simple, woodblock-printed decks were to be destroyed after one use to prevent marking and to encourage consumption. Use of unauthorized cards in games with real stakes could be harshly punished. The crown also leased the monopoly on cockfights in later years, but cards seem to have been most popular in Potosí.

Most of what we know about gambling in Potosí in its heyday comes from a curious type of document found in notary records: the "gambler's renunciation." These were sworn promises by self-described gambling addicts to quit playing a range of card games, dice games, and other betting devices for a set period of time. Should they backslide, the men—and they were all men— were to pay substantial fines, set in accordance with their sense of honor and wealth, to a religious charity.

Most of the gamblers' renunciations from seventeenth-century Potosí pledge a few hundred to several thousand pesos to help take care of the prisoners held by the Holy Inquisition in its jail in Lima. Although the Inquisition did not actively pursue chronic gamblers as far as I can tell,

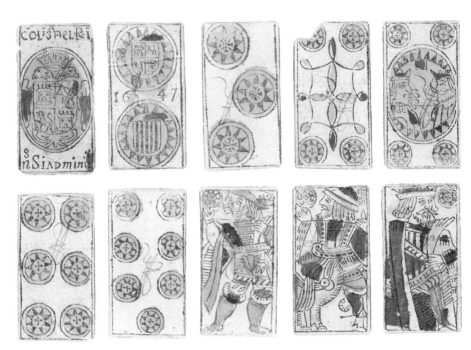

Spanish playing cards, Seville, 1647. Courtesy of the Museo Fournier de Naipes, Vitoria-Gasteiz.

income from such renunciations was a reliable revenue stream, collected by Holy Office commissioners and sent to Lima.[37] Other problem gamblers promised to pay fines to local religious brotherhoods and hospitals. Many also offered substantial bounties to the person who spotted their recidivism and turned them in.

Gamblers in seventeenth-century Potosí tended to swear off card games with names like *comexen, hombre, primera, pasadiez, quinolas,* and *pintas.* Some of these games survive in altered form today. Renunciations extended from a few months to a lifetime, and some men renounced all games, including dice and dominoes—and in some instances, "all games invented and to be invented." A barber retained his passion for dominoes but renounced everything else after losing big at *primera.* A petty trader cited the "disquiet of my person" as he renounced gambling on cards, billiards, and the drawing of lots, but he reserved the right to bet on card tricks.

A few repentant gamblers were priests, and some were extremely rich *azogueros* and arbitrageurs or *mercaderes de plata.* According to the documents, the gaming bug did not discriminate. A few major Potosí lenders, including mint fraud mastermind Francisco Gómez de la Rocha, discussed in the next chapter, made similar pledges not to back risky borrowers. Loan-sharking in Potosí was a dangerous game. I have not found any self-denunciations made by enslaved men, as one would imagine given the usual formula, but they were sometimes denounced by their masters as incorrigible "players" in bills of sale.[38]

## THE SAINT

If there was an exception to Potosí's rule of wickedness, it was Fray Vicente Bernedo. Born in Puente de la Reina, Navarre, about 1562, Bernedo studied at Alcalá de Henares and Salamanca, where he joined the Dominican Order. After preaching in Spain in the 1590s, Bernedo sailed for Cartagena de Indias around 1598. In 1600 he reached Lima after a stopover in Bogotá, and by 1601 he was in Potosí, where he lived in or near the Dominican monastery until his death in 1619. Like his contemporary, St. Rose of Lima, Bernedo turned his back on the world—quite an accomplishment in Potosí—and embraced mortification. According to his hagiographers, who proposed beatification beginning in the early 1660s, Bernedo lived in Santo Domingo's freezing bell tower for two years, then in a rude hut nearby with minimal bedding. Almost a hermit, he scourged himself, starved himself, ignored the elements, and otherwise embraced pious suffering.

Among the special torments of Potosí, aside from perpetual cold and oxygen-poor, polluted air, was the constant din of the stamp mills, crashing throughout the night right next to Bernedo's tiny shelter. According to his supporters, the poor friar had no time to sleep anyway, as he was always praying or reading Thomas Aquinas, on whose writings he commented at length in his notebooks. Some described him as "always in bad health, quite pallid and skinny," all the marks of a Baroque saint, but perhaps also touched by mercury poisoning.[39] In spite of chronic illness, Bernedo routinely visited the sick and collected alms for poor native Andeans. Some elites found him capable of prognostication, as when one confessant learned of the return of her stolen slaves.

At some point, Fray Vicente became known as the (proverbial) saint of the miners. He seems to have preached to native workers in the parish of San Pedro, as well as in neighboring villages. Bernedo's surviving writings are few, but they include a curious opinion piece on trading for captives with the

Chiriguanaes of the eastern frontier, which he experienced during a missionary stint near Tomina. A learned university man, Bernedo was listed as an official consultant or *calificador* for the Holy Office of the Inquisition, closely tied to the Dominicans. After Bernedo's death from a brief illness in 1619, there circulated claims of miracles and of an uncorrupted corpse. During his lifetime, people spoke of casual levitation and sweet smells emanating from his person, but as of this writing Potosí's most pious man has yet to be sainted.

### BASQUES AND VICUÑAS

In the time when by just and secret judgments of God our Lord, the sins of the people, insolences and scandalous excesses, Divine Justice and Providence permitted in the Imperial Villa of Potosí the outbreak of civil wars between Castilian Spaniards and Basque Spaniards.[40]

Despite its high altitude and famously cold winds, something about Potosí, perhaps its volcanic origins, heated the human spirit. The air itself seemed to incite quarrels and violent outbursts from otherwise reasonable people. Indigenous miners were said to be especially prone to drinking, carousing, and quarreling, more so here than in their home villages. Enslaved Africans were charged with outlandish behavior as well, but it was Spaniards and other Europeans, and not only men, as we have seen, who seemed most prone to fight and kill, or at least to plot each others' ruin. Whereas other parts of Spanish America witnessed a tendency toward homogenization of white, peninsular Spaniards (*peninsulares*), who sometimes clashed with native-born and mixed Spaniards (*criollos*), Potosí and much of Upper Peru remained divided into ethnic factions well into the seventeenth century.

It is important to remember that Spain was not a nation-state in the seventeenth century. "España" was an idea, a revival of the old Roman province of Hispania. Iberia under the Habsburgs comprised numerous kingdoms and corporate groups all clamoring for recognition before a part-Austrian monarch who kept a Burgundian court. Andalusians and Extremadurans jockeyed for power against Manchegos, Galicians, and Old Castilians. Northern Iberians, especially the Basques and Navarrese, possessed greater autonomy than most Castilians, and they reminded the king of their concessions. The Catalans and Aragonese, including Murcians and Valencians, also enjoyed distinctions and privileges. The Kingdom of Aragon, barely a day's ride east of Madrid, minted its own currency, and largely stayed out of the affairs of the Americas.

Portugal and its overseas holdings, despite Spanish annexation in 1580, remained largely autonomous until independence in 1640. Portuguese subjects, including so-called New Christians or recent converts from Judaism and their descendants, moved into the Spanish colonies in considerable numbers, and in the case of Potosí many families arrived from the south, having landed at Buenos Aires by way of Rio. Some Portuguese settlers and traveling merchants in greater Charcas, many with connections in Brazil and Atlantic Africa, were suspected of secretly practicing Judaism, and several families, including some of the richest people in the colonies, were tried and convicted by the Inquisition in Lima, most notably in a horrifying auto-da-fé in 1639.[41]

In the Spanish Indies, local identities did not always take precedence. Faced with large populations of native Americans, enslaved Africans, and people of mixed heritage, peninsular Spaniards did at times adopt the moniker "español" to distinguish themselves from people of color. Locally born Spaniards, or creoles, were even more likely to do this, as many were born to parents from different parts of the Peninsula. Over the course of the colonial period, "Spanishness" could come to stand in for "whiteness," although the color spectrum varied greatly by region and over time. Regional identities tended to be most loudly proclaimed in cities with a constant influx of young, competitive, male migrants; Potosí is perhaps the most extreme case.[42]

Merchants and mine owners from Spain's Basque provinces proved highly successful in Potosí by the first decades of the seventeenth century. They spoke a unique language and formed their own religious fraternity devoted to the Virgin of Aránzazu. They introduced the game of handball and an early street in Potosí was called "La Calle de la Pelota." Primarily from Biscay but also from Guipúzcoa, Potosí's Basques aided one another in ways that natives of other parts of Spain disliked. As they grew richer, the Basques purchased and monopolized town council positions as well as crown offices, including those involving oversight of labor allotments, tax collection, mercury distribution, and the minting of coinage. Some of these positions were hereditary, which opened the prospect for an ethnic monopoly on city politics. By the late 1610s, resentment of Basque dominance in Potosí was boiling over. A treasury inquiry begun in 1618 took the lid off the pot.

The Basques' sworn enemies were mostly from southern Spain: Andalusians, Manchegos, and—most importantly—Extremadurans. *Extremeños* often claimed links to the conquistadors, but there had been Basque conquistadors, too. Both groups could also claim rebels in Gonzalo Pizarro and Lope de Aguirre, although no one openly did. These "nations," as they were called, banded together to defend their interests, and also to defend their honor. The non-Basques sometimes called themselves Castilians, implicitly branding the Basques as foreign. As things heated up further in 1620, a group of "Castilians" took the name *vicuñas,* a reference to their hats, made from the wool of this wild Andean camelid. Some creoles and Portuguese joined the vicuñas in challenging Basque dominance, but their interests were diffuse.

Rumbles and assassinations were common in the Imperial Villa and other nearby mining camps, but it was only in June 1622 that Basque-vicuña bickering exploded into gangland warfare. Assassinations and midnight massacres continued to early 1625, stopped only by a controversial royal amnesty. Firsthand accounts of this so-called Civil War are few and partisan, but it is clear that the Basques fell under siege from many sides. They were powerful, but they were also a tiny minority with few friends. Ultimately they would be saved by crown officials, but only after a wave of ambushes and showdowns followed by summary executions. The aftereffects and bitter aftertaste lingered for decades.

The trigger for the gang war was a royal inspection, or *visita general,* led by a royal accountant sent from Lima, Alonso Martínez de Pastrana. His visit had already been delayed ten years. Any crown inspector to Potosí was certain to upset the balance of power, even if he accepted bribes and pretended not to take sides. Pastrana instead sided with the vicuñas and pressed prominent Basques to pay back taxes, fees for office holding, and other debts to the royal treasury. This was his job, but in the process Pastrana exposed a specific type of corruption: vote buying. Powerful Basque mill owners bought votes from Basque town councilmen, which enabled them to avoid paying their debts to the crown for advanced mercury. One could argue that they had sewn up city politics at the crown's expense.

Armed with a royal decree, Pastrana pushed through his plan to exclude many Basques from the town council for their debts, but this was only partially successful, opening up spots for several vicuñas who cleverly bought their way in, but keeping the Basque majority. The Basque faction, which included the large and wealthy Berasátegui clan, braced for conflict. They had the Imperial Villa's corregidor on their side, along with cooperation from weak or corrupt audiencia judges in nearby Charcas. The Basques would not be easily dislodged, although soon many would be forced to flee.

The murder of a burly Basque hitman named San Juan de Urbieta in June of 1622 touched off a series of vendetta cycles, and gangland killings and ambushes continued into early 1624. Initially defiant, some armed Basques allegedly went through the streets calling out in their language (Euskadi): 'Whoever does not respond in Basque shall die!' Outnumbered and out-gunned, however, the Basques got the worst of it. Dozens died, many fled to La Plata and Lima, and relatives in Biscay petitioned Philip IV for aid.

The leader of the vicuñas was the Extremaduran Juan Fernández de Tovar, who in the end became a Franciscan friar and helped broker a truce. Tovar did so in part to head off creation of a permanent military force that was certain to harm his faction. Crown officials stepped in anyway and hunted fugitive vicuñas in the hills around town in late 1624 before the viceroy issued an amnesty at Lima in April 1625. Before the peace, the crown had sent two high officials, Diego de Portugal and Felipe Manrique, to attempt settle-ment. Manrique, who had served in Naples and Morocco, was the less forgiv-ing of the two, and his clear favoritism of the Basques set the stage for later confrontations and assassinations. Even so, Potosí's ethnic gang war was sus-pended by royal decree.

The so-called Basque-vicuña wars of the 1620s were regarded as a major calamity by later observers such as the town historian Arzáns, but for the crown the concern over murderous factions thriving in its most precious silver mining districts became an abiding fiscal worry. Fearing a loss of reve-nue and clinging to the Habsburg notion of governance as the maintenance of peace and concord among a host of rival subjects, Philip IV and his minis-ters proved reluctant to lay down the law in Potosí.

A *visita* in the 1630s was suspended when the inspector-general, an Extremaduran named Juan de Carvajal y Sande, threatened to reopen the investigation of the Basque-vicuña conflict. The same happened to his Catalan successor, Juan de Palacios, in the early 1640s. As will be seen in the next chapter, crown hesitance to follow through on fiscal matters for fear of reigniting ethnic violence helped open the door to massive fraud inside the royal mint, arguably a greater calamity, or "secret judgment of God," than any other to strike Potosí in its long colonial history.

By the time its population topped 120,000 in the early seventeenth century, the Imperial Villa of Potosí had become a global phenomenon, or as Diego de Ocaña grandly put it, "The Eighth Wonder of the World." It boasted a theater, a literate class, great religious processions, and also the Americas' finest brothels, gambling dens, and taverns. Its physicians were among the world's most expensive, if not effective. Potosí was probably the newest city of its size anywhere on the planet, an improbable metropolis at 4,000 meters above sea level and deep in the heart of the South American Andes. To some degree this violent, polluted, and sinful urban agglomeration was Viceroy Toledo's doing, since without the mita, the mills, the reservoirs, and the mint it would not likely have been revitalized after its first bust.

Yet just as clearly, Potosí had by 1600 escaped many of Toledo's plans for it. As will be seen in the next chapter, the city's thousands of restless residents would be harshly punished for their sins, or that is how they described it. For our purposes, we may withhold judgment to observe that Potosí emerged as an accidental alpine city tied to a massive underground mining complex as well as an adjacent quasi-industrial refining sector supplied by dozens of artificial lakes and canals. Its production of silver was huge, to be sure, in terms of money units, but what is often forgotten is how much Potosí *consumed:* the city, the mines, the refineries, all of it together ate up vast resources, from Chinese silk to iron to llama dung. Potosí had over 100,000 mouths to feed, but this was only the beginning; the unique combination of industrial-scale mining, refining, and prodigious wealth took the Imperial Villa far beyond its basic needs as a consumer. This casual wastefulness was what astonished so many early visitors. Rich and syphilitic, Potosí in its prime exemplified globalization's outer limits.

# FIVE

# *Secret Judgments of God*

Sunday, March 15, at 1:30 p.m., the Cari Cari reservoir burst
on the island side, opposite the Río Panga reservoir, and broke
through 22 yards of cutwater; and the speed and violence with
which the water reached town were such that the damage it
caused was irreparable. It was so violent that one saw mountains
of water coming down, higher than the tops of the tallest houses,
and they carried some along for a considerable distance ...
To try and detail the losses incurred would transcend the
brevity of this dispatch. The number of persons drowned would
appear at the present to reach 350; so far it has been impossible
to locate all the missing, who are numerous, both Spaniards and
Indians.

—BARTOLOMÉ ASTETE DE ULLOA, *Royal Factor, to Potosí's*
corregidor, *1626*[1]

ACCORDING TO THE EARLY EIGHTEENTH-CENTURY chronicler
Bartolomé Arzáns de Orsúa y Vela, Potosí began to go bust after 1600 due
to the accumulating sins of its inhabitants. God was angry enough to send
three successive scourges to cripple the city and its mines. First was the so-
called War of the Basques and Vicuñas, treated in the previous chapter.
Second was the 1626 flood described above, caused by heavy rains and poor
maintenance of the reservoirs above town. The third and most crushing
divine scourge, according to Arzáns, was a *visita,* or general inspection, of
the royal mint, which began in earnest in 1649 after almost a decade of
fraud. Scourge three ended only with the death of the special prosecutor in
1660.

W hereas the 1626 flood wiped out half of Potosí's richest mill owners and
drowned 350 people outright, the 1649–60 *visita* was far more sweeping. Led
by an incorruptible former inquisitor from Spain, Dr. Francisco de Nestares
Marín, the royal inspection eliminated many of Potosí's richest miners, merchants, and ranking bureaucrats, including the judges of the nearby Audiencia
of Charcas. Potosí never returned to its former glory despite numerous

Potosí, ca. 1630, Francisco López de Caravantes. Courtesy of the Archivo General de Palacio, Madrid.

attempts to reform the *mita* and to improve supplies of mercury. Instead, the city suffered a continuing sequence of famines, plagues, and other instances of what baroque Spaniards including Arzáns called "secret judgments of God."

The seventeenth century was tough all over, especially the middle decades, and historians have long debated the reasons for this so-called general crisis. Most recently Geoffrey Parker has argued that short-term climate change in the form of an extended cool period, the Little Ice Age, disrupted subsistence patterns worldwide, exacerbating plagues and sparking revolts, mass migrations, and even wars.[2] Potosí's troubles in the seventeenth century were in part related to climate fluctuations, since we have records of disastrous floods followed by multiyear droughts. But if we can trust the documentary record, most of the calamities suffered by Potosí's diverse inhabitants had other, less cosmic causes. Good Catholics blamed themselves and credited "God's wrath" with settling accounts, barely sparing sinful Potosí the fate of Sodom and Gomorrah.

After a brief look at disease, deforestation, and technical innovation, this chapter centers on the two traumatic events that brought Potosí to its knees: the flood of 1626 and the great mint scandal of 1649. Although these were internal dramas, they reverberated globally. Culminating in the mint fraud of the 1640s, the Imperial Villa's time of troubles led to a worldwide currency crisis that took decades to fix. Potosí sent debased silver bars and coins around the world at a time when Spain faced bankruptcy and Europe was embroiled in the Thirty Years War. These years also brought fiscal crisis to the Ottoman and Safavid Empires, and witnessed the fall of the Ming dynasty. These were but a few of the global disruptions that shook the age.

## EPIDEMIC DISEASE

Incurable sickness was common in early modern times, but epidemics still took pious Christians by surprise. Waves of smallpox, influenza, measles, typhus, and many other ailments swept through South America after the arrival of Europeans and Africans, probably facilitated by the introduction of new domestic livestock. A type of hemorrhagic fever raged through the Andes in 1546, the year after Potosí's discovery, followed by a similar ailment in 1560–61. These fevers killed most victims within a few days of falling ill. Another epidemic struck in 1588–89, possibly smallpox plus influenza; it was said to have sickened 10,000 native Andeans in Potosí alone. Demographic and epidemiological historians believe diphtheria struck in 1615, followed by measles outbreaks in 1619 and 1630.[3] Potosí was hit by yet another deadly epidemic in 1649, possibly plague.

The cumulative effect of these waves of disease was simple: "demographic collapse." In warmer lowland regions such as Bolivia's Mizque Valley and Peru's eastern coca zone, this meant population drops of 90 percent or more, exacerbated in some places by the arrival of malaria and other mosquito-borne fevers by the early seventeenth century. Some of the warm valleys southeast of Potosí where vineyards had been planted may have become malarial by 1650 as well, although this is difficult to prove.[4]

Yet even in the cold highland provinces, where mosquitoes dared not fly, disease took a heavy toll. It is difficult to separate the effects of epidemic disease from other factors, such as overwork, interpersonal violence, low birthrates due to malnutrition, and forced marches, but all told, the highland provinces subject to the Potosí mita appear to have lost some 45 percent of their indigenous population by 1620, down 60 percent by 1683. By this time, populations in some areas were starting to rebound, and the number of people of mixed heritage was also rising. Acquired immunity was taking root among all populations, but the cumulative effect of disease on native Andean villagers remained devastating.

Spanish crown officials under Peru's viceroy, the duke of La Palata, finally organized a census to update Potosí's mita allotments in 1689. It was discovered that a large proportion of tribute-paying indigenous men in the southern Andes were now *forasteros,* that is, almost half were migrant workers no longer attached to home villages as peasants.[5] Peru's next viceroy, the count of Monclova, followed by ordering an investigation into the causes for the disappearance of *ayllu* or village residents (aside from disease) and it was found that many indigenous men living within the Potosí mita net found themselves between a rock and a hard place. On one hand, village life provided minimal income and high demands from caciques and *corregidores,* yet on the other, the trek to Potosí could prove disruptive at best, deadly at worst. It became wise to float freely.

Paradoxically, as we have already seen, staying in Potosí and gaining skills as a miner or artisan offered a kind of escape from the rigors of country life. Becoming a forastero, and perhaps migrating to some ranch or farm beyond Potosí, was always risky, but at least it offered hope for survival. Many southern Andeans who escaped the Potosí mita made their way to the vineyards and farms of the Pilaya and Paspaya region, near the modern border with Argentina. Labor-hungry landowners there paid wages and covered tribute obligations.[6] One might get ensnared in debt peonage on a hacienda, but indigenous mobility combined with consistent demand for workers often made such traps difficult to set. Either way, one "worked for Potosí" since the wine produced in the southern vineyards was sold in the Imperial Villa.

As we have seen, caciques and *kurakas,* those men and occasionally women who were responsible for rounding up and sending off mita workers to Potosí, sometimes abused power. Not all were bad, but more than a few were denounced for withholding tribute items to sell for their own profit. Others made shady rental and sales deals with landowners and merchants or collaborated with corrupt corregidores and priests. Many caciques were not from the original lines of native lords acknowledged after the conquest, and several prominent hereditary posts had been taken over by pretenders, including some mestizos.

Before we blame immoral caciques for the ills of Upper Peru, it is wise to remember that the demands of the mita in Potosí had shifted in the seventeenth century toward cash exemption payments. Since these payments were pocketed, those exempted were called "Indians in the pocket" or *indios de faltriquera.* A cacique on the shores of Lake Titicaca, for example, was expected to either come up with the workers expected of him according to an outdated census or to produce a cash exemption package that would satisfy Potosí's mill owners and royal officials. By 1690, some native Andeans from the greater Titicaca provinces were paying over 200 pesos *not to go* to the Cerro Rico. Some complained that they were forced to raise and sell whole herds of livestock, along with whatever else they could manage, just to come up with the cash. Such demands, particularly in years of harsh weather, were strong incentive to leave the village and seek a wage, however small, elsewhere.

A reminder of the rising pain of the Potosí mita net is the case of Gabriel Fernández Guarache, who petitioned the Charcas circuit court repeatedly beginning in the 1640s in hopes of a demotion. Guarache had inherited the title of *capitán mayor de la mita de Potosí,* which made him responsible for rounding up draftees from multiple districts. In the past it had been a lucrative as well as honorable post, but by 1640 Guarache was one of the last native Andean headmen to hold this title, and region-wide population decline had made it so onerous that he was selling his livestock and running wine to the Imperial Villa on mules from the coast in order to come up with the cash exemptions demanded by Potosí's refinery guild. The guild, which relied on Potosí's corregidor for enforcement, countered Guarache's petitions for two decades without relief. The case finally went to the Council of the Indies in Spain, where it became entangled in a new debate over the mita. Guarache remained a pawn despite his powerful-sounding title, and it was only in the 1660s that his and similar demands for mercy started to be heard.[7]

### DENUDING THE LANDSCAPE

This town has a huge expenditure on wood, such that the amount consumed cannot be determined, as there are so many dealers in it; but so that one may get an idea of how large the expenditure is, I will say that one beam that they call an axle, which is 22 feet long and two-feet square in width, is worth 900 and even 1,000 assayed pesos.[8]

Sustaining a city of over 100,000 inhabitants in an alpine setting is a daunting environmental challenge. Anyone who has visited a ski town knows this. Much more demanding are alpine mining towns, which consume a wider range of resources and produce a plethora of toxins. The problem of mercury pollution alone was enough to curse Potosí forever after the arrival of Viceroy Toledo in the early 1570s.[9] But added to this were many other concerns, among them fuel for cooking, construction materials, and access to potable water. With this last concern came the problem of contamination by human and animal feces. Not only was Potosí high and dry, it was above the tree line and experiencing the full effects of the Little Ice Age. How could life in Potosí be sustained, and at what cost to the fragile Andean environment?

Potosí's notary books contain contracts for timber to be brought from as far away as the Argentine district of Tucumán, dragged by mules or carried by natives of that province. More common wood sources included inter-Andean river valleys to the north of Potosí. One contract from 1588 specifically names the Pitantora Valley. Three workers were to receive a truly minimal wage: between 8 and 14 pesos for four round trips.[10] We lack exhaustive studies, but it is clear from colonial accounts that Potosí's wood and charcoal consumption continued to stress forests lying a great distance away. We have seen how Viceroy Toledo noted the problem in the early 1570s. Only *polylepis* trees, a kind of gnarled and resinous dwarf, can survive in the Andes above 4,000 meters, but these trees appear to have been eliminated soon after Potosí was settled.[11] Potosí's fuel demands alone wiped out brush stands for hundreds of kilometers around, leading to collection of everything down to human feces for the refining furnaces.

Mercury amalgamation was less demanding of fuel than the *guairas,* but charcoal was still needed to supply furnaces at the refineries. Potosí's notary records include contracts for charcoal delivery. The royal mint also consumed considerable charcoal to smelt coin metal and burnish blanks, as its internal accounts show. Llama dung was also regularly delivered to the city, although I have not found contracts for it. Another, less noxious fuel was *yareta,* a spongy green moss with a woody root system that grows amid rocks at extreme altitudes. A contract for fifty loads of yareta appears in notary books from 1648, suggesting this kind of collection continued for many years after Potosí's discovery. The 1648 contract says the moss would be collected in a region high above the salt springs of Yocalla and taken to a silver refinery in Cantumarca, just below the Imperial Villa.[12] Deforestation and removal of plants like yareta increased erosion during the cycles of extreme weather typical of the Little Ice Age, and this probably sped sedimentation in the Kari-Kari reservoirs on which the city and mines depended.

## THE GREAT 1626 FLOOD

On Sunday the 15th current, the Cari Cari reservoir burst; they say that at that time people heard and saw some subterranean tremblings and other presentiments. Certain it is that God wished to chastise us, it may be for the offense given him by the multiplicity of our manifold sins; but leaving miracles aside, the reason might be that that side of the reservoir, which was considered safe, had dried out on account of the long drought, and cracked under the great pressure of the water; considering the location of the break, it might have destroyed the whole town; but Divine mercy always prevails over Divine justice.

—BARTOLOMÉ ASTETE DE ULLOA, 1626[13]

Writing a century later, town historian Bartolomé Arzáns called it the "second great thunderbolt discharged by God upon the Imperial Villa of Potosí." The creator had mercifully ended the Basque-Vicuña wars, but the city's inhabitants remained, according to Arzáns, "ungrateful." Returning to prosperity, they forgot piety and embraced vice as never before. Though given to hyperbole, Arzáns's long and painful description of the Holy Week 1626 dam burst is to some extent supported by contemporary accounts such as that of royal factor Bartolomé Astete de Ulloa, quoted above. The Potosí town council met within days of the flood to organize relief even as the aldermen worried about looting. They hinted darkly at native Andeans making off with silver bars and ingots left amid the rubble of the city's refining mills. Such were the worries of the rich.[14]

What had happened? It was mid-March, nearing the end of the rainy season, and the San Ildefonso reservoir, or *laguna de Caricari,* was full. About midday on Sunday a small section of its dam, a tamped-earth structure, gave way. It had apparently been opened as a spillway back in 1599 and afterwards was improperly repaired or badly maintained. Once the dam was breached, the outflow quickly scoured away a larger opening and a wave of water, mud, and rocks swept through the city's main gulch, La Ribera. Dozens of ore-crushing mills and adjacent mercury amalgamation refineries were wiped out in an instant, along with a number of Spanish and indigenous dwellings. The loss of life, estimated in the hundreds of souls, could not be priced, but losses of equipment, plant, and partially refined silver ores quickly reached the hundreds of thousands of pesos. Writing only two days after the disaster, Astete de Ulloa estimated losses exceeding four *million* pesos "in buildings, ore, and quicksilver."[15]

Potosí's town council called for a religious procession "to placate the ire of God and plead for mercy." A committee of *azogueros* or refinery owners was then named and charged with repairing all the dams above town, overseeing the installation of "walls and counter walls." There were sixteen reservoirs in use at this time, all of them desperately needed to keep the mills running day and night, year-round. A new "enclosure and cutwater" was to be built of cement (*calicanto*) where the old Kari-Kari dam had failed. This was after a second scare occurred on the night of April 22 when another, smaller rush of water came down along the same flood path, with "many people exiting their houses naked and spreading panic."[16]

Several mill owners won debt relief from the king as they tried to reconstruct their machines from scattered and broken parts. Some two dozen azogueros lost everything, and another two dozen suffered serious damages. Doña Mariana Maldonado was among the second group. Unluckier still was Isidro Garabito, whose mill was "badly damaged, and he was carried off by the flood and is missing."[17] Well represented on the town council, Potosí's azogueros stuck it to the Indians by asking the Charcas *audiencia* to suspend all suits against them for worker mistreatment and mine accident claims since they were so invested in mill repairs. The city finally enacted plans to clear mud and boulders, repave damaged streets with cobblestones, and replace broken ceramic sewer pipes in September 1626. Crews of stonemasons and peons were hired in October.[18]

God may not have been finished with the iniquitous *potosinos,* as drought returned in early 1627, followed by new floods. In 1628 a blast of smallpox and malignant fever (*tabardillo*) swept through town, followed by a wave of lawsuits against contractors who were supposed to have repaired the Kari-Kari dams. It was now May, tail end of the rainy season, and the new works were full of rainwater and leaking.[19]

For Arzáns, the great 1626 flood was proof of Potosí's sinfulness, and he fills his account of it with horrors and miracles. In his telling, a brothel full of hungover carnival partiers was wiped out entirely as they were unable to find the key to the front door. They stretched their arms in vain as voices murmured: "The lakes are rumbling"; then—wham! Another house was leveled by the torrent, leaving only an adobe wall adorned with a crucifix.

Cinematic as ever, Arzáns describes how novitiates at the Franciscan monastery escaped with their lives amid tumbling boulders as they scurried to save their relics. Meanwhile dozens of young women, enslaved and free, were caught in the swirling waters and drowned. A reminder of God's fury, innocents were slain alongside unrepentant sinners.

For the beleaguered city of Potosí, the 1626 flood was a major setback, but in some ways it only postponed the decline of the Cerro Rico. The chronicler Vázquez de Espinosa asked the king to relieve Potosí's azogueros by lifting the official price of silver, raising its value from 65 reals per mark to 77.[20] This proposal fell on deaf ears, but complaints about rising costs of production amid crushing taxes grew more shrill with each passing year. Potosí's azogueros paid a full-time lobbyist to press their claims in Madrid. As will be seen, some potosinos turned to fraud. The 1630s provided a diversion in the form of a rush to the newly revived mines of Chocaya, in the southern highlands between Uyuni and Tupiza. Suddenly, a whole new cycle of murder and mayhem began, typical of boom times. To astonished chroniclers like Arzáns, it seemed that Potosí's capacity for new cycles of sin and vengeance, amid new lucky strikes, were endless.

## A SILVER LINING: TECHNICAL INNOVATION

All was not darkness, death, and environmental degradation in early seventeenth-century Potosí. Among the unexpected bright spots was Álvaro Alonso Barba, a parish priest whose 1640 treatise, *The Art of Metals,* continues to intrigue scientists and historians. Known as Barba although his paternal surname was Alonso, Potosí's most famous metallurgist was born in the Andalusian town of Lepe, near the Atlantic port of Huelva. Huelva province was home to Spain's famous Río Tinto mines. These polymetallic deposits that stained a river had been worked since pre-Roman times, yielding considerable silver along with copper and lead. We do not know if Barba visited the Río Tinto mines as a youth, but he was called back to Spain as an elderly man to attempt their revival. Based on years of experiments with different ore types in and around Potosí, he believed he could do so.

Ordained some time before 1610, Barba sailed for Peru, and by 1615 he was serving in Tiahuanaco, near Lake Titicaca. Later appointments took him to the remote silver camps of Los Lípes, in what is today southwestern Bolivia, then to booming Oruro. Only in the late 1630s did Barba land in the Imperial

Villa of Potosí, where he oversaw the parish of St. Bernard. He appears in the Potosí notary books in January of 1640 purchasing two enslaved Angolan men from a Portuguese dealer just arrived from Buenos Aires.[21] As Barba's own writings suggest, he brought considerable knowledge of silver ores from other mining districts, including those of nearby Porco, to his laboratory work in Potosí. He was an inveterate experimenter, and he won the patronage of Juan de Lizarazu, president of the Audiencia of Charcas, to whom he dedicated his book.

Barba's aim was to develop and disseminate new methods for refining difficult or refractory silver ores, yet his treatise does more than record his recipes. In it, Barba makes reference to a wide range of classical and alchemical texts, all of which would suggest a typical scholastic adherence to received wisdom, yet he also notes the then-recent findings of Galileo Galilei published as *Sidereus Nuncius,* which documented the discovery of Jupiter's moons. Barba was clearly aware of new trends in science, and as a result his work was partly censored by the Inquisition.

Significantly, Barba directly challenged authorities when analyzing the results of his own experiments. Part maverick experimenter, part baroque alchemist, Barba resists categorization. What is certain is that he was an innovator, and his methods for refining some of the Andes's most difficult ores persisted into the nineteenth century. When a school of mines was first established in Potosí in 1780, students were required to copy his work verbatim in hopes that they might absorb his wisdom.

Barba left Potosí in 1644 to serve in the La Plata cathedral, where he slowly advanced in rank and eventually sought the archbishop's mitre. He did not win it, and it appears that Barba continued to read scientific treatises and experiment with ores. After hearing from a dying Potosí miner who recalled seeing similar ores back home in Spain, Barba petitioned Philip IV for license to return to the Iberian Peninsula in search of these deposits.[22]

Desperate for silver, the king agreed and in 1657 Barba sailed to Spain in a Dutch vessel from Buenos Aires. The lost mines of Niebla, not far from his hometown near Huelva, turned out to be a mirage, but Barba spent the last five years of his life attempting to revive known Spanish silver mines in the interior, including those of Guadalcanal and Río Tinto. Unfortunately, even his most innovative techniques, so well proven in Alto Peru, did not yield results at home. Barba died in 1662 in Seville's Triana neighborhood, his inventory chock-full of arcane books and laboratory equipment. He had won permission to return to his beloved Andes, but he fell ill and expired before the fleet was ready. For Potosí, Barba left a legacy of innovation and experimentation on par with earth sciences and metallurgy as practiced in Europe. Yet like many contemporary European tinkerers, including Isaac Newton, Barba was reluctant to abandon the mystical attractions of alchemy.[23]

## THE MINT SCANDAL

John Elliott has stressed the importance of reputation in the Spanish monarchy of the seventeenth century, particularly during the long and troubled reign of Philip IV (1621–65).[24] Few symbols of the king's reputation were more visible than the silver coins of Potosí. The piece of eight with the mintmark "P" had been an instant hit worldwide, at times a bit richer in silver or slightly heavier than expected. To hold a *peso de a ocho* or *patacón* of Potosí silver was to feel the global reach of the king of Spain. To touch his coat of arms and read his name was to know that to him alone belonged the Treasury of the World.

But like bagels in hard times, Potosí coins soon shrank below their standard weight and purity. The problem worsened as Philip IV's reign reached midpoint. Already by 1630 the Cerro Rico's mines were failing, and the Imperial Villa's mill owners were as insolvent as they had been before the great 1626 flood. Yet not everyone knew this, and many who did know chose not to face reality. Potosí silver was globally recognized, and this *ought* to mean that its coins remained good. The "rial of eight," as the English called it, might be a crudely fashioned, clipped, or tarnished hunk of change, but it was widely assumed to be richer than a handsome Dutch *rijksdaler* or even a Venetian ducat.

The Potosí peso, bearing the Habsburg coat of arms and a Greek cross interspersed with lions and castles, was traded worldwide. When accepted as ransom payment in North Africa, scribes wrote the necessary disclaimer: "Minted by the enemy of religion, the Christian; may God destroy him." It was a backhanded compliment. Writing in 1612, the priest Antonio de Sosa, who spent several years with Miguel de Cervantes as a captive in Algiers, noted of the Barbary corsairs:

> But the foreign money that they most treasure, brag about, and benefit from are the *reales* of Spain, silver coins of four and eight, because they send and carry them even to Turkey and the great Cairo, and from there they move eastward to the great Oriental India, and even up to Cathay, China, and

Tartary, always bringing a profit to those who carry them. And thus no merchandise is more precious, nor can anything of more worth be taken to Algiers, Barbary, or Turkey, than the *reales* of Spain.[25]

The *"reales* of Spain" included the abundant *pesos de a ocho* of Potosí, but even when minted in Seville these global trade coins were frequently made from Potosí silver. According to our best estimates, the Cerro Rico alone produced 20 percent of world silver between 1545 and 1825. The share during the Toledo-driven 1575–1640 boom was closer to 50 percent. During these years, most Potosí silver did not reach Spain as coin but rather in the form of brick-sized bars. An additional, unknown amount was exported from Peru illegally as untaxed ingots. But by the 1620s a growing share of Potosí silver was coined, and the royal mint established by Viceroy Toledo in 1574 was expanding. That the mint's expansion coincided with a steep drop in silver production at the Cerro Rico should have given royal treasury officials pause.

As early as 1630, Seville's wholesale merchants encountered debased silver bars with Potosí marks. Ordered to investigate, Peru's Viceroy Count of Chinchón suspected untrained royal treasury officials in Potosí and Oruro. Unsolved, the problem persisted after Chinchón left for Spain and by 1640 word got out that something worse was happening. Potosí's famous pieces of eight were coming up short of weight and purity as well, far beyond the bounds of ordinary tolerance.

Like most European coins at the time, those of Potosí were made by hand, and thus no two were exactly alike and many were misshapen or ill struck. This did not mean there was no quality control. Mint inspectors culled unacceptable coins for refounding, and passable coins were put in bags of a hundred or so, to average out according to strict royal guidelines. It was no small task to make millions of roughly one-ounce silver coins of consistent weight and purity each year. In Potosí, this was the task of over a hundred enslaved Africans.[26]

By 1641, city officials in Genoa and Antwerp began issuing bans on all coins with Potosí mintmarks, as they could no longer be trusted.[27] The Genoese, long famous for funneling huge sums of cash to Spanish troops in Flanders while serving as the main bankers to Kings Philip III and IV, had reason to protest. Yet like the Antwerpers and a growing number of international traders who handled Spanish American silver, the Genoese found this sudden debasement of Potosí coins puzzling. Foreigners often slipped counterfeits into large batches of coins, but wild variations in general coin purity

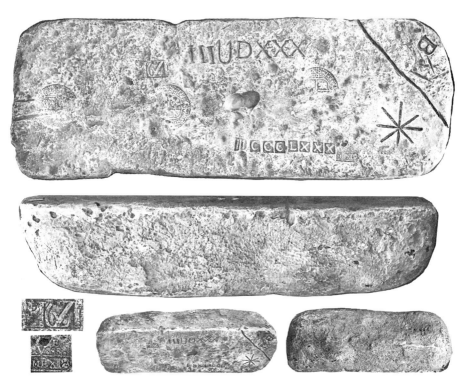

Potosí silver bar from wreck of the *Atocha,* 1622. Courtesy of Daniel Frank Sedwick, LLC, Auction #19, Lot 300.

were something new. It made no sense. Spanish authorities were similarly perplexed, and as in the case of the bad Potosí bars, they ordered Peru's viceroy, now the Marquis of Mancera, to investigate.

It should have been easy, but Mancera was busy with his own projects, which included corraling Portuguese residents scattered throughout Peru following the 1640 Braganza revolt and confronting the Dutch in southern Chile, where they attempted to plant a colony in 1643. Driven to make his mark as the great defender of the king's American treasury amid global panic, Mancera failed to confront rot and sedition inside the realm. Under intense pressure from the Council of the Indies, he ordered an investigator to Potosí, the audiencia judge Blas Robles de Salcedo. Terrified and alone, Robles was quickly compromised by members of an entrenched mint fraud ring. In one 1644 letter to the viceroy from the Imperial Villa, Robles lamented his lack of power and hinted at dark forces. "This matter is most dangerous," he said, as if a knife were at his throat. He all but pleaded with the viceroy to send someone else to investigate. Mancera and the Indies Council pressed for details but by 1646 Robles was dead amid mysterious circumstances.

The following year, two slaves escaped from the Potosí mint and made their way to the Audiencia of Charcas in nearby La Plata. They testified before its judges that their masters and many mint officials and employees were in on a huge debasement scam, along with the city's corregidor and his lieutenant, a nephew, plus many town councilmen. The fraud had a simple product—coins containing far less silver than they were supposed to—but the financial machinations that had led to systematic and massive debasement were complex. They encompassed Potosí's entire credit market, with debasement enabling the continued functioning of the mines and mills despite the Cerro Rico's decline. The great machine of Potosí was now running on desperate futures, its silver shortage filled with copper.

Like Viceroy Mancera, La Plata's audiencia judges dithered and failed to properly investigate, presumably out of fear, but the Indies Council and a frustrated King Philip IV had already made up their minds to send a special prosecutor with broad powers. Dispatched from Spain in September 1647, Dr. Francisco de Nestares Marín was to be the most ardent royal representative in Potosí since Viceroy Toledo. A former inquisitor from Navarre educated at the University of Bologna, Nestares Marín was ordered to clean house in Potosí and to also keep the silver flowing. Spain's foreign enemies had not let up, and the Genoese were returning sacks of cash needed by troops in Italy and Flanders.

When Nestares Marín arrived in Potosí in December 1648 he had already interrogated the fugitive slaves in Charcas and he had also discovered from other witnesses that the judges of the audiencia of which he was now president (one of his special powers granted by the king) were in on the fraud as well. They were not direct perpetrators, but they had been corrupted—tied by debt to the great debasement's principal figures. And who were these villains?

Toledo's royal mint was a blend of Old and New World models, a guild structure expanded to accommodate enslaved Africans and a small number of native Andean draftees. As we saw in chapter 3, the main officers were bonded townsmen who purchased their posts, hoping to recoup their investment from a share of metal coined according to rules created in 1497 under Ferdinand and Isabella. The silver itself came from another class of persons known as *mercaderes de plata* or silver merchants, private citizens who also profited from minting, but at such a narrow margin that it was only worth doing in very high volumes.

By the early 1640s, as the mines sputtered, there were only a handful of men with the necessary capital in Potosí to run silver through the mint at a profitable rate. The silver merchants in turn advanced cash to the mine and mill owners, many of them members of the powerful azogueros' guild and also the town council. Without substantial cash advances from the silver merchants, often on generous terms, the whole machine of the mountain, and thus the city, would collapse in a heap of debt. The news from underground suggested things were getting worse down in the Devil's world, not better.

So it was the silver merchants, headed by Francisco Gómez de la Rocha, who were most inclined to cut corners once they gained access to the mint. Rocha, as he was known, appears to have begun corrupting mint officials around 1641, and he had links to suspicious financiers going back to 1637, when he first arrived in Potosí from Cuzco. Born in northern Extremadura, Rocha had entered the Imperial Villa as a wholesale coca dealer. He had spent his youth running a coca plantation in the jungles east of Paucartambo.

Drug trade profits provided a springboard to high finance in needy Potosí, and by 1644, when Blas Robles de Salcedo wrote his desperate letter to Viceroy Mancera, Rocha was Potosí's richest man. He was probably also the man with a knife at Robles's throat, as he was then sending troops to Chile and loaning money to the king in hopes of winning a noble title. An open secret, the mint fraud grew like a cancer. Rocha's accomplices and competitors also swelled in numbers, all vying to outdo each other in debasing the coinage. It was only natural that many of the principals would turn on each other, and many of Rocha's former friends fled before the king's special prosecutor reached town at the end of 1648.

As Rocha played cat-and-mouse with Nestares Marín, hoping to corrupt him or trip up his investigation, slaves complained under oath that they were working day and night to produce coins so pink they could not be blanched and so brittle that they shattered at a hammer stroke. Interrogated by Nestares Marín, coiners and other junior mint staff broke the silence in hopes of lenient treatment, revealing deeper webs of corruption. Those mint officials not bribed were threatened or forced out, and loans to incoming officials, including the corregidor and the audiencia judges at La Plata, compromised them as well, effectively silencing them.

The Charcas audiencia judges and Potosí's corregidor in turn ran gaming houses that held some of the principal culprits in debt to the tune of tens of thousands of pesos. One merchant lost 20,000 pesos in a single night at cards, the equivalent of sinking a galleon. The fugitive slaves who testified

635

Potosí "piece of eight" or *peso de a ocho* with assayer mark "R," for Felipe Ramírez de Arellano, 1647. Courtesy of Daniel Frank Sedwick, LLC, Auction #18, Lot 635.

spoke of mock inspections that entered the written record as bona fide. One could not trust the books. Like a patient and thorough inquisitor, Nestares Marín compiled a list of 119 culprits as he went after the principals one by one with the king's approval.

The house of cards built by Rocha and his accomplices collapsed by the end of the year 1649, but given the breadth and depth of rot, plus the fragile state of the mining economy, Nestares Marín's options were limited. He had to keep silver flowing or the king would suffer. The new viceroy, the Count of Salvatierra, wanted to take credit for fixing Peru's fiscal problems, too, and to do this he sought support from Lima's powerful merchant guild. This in turn led Nestares Marín to suspect that the viceroy had fallen under the influence of corrupt circles linked to those of Potosí.

Alone in his specially built apartment upstairs in the Potosí mint, Nestares Marín spent all of 1649 taking testimonies, negotiating fines, and ultimately spinning the web that would entrap all the main culprits as well as their affiliates while also seizing their estates. It was a contentious and tense process, and Nestares Marín received numerous death threats; hired thugs fired guns at his window and he was burned in effigy on the main square outside his office. Once it became clear that Rocha, whom he called the worst of the lot and the motor of the fraud, wanted him dead, the ex-inquisitor struck.

In late January 1650, Nestares Marín ordered Rocha executed by strangulation, his body hung from a scaffold on Potosí's main square. Rocha's confession (allegedly taken under torture) has not survived, but he had apparently ordered an enslaved female cook to poison the inspector-general's food with mercury sublimate. Fortunately for him, she had been ratted out by other slaves.[28] Next was the mint's assayer, Felipe Ramírez de Arellano, throttled and strung up in late February 1650. A slew of death sentences followed the two executions, but many of the culprits had already fled to Lima, Chile, Panama, Spain, and even France. Several broke out of jail and were never found.

Nestares Marín was faced with a most difficult task: keeping Potosí's mines and mint running without the established creditors or mint officials, or even the corregidor, whom he exiled to Cuzco only to have him flee to Spain to seek a royal audience. Meanwhile, Nestares Marín had struck a deal with surviving silver producers to keep the coinage slightly below royal standards just so money would flow. Viceroy Salvatierra howled from Lima and the king's councilors sighed in Madrid, but Nestares Marín won a significant concession for Potosí's mine owners, elimination of a 1.5 percent tax on gross silver production (*los cobos*) that had been in place since the reign of Charles V.

THE MINT FRAUD'S GLOBAL CONSEQUENCES

By 1652, Potosí's coinage was back to full weight and purity, and with a new design: the Habsburg shield had been replaced with the Pillars of Hercules. Meanwhile, the old coins, including recent ones produced during the inspection, were officially devalued, called in for restamping and in some cases withdrawn from circulation altogether. The devaluation and recall, begun in 1650, upset currency markets throughout the Spanish Empire, including Mexico, which had its own mint and sources of silver. Hardest hit were cash-poor provinces such as Guatemala, Quito, and Venezuela, but also affected were Tucumán, Buenos Aires, Chile, and the Caribbean islands. Native Andean workers protested the overnight devaluation of their wages in Cuzco, La Paz, and even Potosí, but perhaps the deepest cuts were felt in southern Spain. There the recall spurred riots in Seville, Córdoba, and Granada, already hard-hit by plague and grain shortages.

On the far side of the world, Potosí coins had been routinely rejected in the spice ports of India and Southeast Asia. Frustrated merchants working for the English East India Company complained from Surat to the home office beginning in the early 1640s, but even when the new and improved coins appeared after 1652, pepper kings in Sumatra would not touch them. As far as they were concerned, "P" was for poison. It took decades to restore confidence in the once-famous money of Potosí. Mughal India had another solution: millions of suspect Potosí coins were recycled as rupees, discounted as scrap to bullion dealers happy to extract all the good silver. East Asian arbitrageurs probably did the same among the many ports of China but somebody always got burned. Adjusting to the collapse of the Ming dynasty, Chinese officials wondered aloud if the "fountain of fortune" had dried up.[29]

For Potosí's native son and early eighteenth-century historian Bartolomé Arzáns, God's third and fatal blow to his city was not the mint fraud itself. Rather, it was the overzealous Spanish special prosecutor whom God had sent as scourge: Dr. Francisco de Nestares Marín. Rocha, in Arzáns's telling, was a hapless scapegoat. This version of the story was already in wide circulation in the immediate aftermath of Rocha's execution. That potosinos might see the great debasement as something other than a crime of lese majesty may strike us as bizarre, but such was the distance that had grown between Madrid and the Imperial Villa since the era of Viceroy Toledo.

Somehow by the 1640s it was difficult for many of Potosí's most powerful men—most of them born in Spain—to see the extraordinary idiocy of the debasement scam. By unwittingly damaging their king's reputation, they were fouling worldwide circuits of credit and commerce. Early modern capitalism varied in form and extent from place to place, but much of the world agreed that silver was the standard medium of cross-cultural exchange, and the Potosí piece of eight had up to this point been proverbial. Now the script was flipped: the early champions of globalization had a shared emblem of discontent, of bad faith, of cheating. For them "Potosí" meant "Peru." Both were history.

For his troubles, Dr. Francisco de Nestares Marín was promoted to the Council of the Indies, but he never made it home. In a baroque coda appreciated by Arzáns, Nestares Marín's replacements all died or rejected the post at the last minute. In an era of excruciatingly slow communications years passed before a suitable replacement was sent. When the new man finally came it was too late for Nestares Marín, who left Potosí for La Plata in late 1658 in broken health. He died on 22 April 1660 uttering these last words: "Thus have I served my God and king." Although no evidence of fraud on his part has surfaced in the archives, he was widely slandered in his own time, and it was these stories of the evil inspector that are repeated in Potosí today thanks to Arzáns. Francisco Gómez de la Rocha, by contrast, is a pop-culture figure famous for allegedly burying an enormous treasure.

The great mint scandal of 1649 and its aftermath marked the end of an era in Potosí. Already struggling, silver producers and wholesale merchants went bankrupt by the dozen as the credit bubble burst. The inspector-general Nestares Marín was right to correct the many abuses he found, yet the fact that he was the one to stop them meant that he would be personally blamed for Potosí's decline. Try as he might, he could not revive the mining economy, although in 1651 he had parts of the Kari-Kari reservoir-canal system repaired to offset the effects of drought on milling silver ores. He struggled mightily to bring the currency up to proper fineness, a source of great embarrassment for the crown. A straight man in crooked times, Nestares Marín worked for the king when the Spanish monarchy was facing its darkest hour, roiled by plague, crop failure, conspiracy, and war.

Potosí's troubles mirrored Castile's. The Basque-Vicuña war, the 1626 flood, and the great mint fraud of the 1640s, coupled with a series of epidemics and droughts plus fears of a Portuguese or Dutch invasion, left the Imperial Villa reeling by mid-century. In attempting to offset the decline of the mines after 1640, potosinos opened new mining frontiers, especially in the distant and freezing Carangas and Los Lípes districts. Even that old fraudster Rocha had investments out here in the cold *puna* where Álvaro Alonso Barba had perfected his craft, and Nestares Marín tried to keep the new finds running, supplying silver to the Imperial Villa to offset the problems of the Cerro Rico until new investors could be assembled to drive a new drainage tunnel or invent some new processing method.

The lessons of these "secret judgments of God" may include the global realization that Potosí was not infallible, that even if the Treasury of the World was not inexhaustible, it could sputter, maybe even collapse. Indeed, the great mint fraud showed that when Potosí sneezed, the world caught a cold. For Spain, this string of disasters prompted a last-ditch test of overseas governance. However creaky and inefficient its mechanisms, the Hispanic Monarchy or Spanish Empire was, rather like Potosí, surprisingly durable, capable of staggering back to its feet after a shattering blow. The great mint fraud investigation proved the king was still capable of reining in and punishing rogue subjects in the most remote corner of empire. Even if locals did not interpret Nestares Marín's long *visita* as something positive, it proved that Madrid remained in control. Potosí, for all its pretentions, was not independent.

# SIX

# Decadence and Rebirth

> One day I went to the place where they minted *dinârs,* piasters, halves, and quarters. In this mint house there are forty black slaves and twelve Spaniards working. We saw the pile of coins, like hillocks on one side, the halves on another, and half-quarters still on another, heaped on the floor and being trampled underfoot like dirt that has no value.
>
> —ELIAS AL-MÛSILI[1]

IN 1678, ELIAS AL-MÛSILI, a Chaldean priest from Baghdad, visited Potosí, where he stayed for over a month. The Imperial Villa was his prime destination amid a multiyear Spanish American tour. "Don Elias of Mosul," as his name translates with the honorific "don" he used in Spanish, had received permission from Spain's Queen Mother, Mariana of Austria, to travel to Peru to seek alms for his embattled church. He also carried permission from the pope since he was associated with the mission of the Propaganda Fide. Researchers have discovered that don Elias was a member of Baghdad's Nestorian Christian patriarchate who had converted to Roman Catholicism.

The seventeenth century had been hard on Baghdad as a result of perennial wars between the Ottomans and Safavids. Mesopotamia was an ancient heartland but also a venerable trading crossroads, a region through which considerable silver moved to link the Mediterranean and Europe with Asia and the Indian Ocean basin. Much of the silver that traversed the Middle East in the seventeenth century had originated in Potosí, and it was often carried by Armenian merchants, fellow Christians well known to men like don Elias. In fact, Elias says he was accompanied on his return to Spain by two Armenian servants as well as "four parrots who talked like a human being."[2] Armenian priests had also gathered alms in Potosí amid the great mint fraud of the 1640s.

Elias al-Mûsili's voyage to Potosí was unusually long, but it reinforced the legendary character of the city of silver. Of the Cerro Rico he says: "It is known throughout the world on account of its excessive wealth; countless treasures have been extracted from all four sides of it for a hundred and forty years."[3] This was still true even though the priest from Baghdad arrived when the city was in decline, its mint and mines staffed with less than one third the number of workers employed just a few decades before. Even so, don Elias claims to have met four "very rich men" associated with the mint, one of whom was no doubt Antonio López de Quiroga, a Galician millionaire.

While staying in Potosí's Jesuit compound, don Elias learned some details of the *mita,* of the difficulties of mine work, and of the mercury amalgamation process, which he described. Don Elias eventually left Potosí for La Plata, where he said numerous masses in Syriac (the closest surviving tongue to Aramaic, the language of Jesus). He says he also healed a nun with a potion containing frog ashes.[4] Reciprocity was his game; passing back through Potosí on the way to the Pacific coast, don Elias gave an image of Jesus that he had picked up in Rome to the head of the Mercedarian monastery.

Potosí's town council books record Elias al-Mùsili's petition in an entry for 14 October 1678, calling him "don Elías de San Juan, canon of Babylon." Don Elias asked the town council for alms to support "the rescue of the Holy Church of Babylon, currently in the power of Mohammedan barbarians." He said that many other towns had contributed. The *cabildo* released a donation of 200 pesos and moved on to mundane problems like faulty marketplace weights and measures.[5]

After leaving the Imperial Villa, don Elias says he worried constantly about the safety of his great load of silver. He had reason to be concerned. His voyage was long and complex, with a Pacific leg followed by a trek across New Spain. It appears he barely managed to protect his hoard from the buccaneers who sacked Veracruz, Mexico, in 1683. Somehow, the "canon of Babylon" made it across the Atlantic, but it is uncertain if he ever reached his home. His signature appears in notary records in El Puerto de Santa María near Cádiz in the 1690s, tied to the affairs of other Eastern Christians. It is unlikely that any remnant of Elias al-Mùsili's Potosí silver remains in Baghdad, but his story reminds us of the persistent global reach of the Cerro Rico.

Potosí experienced hard times in the hundred years following the 1649 mint scandal, but not all was darkness and tribulation. Potosí, as don Elias's account reminds us, was surprisingly resilient, somehow living up to its reputation as an inexhaustible fountain of fortune in spite of drawing God's wrath. Other visitors added to the mystique of the Imperial Villa and the Cerro Rico, fueling the dreams of ambitious merchants and envious kings, all hoping to penetrate Potosí's markets or even capture the mountain itself.

Potosí as city of windmills, Arnoldus Montanus, *America,* 1671. Courtesy of the John Carter Brown Library at Brown University.

Meanwhile, local entrepreneurs like the Galician Antonio López de Quiroga made the most of a challenging situation, hiring free workers, introducing black powder blasting, and otherwise rearranging the factors of silver production to improve efficiency.

This chapter traces Potosí's post-1650 decadence, which was offset to some extent by successful figures such as Antonio López de Quiroga, probably the richest man in the colonial Americas in his day. The chapter also sheds more light on the city's ties to surrounding silver camps and new technologies. It was in this era also that great effort went into reforming the mita, with mixed results. Amid crisis, there emerged two major artistic figures, the author Bartolomé Arzáns de Orsúa y Vela and the painter Melchor Pérez Holguín. The chapter also treats the continued belief among outsiders, such as Elias al-Mûsili, that Potosí was inexhaustible. After a widely disseminated late-1650s report by French visitor Accarette du Biscay, a new hype about the Cerro Rico arose that helped inspire the formation of the South Sea Company, a British monopoly trading enterprise intended to pay down the national debt that spawned a huge financial bubble around 1720. Thanks to

Accarette, French interest also peaked under Louis XIV. It began in the 1650s and continued until after the 1702–13 War of the Spanish Succession that put the Sun King's grandson on the Spanish throne. Even in decline, Potosí remained the undisputed treasury of the world.

## THE COLBERT REPORT

For curious kings, travelers' accounts of Potosí were worth their weight in silver. If nothing else, they provided hints of the true wealth of the kings of Spain. Elias al-Mûsili's Arabic account of his voyage to Potosí seems to have languished in obscurity for several centuries, although some part of it may have been read to Ottoman sultans or Persian shahs. We know of it because it was eventually discovered by Jesuit scholars in the early twentieth century.

Far different was the late seventeenth-century traveler known to us as Accarette du Biscay. Possibly a French Basque, Accarette wrote a brief but pithy account of his 1658 visit to Potosí via Buenos Aires. French interest in Potosí was stoked in the early reign of Louis XIV, in part thanks to Accarette, who delivered a copy of his manuscript to Finance Minister Jean-Baptiste Colbert. Plans for a French invasion were made but not pursued, perhaps due to the 1659 Peace of the Pyrenees ending the long war with Spain. Accarette's account was quickly translated from French to English and served to excite the imaginations of buccaneers and investors alike.

Like Elias al-Mûsili, but with the sort of eye for detail one might expect of a spy, Accarette explained the relative ease of travel to Potosí from Buenos Aires despite the great distance. He was impressed by the wealth and lack of defenses of nearly every Spanish American city he visited. He claimed that Córdoba, in central Argentina, sent nearly 30,000 mules a year to Potosí and other parts of Upper Peru. This had made the isolated city rich. Human diversity also caught his eye. Accarette was quick to comment on how native Andeans and enslaved Africans dressed and armed themselves, and how mestizo men seemed to number about the same as Spaniards. This detail does not appear in Spanish records, although we know *mestizaje* was on the rise.

Accarette also notes that Spanish women in Potosí were "generally addicted to excess in taking coca." Apparently he did not understand its effects, adding that: "They are so heated, and sometimes absolutely fuddled by it, that they have no command of themselves at all." As for yerba mate, or the "herb of Paraguay," Accarette says it was consumed in large part by native workers to restore "moisture" after suffering the air of the mines, "which strangely dries them up."[6] Whether or not *potosinos* felt this way, Accarette espoused prevailing galenic notions of the human body.

Historians must approach writers like Accarette with caution, keeping in mind in this case the author's need to impress his patron, Louis XIV (by way of Colbert). Yet the main weakness of this source, its naiveté, is also its strength. When compared with Spanish or indigenous sources, we see that Accarette offers odd details much like don Elias al-Mûsili, the kinds of things that locals found unremarkable. For example, Accarette, perhaps because he was a Basque, was told that the Cerro Rico was called Aránzazu, after the site of an apparition of the Virgin in the mountains of Guipúzcoa. To my knowledge, no one else makes this claim.

Accarette goes on to describe the silver milling and refining process in far greater detail than don Elias, followed by brief discussions of minting and taxation of raw silver bars, followed by their transport to Spain. This was the sort of detail that would interest a statesman like Colbert. More interesting for our purposes is Accarette's awestruck description of a festival celebrated in the Imperial Villa upon receiving news of the birth of Prince Carlos, future king of Spain, last of the Spanish Habsburgs (see appendix). The festivities lasted two weeks, and all work stopped: "And all the people great and small, whether Spaniards, foreigners, Indians, or blacks, minded nothing else but to do something extraordinary for the solemnizing of this festival."[7] There were days of games, balls, parades, and musical performances, with a finale of global pretensions: native Andeans pulled a mock ship complete with sails and live cannons through the streets of the Imperial Villa. At the helm was a prominent potosino dressed as "an emperor of the East," come to pay obeisance to the king of Spain on the birth of his son via his representative, the *audiencia* president.

The ship was then pulled up in front of a mock castle said to house Oliver Cromwell, Spain's most hated Protestant enemy at the time, and after a battle replete with fireworks the ship and castle together went up in flames. After this, a number of wealthy people tossed coins to the poor in the king's name, but the image that most impressed readers of Accarette du Biscay, especially the French and English merchants and officials who would later use his writings as propaganda to drum up investment for overseas trading firms like the South Sea Company, was of the last day of the festivities, when the Holy Sacrament was paraded through Potosí's streets, several of which were temporarily paved with silver bars.

The altar where the Host was to be lodged in the Church of the Recollects was so furnished with figures, vessels, and plates of gold and silver, adorned with pearls, diamonds, and other precious stones that scarce ever could anything be seen more rich, for the citizens brought thither all the rarest jewels they had. The extraordinary charge of this whole time of rejoicing was reckoned to amount to above 500,000 crowns.[8]

Clearly the old Imperial Villa—even in decadence—could still put on a show. Despite decades of poor returns from the mines and a sequence of calamities that wiped out a whole class of elites, the city remained insanely opulent, outrageously inventive, and incurably festive, as it had always been and as it would remain as long as there was something to celebrate and something of value on hand to display. Accarette is invaluable to us in part because the town council books for 1658 are incomplete and say nothing of this celebration.

As Lisa Voigt notes, another celebration from 1663, memorialized by an unknown poet, suggests continued revelry and over-the-top ostentation amid diminishing returns.[9] In this Easter morning festival, the "renovation of the Holy Sacrament," everyone turned out in full regalia, including the president of the Audiencia of Charcas, all twenty-four town councilmen with their silver staffs of office, all the great ladies of the city, and all the clergy in their finest white robes. And although the Cerro Rico at sunrise was "crowned" by rays as "its own monarch, to the amazement of the world," the poet emphasizes parity with Madrid, as if Potosí had for a day become the capital of the empire. A great wall hanging sent by the viceroy helped the partygoers imagine the Escorial, the Buen Retiro, El Pardo, and Aranjuez. Getting back to the sacred, three crucifixes fashioned as fountains flowed with wine, water, and *chicha* from Christ's nail wounds, "from which the Indians, mulattos, and blacks / were obstinately drinking."[10] Sponsored by the city's *azoguero* elite, all this took place as the mita came under severe scrutiny.

### THE MITA'S CRITICS RETURN

As we have seen, the morality of the Potosí mita, formally instituted by Viceroy Francisco de Toledo in the early 1570s, was debated from the start. The mita for the mercury mines of Huancavelica, on which Potosí relied for its survival, was even more controversial. Back in 1629, Padre Pedro de Oñate had offered a forceful opinion. Oñate claimed that the mine mita went against natural law, that mine work was something even the Romans knew to be a deadly punishment, the stuff of martyrdom, and that it ought to be outlawed right away for the good of the royal conscience.

To those who claimed that the Spanish monarchy needed the silver of Potosí, and thus the mercury of Huancavelica, to protect the Catholic Faith amid the chaos of the Thirty Years War, Oñate offered this: "Is it possible that God, with the infinite treasures of his omnipotence and eternal wisdom, has no other means to conserve and defend his Church against heretics than the mercury of Huancavelica . . . ?"[11] Oñate went further, arguing that the silver of the Indies had been a curse on Spain, and that the Faith had been purer and more defensible without it. Young Philip IV may have taken note of this polemic, but he did nothing to mitigate the abuses of the mita either at Potosí or Huancavelica.

Yet over the course of Philip IV's long reign, the Potosí mita had changed considerably as native Andean populations fell and regrouped. As we have seen, by 1640 if not before the mita had become in large degree a cash subsidy for powerful mine and refinery owners lucky enough to have an allotment. For some, Indians "in the pocket" were as good as Indians in the mines. Yet the mine mita was not dead, and it still ate men in the era of the great mint fraud and its aftermath. Thus it continued to draw critical fire from priests and secular officials.

It must be noted, too, that native Andean resistance to the mita continued apace. Most draftees voted with their feet, but some of the mita catchment zone's most powerful native headmen came together to offer new and detailed critiques, pushing hard to have the mita reformed if not abolished. As Luis Miguel Glave and others have shown, the tide of mita criticism rose in the aftermath of the mint fraud and the arrival of a new viceroy, the Conde de Alba de Liste. Viceroy Alba had his own ambitions, and one of them was to rush through a mita overhaul by way of another royal inspector.[12]

The Dominican friar Francisco de la Cruz was arguably the most personally involved critic of the Potosí mita in the seventeenth century, and it appears he paid for it with his life. Recently named bishop of Santa Marta, on Colombia's Caribbean coast, La Cruz was sent to Potosí in 1659 by Viceroy Alba to implement radical reforms. Accarette had just left. Outraged by the abusive practices of Potosí's azogueros, La Cruz suspended mita exemption payments, protected native headmen, and ordered a new census. For his efforts, he was murdered in April 1660, poisoned by his evening chocolate. The local refiners' guild, which depended on the mita both as labor and cash subsidy, was suspected of ordering the hit.[13]

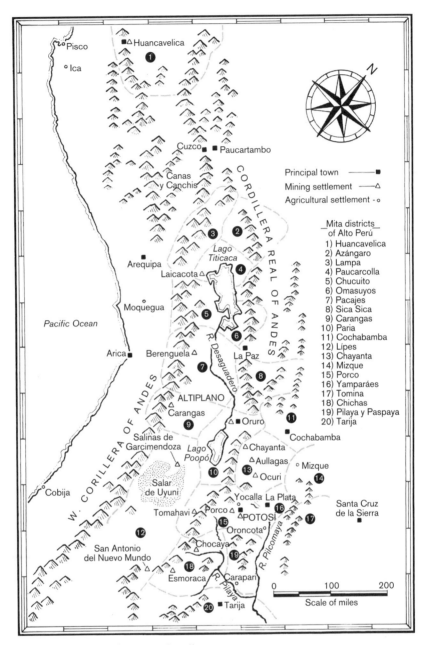

MAP 5. Potosí's *Mita* districts and satellite mining camps.

Yet pangs of guilt soon returned. By 1670, nearly a century after Viceroy Toledo formalized the mita, a new Peruvian viceroy, the Conde de Lemos, wrote an impassioned letter to the Queen Regent, Mariana of Austria. Lemos sketched a brief history of the Potosí mita along with attempts to reform or abolish it. He then related how the system had become an entrenched subsidy for a small group of powerful mine and mill owners who managed to extort the crown by claiming the Spanish monarchy would fall if the mita were altered (the same claim refuted by Oñate in 1629). A group of Jesuits in the highland Peruvian town of Julí echoed the viceroy's lamentations in a letter from 1670, saying that they shielded their native parishioners from the Potosí mita by helping them sell crops for cash to pay for exemption.[14]

Aside from propping up Potosí's old refinery-owning class, the mita continued to depopulate the Andes, reducing the number of Spain's subjects and burdening the royal conscience. Lemos said that over 24,000 native Andeans resided permanently in Potosí, and that they ought to suffice to supply the mines with voluntary workers. Although Queen Regent Mariana was perhaps the most sympathetic of all the Spanish Habsburgs to the suffering of native American peoples, she chose to say a prayer rather than decree reform. Lemos died in office and the mita was not abolished.

To some degree, "the crown's doubts" were assuaged by reforms implemented in the wake of the Lemos administration.[15] A long-overdue census was finally taken in 1689, and it showed the extent to which indigenous populations had suffered from the demands of the mita. A Lima circuit court judge, Matías Lagúnez, argued for near-abolition in a 1691 treatise, which in turn led to a more modest and rule-bound mita allotment in 1692. Additional restrictions decreed in 1697 reduced the mita further, yet even in decline Potosí's azogueros fought back, interfering with enforcement of the new rules. As the House of Bourbon replaced the Habsburgs in 1700, calls for reform clashed with new fiscal demands, and war continued to 1713.

By 1719, critiques of the mita had become so routine they were often less pointed, not even grounded in specific facts.[16] It was as if Viceroy Toledo's great machine had become so naturalized that its worst features were no longer an outrage, or at least not enough to merit abolition. This is one way to read the wide-ranging and seemingly contradictory opinion on the mita offered by Padre Manuel de Toledo y Leiva in 1724. To be fair, Leiva was writing about the mercury mines of Huancavelica, where he served as rector of the Jesuit college, but he also made frequent reference to Potosí, a city whose situation he knew well.[17]

Like those who came before, Toledo y Leiva acknowledged the long and troubled history of theological opinions on the mita and on those who offered them. He vividly described the death of the viceroy who started the Huancavelica mita, presumably referring to Francisco de Toledo. This involved a deathbed vision of "innumerable Indians like atoms in the air" crying out to such a degree that the viceroy exclaimed, "Leave me, Indians of Huancavelica! What do you want?"[18] Leiva seemed to argue that the mita was all but dead in Potosí thanks to the plague of 1719–21 (discussed below), and that many silver miners and workers had moved to Oruro, which was again booming.

As for Huancavelica, Leiva lamented the hardships the mita posed for native workers, but when it came down to it, he believed there was no other way to keep the mines and refineries running. Mercury was essential to the crown and Huancavelica was unique in the Indies. The idea that native Andeans would work here voluntarily, as might be possible in Potosí, struck Leiva as absurd. The mita, as always, lurched onward.

### POTOSÍ'S HARD-TIMES MILLIONAIRE: ANTONIO LÓPEZ DE QUIROGA

Each day one sees in this land great adventurers aiming to get rich by way of mines, and he who was shirtless yesterday may have tomorrow 500,000 pesos and as much on display as a great lord, although in the same space of time we have seen many fall to ruin for their vanities and excessive expenditures made during their prosperity.[19]

In the aftermath of the 1640s mint fraud, Potosí's mining industry struggled but did not collapse. The city was not abandoned, and silver continued to flow, albeit at a slower pace and with few new discoveries to offset the Cerro Rico's declining yields. As sometimes happens in the business world, one of the greatest entrepreneurs to ever inhabit Potosí flourished amid the ruins. Antonio López de Quiroga, a Galician merchant who arrived in Potosí in 1648, would by his death in 1699 be known as one of the richest Spanish Americans of the entire colonial period. He started from relatively modest means and built a personal empire: a vast web of mines, refineries, rural estates, urban townhouses, shops, and even religious chapels. One of the only things López de Quiroga proved unable to buy despite his phenomenal gains was a title of nobility.

Portrait of Antonio López de Quiroga. Courtesy Casa Nacional de Moneda, Potosí.

Antonio López de Quiroga's business success in hard times serves to remind us that enterprising individuals could prosper in a Spanish colonial setting.[20] There was nothing about the culture or the legal system to stifle an ambitious businessman. Even high taxes were not an obstacle. López de Quiroga began his long climb as a silver merchant, essentially assuming the role of the executed mint fraud mastermind, Francisco Gómez de la Rocha. López worked briefly for another merchant in the early 1650s before taking over the business of buying raw silver and advancing loans to mine and mill owners in coin. Upper-level banking was not a bad place to start, although López complained that many of his customers were overdrawn deadbeats.

Having accumulated both capital and knowledge as a silver merchant and financier, López turned to mining and refining by the end of the 1650s, a tough decade for silver producers as a result of droughts and other contingencies. Many mills sat idle thanks to an unpredictable climate. Slowly, López bought moribund or flooded mines, hired skilled workers, introduced black powder blasting to his diggings, and invested in long-range projects, usually expensive but necessary adits or *socavones*. A prudent money manager with deep pockets, he could stomach losses and hold out for profits much longer than other individual mining entrepreneurs.

Importantly, López took advantage of the struggles of others to enter a business—hard-rock mining—that a person without ready money would most likely have avoided. What is more, he had the blessing and encouragement of inspector-general Nestares Marín, who remained in Potosí until 1658, still trying to set the royal finances aright (Accarette du Biscay mentions meeting him personally). Nestares Marín desperately needed men like López de Quiroga to fill the gap left by Rocha and his mint fraud cronies.

Fill the gap he did. In the 1650s alone, Lopez de Quiroga's first decade in Potosí, he moved over 14 million pesos' worth of silver through the treasury and mint. His first rich mine in the Cerro Rico, ironically called "Mala Moneda," or "Bad Coin," had been donated to him by a widow he had treated kindly. López also acquired his first silver refining mills from several of his major debtors. As they went broke and died, he took over and prospered.

López de Quiroga was more than just a lucky vulture, however, and before long he began to invest in distant mining camps such as San Antonio del Nuevo Mundo, high in the province of Los Lípes to the southwest, and Laicacota, a major silver deposit near Puno, Peru, far away to the north overlooking Lake Titicaca. These were not new finds, but rather like the Cerro Rico, they had fallen on hard times and lacked long-term investors willing to take substantial risks. Such a man was Antonio López de Quiroga. López sent trusted subordinates and hired hands who knew his favored methods of operation. His drainage adits paid off handsomely, and by the 1670s López was fabulously rich.

It is worth pointing out how risky these investments were. In the 1660s, Laicacota was wracked by violent feuds reminiscent of the Basque-Vicuña wars of Potosí, necessitating a personal visit by the viceroy, accompanied by troops.[21] San Antonio del Nuevo Mundo, also known as San Antonio de los

Ruins of San Antonio del Nuevo Mundo, Los Lípes, 2016. Photo by author.

Lípes, was similarly famous for murderous violence, although its high-altitude climate was also exceedingly rigorous. The Spanish globetrotter Gregorio de Robles passed through in the 1690s, just as López de Quiroga's last projects panned out, and left a rare description. Coming up from Buenos Aires through Salta and Jujuy, Robles describes the remote mining camp at over 5,000 meters (16,500 feet) above sea level as follows:

> I stayed there for twenty days, and I saw the whole sierra with its silver mines and refining mills, more than sixty of them, worked and populated, as they are the ones that supplement Potosí, whose mining and shortage of ores is notorious. This country is so cold, and the terrain so rugged, that I could not finish my reconnaissance of it, as the cordillera is full of snow all year round, and on the slopes the greater part of it, such that in that country they say that water is carried in gunnysacks, as it is ice that they collect, melted over fires and reduced to water. It is also true there that women who conceive must go to give birth eight leagues away, where there is a settlement, or ravine, with some 100 residents, called the old mine of San Antonio, with a more benign climate.[22]

Clearly, mining at such extreme altitudes, and amid the rigors of the Little Ice Age, was no small feat. For workers, such mining camps marked the outer limits of survival; for investors, they marked the outer limits of entrepreneurship. Luckily for men like López de Quiroga, they did not have to personally live there. López built a lavish mansion off the main square in Potosí that still stands.

Curiously, López de Quiroga found it difficult to win the kind of martial recognition demanded by Baroque Spanish society, both at home and in the colonies. He was of course a captain of finance and industry rather than a commander of troops, but this choice of professions had not stopped others from funding and even personally embarking on campaigns to defend ports against Protestant "heretics," or to put down indigenous uprisings in the backlands. Many lesser men became nobles under Habsburg rule in the seventeenth century.

By the 1670s, López de Quiroga sought to make a name for himself by funding an expedition to the upper Amazon in search of the fabled kingdom of the Great Paitití, a variation of the Eldorado legend. For such a hardheaded businessman to spend money on a scheme of this sort a century after the death of the last Inca would seem quixotic, but this was virtually the only means available by which López might win a noble title. Peter Bakewell suggests that the Galician millionaire's failure to be named count or marquis, or even *adelantado,* were due to his overreaching. The Great Paitití expeditions, led by relatives in Santa Cruz de la Sierra, came to nothing, but they contributed to López de Quiroga's regional fame.

In the end, López de Quiroga had to content himself with the title of *maestre de campo,* or field marshal, yet presumably he could rest at his death in 1699 knowing that no one had ever overseen production of so much silver in a single lifetime, much less in a period of decline rather than boom. According to tax records, López produced over 1.7 million marks (approx. 386,000 kg) or nearly a million pounds of silver between 1661 and 1698. This was about one seventh of all silver registered by Potosí's royal treasury officials in these years. A veritable fountain of fortune in his own right, Antonio López de Quiroga, the lucky Galician merchant turned mining entrepreneur, became a legend, a rare star amid the twilight of Habsburg Potosí. He was buried in Potosí's Franciscan monastery and his portrait hangs in the Royal Mint.

BAD START FOR A NEW CENTURY

As the childless and sickly Habsburg King Charles II breathed his last in Madrid in November 1700, the prospect of a Bourbon monarch on the Spanish throne hung like a dark cloud over much of Europe. Louis XIV was poised to annex Spain and its overseas empire, prompting England, the

Netherlands, and other European powers to form a league against the French-Spanish alliance. They had a Habsburg successor on hand, though not the one favored by Charles. For Potosí, the ensuing War of the Spanish Succession (1702–13) proved a mixed blessing. The mines were moribund in the absence of men like López de Quiroga and mita workers were in short supply. Yet Spain's sudden embrace of France prompted an influx of cheap French goods that stimulated silver production.

As Potosí staggered, the silver mines of Zacatecas, in north-central Mexico, took off. This was also the great age of Brazilian gold, discovered in the southern highlands around 1695. Newly expanded global trade, especially in South and East Asia, drove up demand for all manner of bullion and coin. Both Louis XIV and English speculators investing in the South Sea Company wondered how they might tap the fabled Cerro Rico of Potosí, inexhaustible Treasury of the World. Accarette's now outdated 1658 description was translated and widely disseminated under a phony name, with new renditions of the Cerro Rico made into posters for the South Sea Company.

Much of this international interest remained unknown to elite potosinos, who faced their own cash-flow problems. As was typical, they blamed native Andeans. Many pointed to the perennial matter of high-grading, now called *kajcheo*. When mine owners were short of capital, indigenous miners filled the gap in various ways. Kajcheo first appeared in Potosí records under that name in 1709, and officials claimed that indigenous "high-graders" or *kajchas* were producing considerable silver in primitive, usually horse-powered mills called *trapiches,* the same term used for small sugar mills.[23]

High-grading was hardly a new phenomenon, as we have seen, but its implications had changed with the decline of the big mills and growing scarcity of quality ores. The kajchas only removed about 5 percent of the mountain's ores, according to official estimates, but it was clearly the best 5 percent, estimated to yield 40 percent of Potosí's silver.[24] By law, kajchas who got caught removing ore faced a sentence of six months' forced labor in either a city bakery or in the royal mint, but enforcement was lax.

Potosí silver attracted many foreigners besides the French in this period, including France's nemesis in the War of the Spanish Succession: England. After the 1713 Peace of Utrecht, the South Sea Company won the exclusive right to send enslaved Africans to Buenos Aires. This monopoly, known as the *asiento,* served as cover for contraband commerce in dry goods, most of it exchanged for Potosí silver. Legal or not, French and English traders at Buenos Aires stimulated production at the mines. Unfortunately, disaster soon struck. Historians now believe that one of these European trading ships carried influenza, plague, or both.

The epidemic reached Potosí in 1719, killing, according to local chronicler and survivor Bartolomé Arzáns de Orsúa y Vela, some 22,000 persons by the time it let up in 1721. This seems a high number given the population of the city at the time (at most 50,000), but this was probably the most devastating epidemic to hit the city and its surrounding region in colonial times. A similar number of dead was reported in Cuzco, and a staggering 72,000 fell victim in the Archbishopric of Lima.[25]

It took decades for Potosí to recover from the great epidemic of 1719–21, but two contrasting and sometimes complementary social groups surged: the mill owners or azogueros, and the kajchas, or "ore thieves." Azoguero pressure led the Bourbon king Philip V to reduce the *quinto real* to 10 percent in 1735, a major stimulus for large-scale silver producers who relied on mostly low-grade ore. As the indigenous population began to rebound, Potosí's labor shortage eased somewhat, but without the mita the azogueros claimed they could never survive. As seen above, despite centuries of criticism, Viceroy Toledo's most shameful legacy remained in place.

One indigenous response was to organize, in part by way of religious sodalities or confraternities. An inspection of Potosí's fourteen native parishes from 1690 had found an astonishing 112 of them.[26] On Huayna Potosí, even the kajchas had their own religious fraternity, complete with a shrine. Penalties for stealing ore grew harsher, and kajchas also faced off against a new class of mine entrance guards hired by Potosí's richest men. As will be seen in the next chapter, the stage was set for rebellion.

LOCAL TALENT: BARTOLOMÉ ARZÁNS
AND MELCHOR PÉREZ HOLGUÍN

And if this Imperial Villa of Potosí, my *patria,* has managed to survive after so many calamities, it is only due to the veneration that its residents, although sinners, have had for the divine cult.[27]

It was precisely in these dark years that Potosí produced its greatest literary figure: Bartolomé Arzáns de Orsúa y Vela, born in the city in 1676. Arzáns began writing his massive, million-word *Historia de la Villa Imperial de Potosí* about 1705. He only stopped writing when death stilled his pen in 1736. Arzáns's *History,* sent to Spain for a publication that would not occur

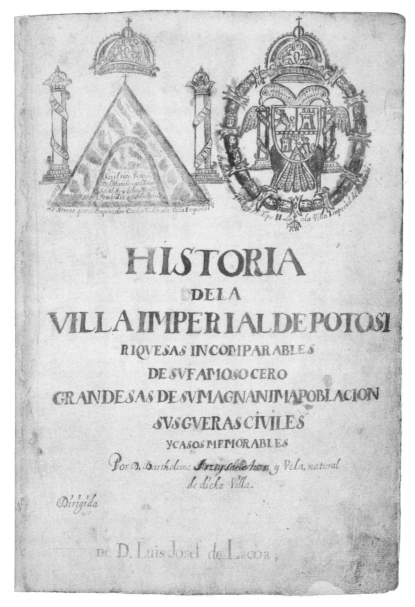

"Historia de la Villa Imperial de Potosí," Bartolomé Arzáns de Orsúa y Vela, frontispiece, ca. 1736. Courtesy of the John Hay Library at Brown University.

"Entry of the Viceroy Morcillo," ca. 1716, Melchor Pérez Holguín. Courtesy of the Museo de América, Madrid.

for over two centuries, devotes several pages to each year of Potosí's history, but the annalistic format is soon overwhelmed by what one modern editor has called "tales," fabulous accounts of witchcraft, cross-dressing, gang warfare, and much more. We have summarized his account of Potosí's "warrior maidens" in chapter 4. Arzáns pauses occasionally to moralize, as in the cases of the 1626 flood and the mint fraud of the 1640s, but mostly he marvels at the strange deeds that marked the passing of time in his rough-and-tumble hometown.

Arzáns has frustrated modern historians since he blends fact and fiction, not a rare practice among baroque writers whose aim was to entertain as well

as edify. Even so, Arzáns goes well beyond his contemporaries, approaching magical realism. Perhaps most curious is Arzáns's apparent invention of numerous prior historians of Potosí whom he cites liberally. Most of these "authorities" have not been discovered, but a few have shown up, making it all the more difficult to discount the truth of Arzáns's tales. We distrust him at our peril. As a literary figure, Arzáns has drawn sustained interest from scholars but much more remains to be learned.[28]

Melchor Pérez Holguín has been hailed by art historians as a local genius on par with the chronicler Arzáns.[29] His style, devout yet personal, is distinctive. Most of his paintings, many of which hang in Potosí's mint museum, employ a silver-gray palette, and his human figures often have a gnarled quality. Holguín, as he is often known, was born in Cochabamba around 1660 and was active as a painter and later sculptor in Potosí by 1676. Starting as a teenage prodigy, he produced a vast body of work until his death sometime in the 1730s. Like other painters and sculptors in his day, Holguín's oeuvre is almost entirely religious, mostly created to decorate chapels and altars.

A notable exception to Holguín's religious art is the 1716 painting *The Entrance of the Archbishop-Viceroy Morcillo in the Imperial Villa of Potosí*, a massive canvas now housed in Madrid's Museo de América. It was apparently a gift to King Philip V. Pérez Holguín even includes himself in the foreground, palette and brush in hand, but the aim of the painting is to capture the grandeur of the archbishop-viceroy's retinue, along with the welcoming display put on by the city's diverse population.[30]

It was the first time a viceroy had personally visited Potosí since Francisco de Toledo camped out and transformed the city in the early 1570s. In the painting, wealthy women stand peering from balconies, accompanied by indigenous servants and enslaved African women. Those looking down on the procession have hung out their favorite paintings or draped their finest textiles on their balconies, making for the most conspicuous possible display.

Struggling to get everything into the picture, Holguín adds two inset images depicting the archbishop-viceroy's reception on the main plaza by day and by night. The Cerro Rico looms behind. The archbishop-viceroy himself is almost a lost figure amid the armies of local nobles, priests, grooms, and militiamen marching along with their muskets on their shoulders in their finest outfits. Many turn their heads to the viewer, further distracting from the archbishop-viceroy. Speech scrolls emanate from the mouths of an elderly man and woman in the foreground near the painter. He asks: "Little lady, have you ever seen such a marvel?" She replies: "Ah, Louie, not in a hundred-and-some years have I seen a grand show of this size."

If Potosí hit bottom in the early eighteenth century, beaten down by plague and overrun with freelance indigenous miners whose silver escaped taxation, the works of Arzáns and Pérez Holguín remind us, along with the intricately carved stone facade of the San Lorenzo de los Carangas church and many other architectural jewels, that artistic fluorescence need not coincide with high silver production. Before these great artistic figures appeared we find the personage of Antonio López de Quiroga, the Galician millionaire who made the mines produce against the odds thanks to new technologies, hard-nosed business practices, careful money management, and harsh treatment of subordinates.

Potosí remained a global city, still firing the imaginations of envious monarchs as the Habsburg dynasty faded in Spain. Foreign visitors like Elias al-Mûsili and Accarette du Biscay relayed their tales of Potosí's continued opulence to distant readers in the Middle East and northern Europe. Who knows what images don Elias's manuscript inspired in and beyond Baghdad. Accarette's account drove French and English intervention, if only through aggressive trade. Stoked by new if deceitful images of the Cerro Rico, European and Asian monarchs would continue to dream of taking Potosí for themselves.

But the Baroque age in Potosí so well represented by the words of Arzáns and the images of Pérez Holguín was about to be challenged by a series of Enlightenment-inspired bureaucrats and scientists from Spain and other parts of Europe. They believed that the once-great Cerro Rico had fallen into the hands of superstitious rubes who sat like fools on mountains of untapped silver. Desperate for revenue to fund colossal new armies and navies, Spain's Bourbon kings blessed these secular missionaries as they left for Potosí.

# SEVEN

# From Revival to Revolution

The inhabitants of this Villa and its riverbank are made up of outsiders who come and go, of all classes of folk. The frigidity of the site comes from its elevation and the snow peaks that surround it, and this makes windy days bothersome, but the Spaniards and mestizos are well sheltered by their narrow rooms and dividers, adding to their succor with smoking braziers and gourds of hot water, which are continually taken by the women, and which is the treat they offer to men at all hours. They say that after the discovery of the riches of that great mountain they ordered 15,000 Indians to supply its labor and that of the silver refineries. The declining richness of the ores, among other causes, reduced this number to 3,500, which is how many are assigned nowadays, most of them accompanied by their women and children, which in all would number more than 12,000 souls, including those who remain and employ themselves in the honorable exercise of Chalcas [*Kajchas*], which are certain ore thieves who enter the mines at night, and being expert in them, they get the most precious part, which they refine and take to the king's exchange bank, it being certain that these "permitted pirates" extract more silver than the mine owners.

— CONCOLORCORVO,
*El Lazarillo de Ciegos Caminantes*, 1773[1]

WHEN A POSTAL INSPECTOR CALLING himself "the man in black" (*Concolorcorvo*) visited Potosí on his way from Buenos Aires to Lima in 1773, the city's decadence was on full display. Yet the chilly Imperial Villa still lived, and the Cerro Rico still yielded up treasures to the "permitted pirates" called *kajchas*. Things were turning around. Potosí experienced its greatest boom-and-bust cycle between discovery in 1545 and the mint crisis of 1649. Silver production peaked in 1592 at 444,000 pounds, a level never reached again in colonial times. The next ninety years or so, from roughly 1650 to 1740, marked a long period of decline, interrupted by a few minor upswings spurred by contraband traders and slavers. The seventy years or so following, from about 1740 to 1810, witnessed a notable revival, peaking in the 1790s, but ending in an abrupt crash around 1800.

We know much about Potosí in the later eighteenth century, the age of reforms treated in this chapter, thanks in large part to Spain's self-conscious and often ambitious Bourbon officials. Although their efforts rarely yielded the dramatic results they hoped for, these men spent their careers trying to mend what they regarded as a broken money machine. Luckily for historians, they wrote about Potosí, both the Cerro Rico and the Imperial Villa, at length, often after consulting manuscript records that no longer exist. We are less fortunate in that local sources like that of Arzáns remain so rare, and that indigenous voices are far more muted than in the records of previous centuries.

This chapter focuses on Bourbon attempts to revive Potosí in the eighteenth century. For starters, reformers established a miners' guild, a savings bank, and a new mint. The chapter shows how Potosí became key to the new Viceroyalty of Río de la Plata, centered on Buenos Aires beginning in 1776, and what role it played in independence in the 1810s and 1820s. The chapter also returns to the issue of foreign technological expertise versus local knowledge, as the Spanish crown sent German and other northern European technicians to upgrade the mines and refineries, with limited success.

EARLY REFORMS

We saw in the previous chapter how the 1702–13 War of the Spanish Succession revived global interest in Potosí. The French and English, in particular, envied its legendary wealth. Strapped for cash to defend against these and other European powers, Spain's new Bourbon king, Philip V, began investigating ways of stimulating silver production in the high Andes. Mercury supply was a perennial issue, but troubles at the Huancavelica mines in Peru were overcome by the 1730s, lifting production into the early 1760s. The king had given Potosí's mill owners a gift in the form of mercury purchase on credit in 1725. Abuse of this privilege was perennial, and mercury policy remained contentious to the end of colonial times.

Crown intervention in the labor supply was even more controversial. The late-Habsburg wave of criticism of the *mita* continued after the Bourbon succession, and some well-connected observers in Madrid expected the draft to be abolished in the early 1720s, when a number of indigenous headmen organized and demanded enforcement of checks. Potosí's still-powerful *azogueros* responded by staging a lockout in 1727, which shut off production and prompted the crown to respond by guaranteeing the mita by decree in 1732. More enslaved Africans also reached Potosí in these years, now supplied to Buenos Aires factors by the British South Sea Company. Most were destined for domestic service or skilled trades, as slave prices remained almost as high as in the 1640s.[2]

On 28 January 1735, the azogueros won another major break, perhaps the biggest one in the city's history. Royal taxes on gross silver production dropped from 20 to 10 percent overnight. News traveled slowly, so the decree was only issued in Lima in July 1736. Silver mining towns all over Spanish America had enjoyed the lower tax rate for years, but the crown had resisted calls to do the same for Potosí, apparently because of the mita labor subsidy. That was the pact, or Devil's bargain, as critics would have it, for over a century and a half: Andean blood for Potosí silver.

Along with halving the severance tax, the king allowed Potosí's mill and mine owners to charter a savings bank, the Royal Bank of San Carlos, in 1751 (it had been established in 1746 as an exchange bank). The fund grew from a trickle of cash as silver bars were taxed, and the accumulated money was lent at low interest to needy but qualified (i.e., propertied and well-connected) borrowers. This was how the bank worked in theory. Unfortunately, leaving the azogueros in charge of the strongbox was like letting foxes into a henhouse. Chronic embezzlers dug in within a few years of the bank's founding, and mismanagement continued despite periodic crown inspections.

ANOTHER ROYAL PAIN

If Potosí had been brought to its knees by special prosecutor Francisco de Nestares Marín back in 1649, the city must have suffered dejà-vu with the arrival, exactly a century later, of Governor Ventura de Santelices y Venero in 1749. Going straight to the bank, Santelices discovered a measly 14 pesos in an account that should have contained over 175,000.[3] Santelices used his broad authority to go after embezzlers, but he discovered that Potosí's two main azoguero factions, despite their periodic thefts and chronic tax evasion, were going bankrupt. It took a decade for the magistrate to rehabilitate the Bank of San Carlos, only to have its funds fall into the less competent hands of his successor, who allowed the accumulated capital to dissipate again in the 1760s.

Like his seventeenth-century predecessor Nestares Marín, Santelices was a reformer on all fronts. Even so, he more closely resembled Nestares Marín's contemporary, Fray Francisco de la Cruz, in declaring himself a protector of native Andeans. One of Santelices's aims was to eliminate production quotas for mita laborers. These were being ratcheted up in lieu of the crown-mandated daily or weekly wage. In 1749 there were about 3,000 Andean men from twelve highland provinces still being drafted into Potosí's mita, and each was required to extract a considerable amount of ore.

Against loud and sometimes threatening mine owner objections, Santelices returned the mita to the wage system. He also halted some clerical abuses of *mitayos*. Such abuses were not new, but they apparently worsened in the desperate years of the early eighteenth century. Potosí had more than a dozen indigenous parishes inherited from its boom days, and supporting each church and its priest had become burdensome, especially after the epidemic of 1719–21. Santelices reduced the number of parishes to eight and then tried to reduce individual priests' demands on native parishioners. This was standard Bourbon regalism, curbing church power by pinching its income streams in the name of native welfare.[4]

Even with Santelices's reforms, however, mitayos suffered significant wage deductions for various church-related affairs. They paid for specific feasts and sermons, along with supplies such as palms, oil, mats, roof tiles, and even chili peppers for priests and their assistants. Hospital fees were higher still, despite these institutions' ostensible charity mission. Even Santelices's wage reform did not function as he intended. Mine owners simply upped worker production quotas. Thus, ore carrying mitayos who extracted fifteen loads per night in 1750 found their quota doubled to thirty loads by 1767.[5]

Other laborers, the *mingas,* or free hires, were by this time a varied lot that included non-village Andeans, mestizos, mulattos, and free blacks. Potosí's mingas now ran the gamut from skilled pick-men to totally untrained amalgam stirrers (*repasiris*) and ore carriers (*apiris*). Many of the latter were indebted peons hoodwinked into service with advances of brandy and coca. When mitayos and mingas exited the mines on weekends to visit families and relax in the eight parishes below, the "ore thieves," or *kajchas,* went to work.

As we have seen, the kajchas, often the most skilled mingas, extracted small amounts of high-grade ore that was then processed by owners of rudimentary mills, or *trapiches*. It appears there were about 3,000 kajchas active in Potosí in 1750, and there were probably over 200 trapiches, owned by all sorts of people, including Spaniards and Indians, among them native headmen. Although the azogueros lost out by this arrangement, crown officials remained ambivalent despite suppression attempts in the mid-1730s. From the king's perspective, a steady stream of silver was being produced, and *kajcheo* could be seen as a weekend wage supplement that kept the mines operating through the weekdays. The azogueros in turn stayed in business by processing huge amounts of low-grade ore along with mounds of tailings, which their large-scale operations made marginally profitable.

## A BALANCED SYSTEM OR A POWDER KEG?

How might Spain's allegedly enlightened royal officials improve on this seemingly jury-rigged yet somehow functional system of silver production? Not easily, or without violence. Obstacles to reform were manifold. One was the resistance of the kajchas and trapiche owners to any kind of intervention, since they had literally carved out niches that served their livelihoods. Both kajchas and trapiche operators were treated as enemies by Potosí's elite mine and mill owners, who sought a crown crackdown. Yet the azogueros were divided into competing factions. In Santelices's time, two factions stood out, one led by Francisco Velarde, the other by Geronimo Gómez Trigoso. It was Velarde who provoked a near-riot by the kajchas in January 1751. His intention was to force Governor Santelices to militarize the city and punish ore theft. The 1751 disturbance is worth recounting briefly.[6]

The trigger event occurred when a teenage kajcha was shot and killed by one of Francisco Velarde's mine guards. Three others were wounded. Days later, 200 kajchas protested at the mine entrance, and soon after, one of the guards was chased into a tavern amid a hail of stones while another sought shelter in the Franciscan monastery. A rumor quickly spread that the kajchas were planning to take over the city, prompting panic and a militia muster. All of this seems to have been a misunderstanding, with the mine owner Velarde cynically playing to the fears of Potosí's new crown officials freshly arrived from Spain.

It was carnival time in Potosí, and the kajchas were in the midst of their main annual ritual: bringing the cross of their confraternity from the mines down into town, where they would hear mass at the parish churches of Santa Barbara and Santa Cruz. It was in the midst of the so-called Caccha [Kajcha] Cruz Festival on 3 February 1751 that a rumor spread among the kajchas to the effect that some of their members had been jailed. A confused and noisy response continuing into the next day convinced Governor Santelices that a violent revolt was imminent, so he ordered a militia muster and placed the city under martial law.

Several alleged kajcha ringleaders were captured and jailed, but in the aftermath Governor Santelices quickly discovered that he had been tricked into overreacting. The alleged revolt was the creation of Francisco Velarde and former inspector-general José de Herboso, who both stoked rumors and heartily participated in the militia musters. For them, the phony tumult was a chance to settle scores. Once it was clear that Santelices was onto them, an intimidation campaign began, reminiscent of the one used against Inspector-General Nestares Marín back in 1649–50. A threatening broadside was posted on Santelices's door. The crown official feared for his life, but he held firm and prosecuted Velarde's guards. For balance, two of the kajchas were sentenced to several months' labor in the royal mint.[7]

Some of Potosí's richest men gave Santelices cause for worry, but it should be noted that he was no friend of the kajchas. When one of them killed a mine guard in November 1751, Santelices reacted harshly. Two kajchas were captured and jailed, and one of them, Asensio Patapata, was executed in Potosí's main square in March of 1752. Church authorities also sought to crack down on the kajchas' unauthorized procession of the cross. These events combined to minimize the workers' power as a bloc, but how could the embattled Santelices steer the outcome of the 1751 disturbance toward lasting reform? A plan to establish a permanent military force to patrol the city and Cerro proved unworkable. Simply put, no one wanted to pay for it, and few believed the kajchas presented enough of a threat to warrant martial law. If anything, most *potosinos* believed that the kajchas were the workers who sustained the city in hard times, and in this they were probably right.

Another of Santelices's reform efforts centered on the reservoirs and canals established nearly two centuries before by Viceroy Toledo. Santelices relied on an old Basque military colonel to organize the repair of eighteen *lagunas,* or reservoirs, which were technically overseen by salaried officials (who never visited).[8] By 1750 only five lakes were functional, and even these dried up before the end of the milling year. This was a far cry from Toledo's renaissance "machine," which at its optimum supplied water through two years, bridging a year of drought when needed. Only 45 mill heads were left of the 150 built in Toledo's day, and most were nonfunctional. Repair costs for the lakes and aqueducts were estimated at 50,000 pesos; labor would be supplied by mita draftees. King Ferdinand VI approved Santelices's plan in July 1750, ordering that it be funded with city market taxes on comestibles.

"Villa Imperial de Potosí y Serro Rico con 21 lagunas . . . ," ca. 1755–75, Francisco Javier Mendizábal. Courtesy of the Museo del Ejército, Toledo, Spain.

It was a wise investment, as Potosí's share of world silver production climbed back above 10 percent of the world total in the 1750s, a level it roughly maintained to the end of the century even as Mexican mining took off.

### OLD MERCURY IN NEW BOTTLES

Suppression of the kajchas after 1751 naturally led to the decline of the trapiches, which relied on the weekend high-graders' ores to be profitable. Even so, it seems that within a decade the number of trapiches had bounced back to pre-"revolt" times, and Potosí was again faced with the problem of what to do about kajcheo. Crown officials' continued ambivalence centered on one thing: silver production. The crown bought trapiche silver at discount, and treasury and mint officials were thus loath to kill a goose that laid silver eggs. Jaime St. Just, Potosí's new governor, complained to the crown in 1762 that there were 4,000 kajchas invading the Cerro and 235 trapiches scattered around the hinterland, many of them operated by indigenous headmen. Silver production had in effect reverted to Indian hands, much as in the times before Viceroy Toledo.[9]

For the long-entitled azogueros, tax breaks, subsidized mercury, access to mita workers, and bank credit kept things going. Yet without major new mining initiatives the business of these large-scale operators was bound to yield low rents. The milling and refining of low-grade ores and tailings could only be made profitable through financial gimmicks. The most popular of these was to rent marginally profitable mines and refineries to Spanish green-horns. Fresh dupes from Spain kept the pyramid from collapsing for a time, but waves of bankruptcies destabilized the overall mining economy.

The other way to increase profits was to demand more of workers, and there is abundant evidence of this after 1750.[10] With the aid of crown officials, mine and mill owners steadily increased ore quotas and work hours while keeping wages low and withholding them as long as possible. It appears that despite all the reforms instituted by the Bourbons, the only thing that actually lifted Potosí's silver production in the later eighteenth century was more intense exploitation of Andean workers—no surprise to the mita's critics.[11] In the 1770s, registered silver output rose above 30 million pesos per decade for the first time since the 1680s.

Potosí's famously corrupt royal mint also drew the attention of Bourbon reformers. The model was Mexico City, where a mechanized and professionally staffed mint opened to great fanfare in 1733. Despite some cyclical mining crises, Mexico City's mint was a huge success, pumping more cash into the global economy than even Potosí had in its heyday. Plans to reform Potosí's mint stalled until the early 1750s, when the idea of creating a new structure in the old *plaza del qhatu,* or female indigenous market square, gained support. Local mint officials dragged their feet, as did others who benefited from the old artisanal guild system, and so it was not until 1773 that the new mint opened. It was a huge and expensive structure, but as in Mexico City, Potosí's new Casa de la Moneda quickly became a source of pride, symbol of the Imperial Villa's regeneration.

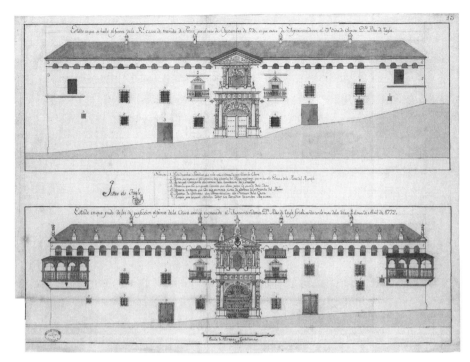

Two façade plans for Potosí's new royal mint, ca. 1772. Courtesy of the Archivo General de Indias, Seville.

## POTOSÍ AND THE GREAT ANDEAN
## REBELLION OF 1780–82

In view of the Chayanta movements from October 1780, I asked the viceroy for 500 rifles; I had ten cannons and a light cannon founded; I stockpiled powder, munitions, 100 machetes, and some lances. In December the Villa was prepared. I fixed the city's two decrepit militia companies by forming three new companies of merchants, cavaliers, and artillerymen, and set up arms training for all. At the end of January the alert level rose with news of the murder of the corregidor of Paria.

—*Letter from Potosí's governor to Buenos Aires officials, 1781*[12]

Thus did Potosí governor Jorge de Escobedo describe the Imperial Villa's military preparations as indigenous peasants rose up against oppression. It was not the mita that the Chayanta district's villagers were rejecting, but rather moves by regional elites to impede their subsistence, their means to supply their own mitayos during their service in Potosí's mines and mills.

Governor Escobedo ignored the causes of the disturbances to stress his heroic efforts to protect the Imperial Villa and the king's treasure. Escobedo went on to describe how he had ordered trenches built, how sentinels were posted and night watches increased. Even the system of reservoirs and aqueducts above the city was being closely watched, as Potosí's refinery owners had always feared an act of sabotage that would repeat the horrors of the great flood of 1626.

Governor Escobedo said confidently that steps had been taken to protect the city's women—by which he meant elite Spanish women—and also the treasures of the new mint, the Casa Real de la Moneda. Meanwhile, refugees from the countryside were streaming into town, and one rebel, "the famous Andrés Tola," had been captured only a short distance away and executed in the main plaza, "in presence of all the Indians of the city."[13] Churchmen and azogueros had piously offered financial support such that the defense of the Imperial Villa against native insurrection would not strain the royal treasury.

It was in part the ratcheting up of demands on workers in Potosí that sparked the largest indigenous uprisings in all of colonial Latin America. Known to scholars as the Great Andean Rebellion or more recently as the "Tupamarista Revolution," there occurred a cascade of revolts led by indigenous headmen protesting a variety of abuses, from excessive taxes to forced sales of merchandise to priestly corruption.[14] Potosí remained the linchpin of the southern Andean economy, and as such its symbolism was reinforced by the tumults of the early 1780s. Mita service was by this time seen paradoxically as a show of fealty to the king and as a cruel and unbearable burden. The city of Potosí itself was spared from revolutionary violence, but when the dust settled in the countryside and in the city of La Paz, tens of thousands lay dead, either from fighting, execution, or starvation.

The first stirrings of rebellion had occurred in the tiny village of Pocoata, several days' walk north of Potosí in the subdistrict of Chayanta.[15] Several thousand indigenous residents from the Macha ethnic group assembled in Pocoata on 24 August 1780 to celebrate the feast day of St. Bartholomew. The Machas were to send off a troop of mitayos to the Potosí mines, as they did every year. A skirmish occurred when Spanish authorities failed to free a jailed indigenous spokesman named Tomás Katari, soon to be the leader of a violent rebellion but up to this time a peaceful petitioner who had walked all the way to Buenos Aires to gain an audience with the viceroy. Not only had Katari gotten the viceroy's attention, he had also won his support. Katari had returned to his hometown of Pocoata with an order to have an unpopular *corregidor,* Joaquín Alos, removed from office for overstepping his authority.[16]

On 4 November 1780, to the south of Cuzco in the province of Canas y Canchis, in the village of Tinta, a relatively wealthy cacique named José Gabriel Condorcanqui seized the Spanish corregidor responsible for his district, José de Arriaga, with the aid of followers who had set an ambush. Arriaga was declared a failed official whose punishment, death by hanging, had been ordered by the King of Spain, Charles III. A monarch in his own right, Condorcanqui took the name Túpac Amaru II, once and future Inca.[17] Corregidor Arriaga's execution on 9 November 1780 triggered a far more violent and uncontrollable uprising than the disturbances in Chayanta, far away to the south. What these disparate but eventually overlapping revolts had in common was the Potosí mita.

Whereas the villagers at Pocoata chose to use conspicuous mita service to show loyalty to the king, leveraging it for future bargains, the followers of Túpac Amaru in southern Peru rejected their mita obligations altogether. Túpac Amaru knew Potosí as well as anyone from his home district: he owned mule trains that transported mercury and coca to the Imperial Villa. Like Tomás Katari, he had trekked to the viceregal capital, for him Lima rather than Buenos Aires, in part to request that his subjects be exempted from mita service in Potosí—a burden he likened to a death sentence. The fact of these rebel leaders' long struggles within the Spanish colonial justice system prefigured their later demands. They did not seek independence; they sought justice.

But rebellions have a way of opening spaces for new ideas and assertions of power as well as offering the chance to settle old scores. The Túpac Katari rebellion soon developed into a multistage revolution throughout the broad hinterland of Potosí, punctuated by attempts to seize the cities of Chuquisaca and Cochabamba. Several provincial corregidors were killed, and after them many townsfolk as well, including numerous women and children. Those who were spared were often forced to wear indigenous clothing and chew coca to demonstrate their loyalty to the new authorities, sometimes styled as Inca kings.

In Peru, Túpac Amaru II came to be seen as a traitor of the first order, and after a failed siege of Cuzco he was captured in the highlands to the south, brought back to Cuzco, and put to death along with his wife and relatives. Body parts were shared out as warnings. Tomás Katari also died violently, and yet like Túpac Amaru II he was quickly succeeded as rebel leader by close relatives. The Peruvian rebellion shifted to guerrilla fighting in the Puno region, whereas the Bolivian uprising continued to flare up all around Potosí and eventually in the silver mining town of Oruro. A combined siege of La Paz soon followed.

The Oruro uprising of 1781 involved local elites as well as indigenous rebels.[18] Mining equipment was destroyed, but except perhaps in certain places such as Aullagas, high in the mountains east of Oruro, the revolt was not in itself a protest against mine labor abuses. The crux issues included forced resale of goods, the so-called *reparto de mercancías,* and heavy tax burdens pushed onto the populace by Spanish-born crown officials. Significantly, when royalists retook Oruro native workers went to Potosí to serve as mitayos as a means of guaranteeing crown forgiveness. The mita had become a kind of pilgrimage of penance. Unfortunately for Oruro's local mine owners, several of whom had also defied crown authority, Potosí was where they were sent to jail before being transferred to Buenos Aires for execution.

More blood would flow as a result of the Spanish king's hunger for silver. The siege of La Paz in early 1781 was led by an indigenous commoner calling himself Túpac Katari, a clever combination of Túpac Amaru and Tomás Katari, both dead by this time.[19] Túpac Katari was perhaps the most radical native rebel thus far, and yet he resembled his predecessors in having traveled as a petty coca dealer. He knew his way around the rugged Andean landscape, and also around both white and indigenous elites. Thousands died during the months-long siege of La Paz, but eventually the rebels, in the end a mix of Túpac Katari's and Túpac Amaru's followers, retreated in the face of Spanish royalist firepower.

Túpac Katari was captured in October 1781 and executed the following month. Like his predecessors, he was torn apart by horses and his body parts displayed in the places where his crimes were considered most heinous. The lesson learned from all this bloodshed was not to underestimate the power of native Andeans. Terrified and awakened to the weight of 200 years of resentment of mita abuses, crown officials and rich potosinos would do all they could to keep a lid on the powder keg.

REFORM IN THE NEW INTENDANCY OF POTOSÍ

As one of his centralizing reforms, the Bourbon king Charles III (1759–88) ordered the creation of French-style intendancies throughout Spanish America. Established in the 1780s, these administrative units, headed by a crown-appointed *intendente,* replaced the older *corregimientos, alcaldías mayores,* and similar jurisdictions. Potosí's first intendant, Juan del Pino Manrique de Lara, took office in 1781, first as governor and after 1783 as intendant. Governor Manrique quickly set about reordering his district so that he might better serve his king—and also his personal career.

Potosí, though a shadow of its former self, still produced the lion's share of crown revenue in Greater Peru, and the recently created Viceroyalty of Río de la Plata, established in 1776 with its capital at Buenos Aires, was utterly dependent on Potosí silver.[20] Manrique's first job was to deal with an emerging rental crisis in Potosí, but he soon turned to reforming the district's mining codes. He also sought cheaper steel tools, a stronger mita, and better mining and milling techniques. Manrique considered himself a man of science.[21]

The rental crisis, if it may be called that, concerned recently arrived Spaniards (for the most part) who rented mines and mills and tried to eke out enough profit to make it worth their while. Many barely did, and bankruptcies were frequent, disrupting the flow of silver. Manrique responded to the renters' requests by attempting to cap rents, but owner opposition and fluctuating mercury prices stopped him cold. Manrique's request for prefabricated tools from Biscay also won no response, probably thanks to entrenched merchant-ironmonger interests. Even his hopes for local mining laws were stalled by a crown order to adopt Mexico's mining code in 1785.

In the midst of these halting attempts at reform, a most interesting person arrived on the scene: Pedro Vicente Cañete y Domínguez. A native of Paraguay educated in the Southern Cone universities at Córdoba and Santiago de Chile, Cañete reached Potosí in 1785 at age 31, an ambitious and wildly energetic young bureaucrat. He would soon produce the longest and most detailed report on Potosí and its hinterland to survive from the colonial period. Cañete worked closely with Intendant Manrique on proposed legal reforms and the two agreed on most things. But it was Cañete who recognized the critical importance of concentrating reform efforts on the mita.

A shrewd politician, Cañete was not the consistent critic of the mita that he made himself out to be.[22] He knew that he would be favored by the crown for criticizing the inhumanity of the mine and refinery owners and for lamenting the general misery of native Andeans, while also proposing a way to "reform" the mita and therefore keep the crown's tax revenues flowing. In this, Cañete was no more enlightened or morally troubled than his many Habsburg predecessors, and indeed he considered Viceroy Toledo's organization of the mita, now more than two centuries old, an extraordinary achievement.

Cañete and Intendant Manrique drafted a plan in 1786 for legal codes that differed from those of Mexico with regard to the rental of mines and refineries, as well as mita work quotas. The Mexican mining code said virtually nothing about draft labor, since Mexico's *repartimiento* had all but disappeared by the eighteenth century. For Cañete and Manrique, writing the mita into law was an important change. The proposed laws also laid out the means to support a new mining college to be established in the Imperial Villa. The ordinances stalled with the death of Spain's Indies minister José de Gálvez in 1787, so Manrique tried again in 1790, producing the massive Caroline Code, treated further below. In the meanwhile, residents of the Imperial Villa took time out to entertain a group of scientists from northern Europe. The foreigners were yet another face of the so-called Bourbon reforms.

### REFORM STILLBORN: THE NORDENFLICHT EXPEDITION

In the late eighteenth century, many educated Spaniards believed themselves far behind the rest of the world in matters of science and technology. Among these scientific matters were advances in mining and metallurgy, most developed in central and northern European university cities such as Freiberg and Uppsala. The Basque brothers Fausto and Juan José D'Elhúyar were trained abroad at crown expense, and upon their return to Spain they recommended sending German-speaking technicians and skilled workers directly to Mexico, Upper Peru, and New Granada. These enlightened foreigners, it was believed, would personally turn the baroque art of American mining into a modern, European science.

Officials under Charles III, most importantly Indies minister Gálvez (in his last years), heeded the Elhúyar brothers' recommendations and sent three expeditions to Spanish America. Greater Peru's mining mission reached Buenos Aires in July 1788. It was led by Baron Thaddeus von Nordenflicht, one of Fausto de Elhúyar's old schoolmates from Freiberg.[23] When the Spanish first called on Nordenflicht, he was working in the mines of Poland. As expected of a self-important baron, he demanded and received lavish compensation.

The Nordenflicht expedition included fifteen Germans, most of them, like Baron Nordenflicht, Protestants. Traveling to Peru required special permission from King Charles and also restrictions on the Germans' behavior. In short, they were not to preach. Initially, the Nordenflicht mission was to sail around the southern tip of South America and approach the Andes from Lima, but Potosí's new intendant, Francisco de Paula Sanz, arranged for the group to march overland from Buenos Aires, making Potosí the first destination worthy of their technical expertise.

The Nordenflicht expedition succeeded in surveying and redirecting crown-sponsored drainage adits, or *socavones*, in the Cerro Rico. The old Berrío adit was deemed too high on the Rich Hill to merit continuation, despite having already "drained" the king's purse of nearly 180,000 pesos. A new adit, named for the Immaculate Conception, was begun in July 1789. It also proved a better drain of the king's purse than of the Cerro Rico's veins. Workers were still chipping along without reaching paying ore bodies in 1800, long after the Protestant engineers' departure.

Nordenflicht was generally appalled by the crude and seemingly inefficient state of mining in Potosí, and he and his companions did not withhold disdain. Nordenflicht called for careful inspections and better management, and for a brief time his efforts lifted production. Even so, Nordenflicht left Potosí to visit other mining districts to the north after only nine months. One of the German miners in the expedition, Johann Daniel Weber, stayed behind at the mines of Colquechaca, a lofty and desolate site in the northern province of Potosí east of Oruro, where he oversaw the excavation of a drainage adit. The work yielded impressive results, and great profits were taken by 1806. It was a rare success, but not a technical marvel.

### THE BORN PROCESS

The Nordenflicht expedition was meant to introduce new methods of assaying, underground surveying, and minting, but most anticipated was a sophisticated silver refining process developed by the Austrian scientist Ignaz von Born—like many learned men of his day a harsh critic of the Spanish Inquisition (alleged killer of enlightened scientific inquiry). The Born method, which consisted of mercury amalgamation in heated, rotating barrels, was expected to make even very low-grade ores profitable. Potosí had nothing *but* low-grade or at least hard-to-refine ores by the time Nordenflicht and his assistants arrived in 1789, but construction of Born-type machines proved costly and difficult. In this new world of "global," enlightened science, Potosí's awestruck locals hoped the foreigners' machines would save the city.

Champions of the Born method gushed with enthusiasm, and despite cost overruns the first machine built in Potosí seemed promising, so much so that crown officials agreed to lend considerable sums to private refinery owners hoping to "upgrade" to the new system. Hopes were soon dashed, however. Within a year of Nordenflicht's departure, Potosí's powerful mining guild pulled out of the project, claiming that money they had invested in the city's first Born barrels had been wasted. They had spent 40,000 pesos to build a machine initially quoted to them at just over 8,000 pesos, and worse, the first refining trials caused the equipment to collapse.

It appears that building such a heavy-duty contraption in a barren place where limited smithing and carpentry skills and equipment were the norm was asking for trouble. As always, premium timber had to be brought in from great distances, along with all iron and steel, not to mention tons of charcoal. To boot, casting bronze components and tempering iron and steel straps proved difficult at 4,000 meters (13,200 feet) above sea level. The crown might have done well to listen to Intendant Manrique's call for imports of prefabricated iron and steel tools and components.

Even so, the azoguero guild's prototype machine was repaired, and three copies were built. Local innovators supplied wooden parts to substitute bronze ones recommended by Born, and with experimentation it became clear that although the Born barrels were not miraculous as promised, they did consume less mercury than the older *buitrón,* or basin, method by at least half.

Despite crown attempts to publicize these successes in 1791 in Peru's first newspaper, the *Mercurio Peruano,* Potosí's mining guild managed to undermine the project.[24] Apparently, the old-school master refiners, or *beneficiadores,* had struck back. The new machines threatened their livelihood, and their employers were too dependent on them to risk alienation. It was an age-old battle, made worse by the arrogant attitudes of Nordenflicht, Anton Zacharias Helms, and other members of the expedition. The German "mineralogists," hailed as miracle workers on their arrival, risked, according to Helms, "stoning and crucifixion" by the time they left.[25]

NEW LAWS FOR OLD MINES: THE CAROLINE CODE

The failed Nordenflicht expedition's Spanish promoters did not give up hope. Key was Potosí intendant Francisco de Paula Sanz, who replaced Manrique in 1789. What could be done to increase Potosí silver production if labor-saving foreign technologies failed? As in the past, the most obvious answer was to increase the supply of cheap labor. In Potosí, this meant reviving or ratcheting up the mita.[26]

Another potential aid to struggling silver producers was—as we have seen in the case of Intendant Manrique—to update legal codes to match those of Mexico, where the silver industry was booming. But it was only new rules about the mita, and maybe taxation, that interested Potosí's old guard. What Intendant Sanz soon discovered was that the mita was still a touchy issue, now in ways influenced by Enlightenment ideals regarding human capacity and individual freedom. Some priests in the regions affected by the Potosí mita spoke out against its revival in an updated humanitarian language, but it was the crown-appointed Protector of the Natives, Victorián de Villava, who offered the sharpest critique of Sanz's so-called Mita Nueva, or "New Mita."[27]

The New Mita was part of the so-called Caroline Code (named for Charles IV), which Cañete y Domínguez and Sanz had attempted to push through since 1791. Local mine and mill owners initially favored the code, as did the viceroy of the Río de la Plata, but upon reading the fine print (the 700-page document contained 1,300 ordinances), howls went up. These were amplified such that Potosí's azogueros roundly rejected the entire Caroline Code by 1794. The sticking points were rent controls and reworked mita allotments. The reforms favored mine renters over owners, especially absentee owners, and thus the old pattern of conservative rent seeking stayed in place. Cañete's attempts to help less risk-averse entrepreneurs were scuttled.

Arguments against the mita re-allotment focused on two things. First, the Mita Nueva would reduce the number of mitayos to individual mine and refinery owners, an obvious concern since mita allotments were used to assess overall property values, as if mitayos were slaves. And yet, in the second place, the Mita Nueva would increase overall mitayo numbers by expanding recruitment, delivering workers to a broader pool of refiners and mine owners (Cañete's hoped-for entrepreneurs). The arguments against this second feature of Cañete's brainchild were largely moral, and it was Victorián de Villava who led the charge.

Cañete argued that a rising indigenous population meant that he was not actually proposing expanding the mita to bring in 8,000 laborers, but rather simply complying with the one-seventh proportion stipulated in the favored 1574 laws of Francisco de Toledo. Villava would have none of it, and he flatly called the mita a sin and crime—in a word, "homicide." Sanz and Cañete expected the backing of the viceroy to override the protests of "Indian Protector" Villava, but they underestimated him. Villava organized rural and church opposition to the Mita Nueva and used his position in the Audiencia of Charcas to trumpet his claims.

All this publicity opened a forum for long-brewing indigenous opposition as well, and the list of critics expanded to include intendants whose jurisdictions reluctantly supplied workers to Potosí. As Sanz and Cañete struggled to win the rhetorical battle against Villava and his supporters, royal officials in Spain sided with the Protector. As of 8 March 1797, the Caroline Code was dead. By coincidence, the viceroy of Río de la Plata who had supported it was also dead.

## RETURN TO CRISIS

In the midst of all the shouting about the New Mita, a new crisis arose: by the mid-1790s profitable ores and tailings were running out and mercury was suddenly short. Piles of low-grade ore seemed always to show up sooner or later, but the lack of mercury was critical. Production at Huancavelica fell abruptly, and wars in Europe cut off supplies from Almadén in Spain and Idria in Habsburg Slovenia.[28] Starved of their most needed reagent, Potosí's "mercury men," the azogueros, faced bankruptcy. Sanz and Cañete were forced to extend loans from the royal treasury to the mine and mill owners just so they could meet payroll. Mita workers continued to arrive in Potosí, but their numbers were reduced by several factors. One was indigenous resistance, stoked by Villava's condemnations. Another was the redistricting of the provinces around Lake Titicaca in the 1780s and 1790s, placing them under jurisdiction of Cuzco's new appeals court, or *audiencia,* created in 1787.

A drought in 1801 stopped Potosí's mills for over a year, the longest stoppage since the great 1626 flood. Even if mita workers had been sufficient, without water and without mercury the venerable machine of Potosí simply could not run. Royal loans to the mine and mill owners exceeded 1 million pesos, raising tensions between Sanz and officials in Buenos Aires, who believed he was stupidly bankrupting the treasury.

Despite their long-standing differences with the intendant, local mine and mill owners praised Sanz for understanding their predicament. Meanwhile,

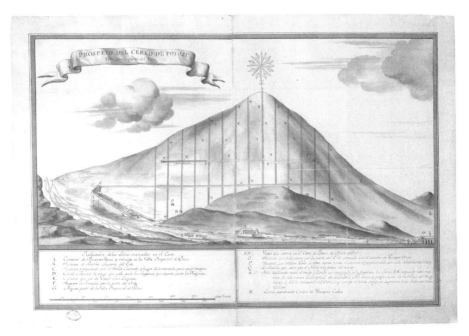

"View of the Cerro de Potosí" with Berrío adit at left, ca. 1779. Courtesy of the Archivo General de Indias, Seville.

the costs of drilling the Immaculate Conception adit and reopening the Berrío adit (in 1790, at Sanz's order) remained high. The price of work on the two tunnels averaged over 18,000 pesos per year in the 1790s, dropping only slightly to about 16,500 pesos annually through 1810. A lot of money was going into these holes and none was coming out.[29]

The years 1800–05 were not just years of drought, but also of widespread famine in the Andes. Food prices skyrocketed in Potosí, leaving numerous destitute mitayos and free workers to beg in the streets. Many starved. A disease epidemic hit just as the rains began to return in 1804 and 1805.

Desperate for workers, Potosí's mine and mill owners revealed their long-held prejudices toward native Andeans. Some argued that they ought to be shackled and forced to work like convicts, others that they be made to hire themselves out like slaves, to yield a rent to their "masters" on a daily or weekly basis. No such actions seem to have been taken, but the extraordinary history of Potosí's mita was here cast in sharpest relief. Its inherent inhumanity and racism could no longer be hidden.[30]

Like a dying person struggling for a last breath, Potosí's mining fortunes seemed to improve unexpectedly after 1806, if only briefly. One crown-sponsored adit reached the mother lode that its workers had been tunneling toward for over twenty years. In coordination with the new viceroy at Buenos Aires, Intendant Sanz managed to restructure the mine and mill owners' debts in a way that seemed to satisfy all parties. Even the price of mercury dropped to a level that pleased the azogueros. But fate was fickle. Napoleon's troops sacked Madrid in 1808 and by 1809 the first stirrings of independence were heard in Potosí. After 1810, when Buenos Aires rebelled against the Spanish crown, the mining industry was doomed.

Amid the turmoil an interesting thing happened with regard to the mita, that most resilient and controversial of Spain's labor institutions. With the announcement of independence in Buenos Aires, many of Potosí's mita workers fled. Royalist occupiers reported as much in 1811. A festival in honor of the loyalist "American General" and "Peruvian reconqueror" Marshal José Manuel de Goyeneche tried to revive the city's old spirit, but the oligarchy's celebrations were short-lived.[31] When Potosí fell back into rebel hands in 1813, they declared the mita abolished, but they created no mechanism for enforcement. As it happened, the mita had also been abolished in November 1812 by the liberal Cortes of Cádiz, Spain's government-in-exile during the Napoleonic occupation.

Potosí's azogueros did everything in their power to hang onto their prized worker allotments, and it seems they succeeded in part through 1819.[32] But by that time the industry had shrunk considerably; only fourteen mills were operating. Other problems compounded the disappearance of the mita. The Royal Bank of San Carlos collapsed, its lending policies and holdings having been abused by rebels and royalists alike, and mercury prices soared in wartime. Potosí entered a period of crisis unlike any seen before, and mining reverted to a kind of subsistence activity: low risk, low return, dominated by indigenous agents, the kajchas.

A public figure whose fortunes in these turbulent years epitomizes the state of Potosí at independence is don Indalecio González de Socasa.[33] Socasa, as he was sometimes known, was born in 1755 near the coastal city of Santander, in northern Spain. He came to Peru as a young man, one of a new wave of fortune-seekers hoping to make their mark in the era of Bourbon reforms. Socasa appears to have served in a military unit in Cuzco, possibly as a member of the forces sent to put down the Túpac Amaru II revolt of 1780–81. In any case, Socasa was in Potosí by the early 1790s. Soon after arriving, he married the daughter and sole heir of a wealthy family and before long he became one of the Imperial Villa's richest and most powerful men.

Socasa did what predecessors such as Antonio López de Quiroga had done: he found a rich match, then made money in commerce, entered into mining and refining, and backed everything up with agricultural properties, including vineyards. Socasa's main vineyards, near Cinti south of Potosí, produced substantial quantities of brandy, today's *singani*. Socasa competed with the many brandy producers of Arequipa, in southwest Peru, whom he hoped to undersell. Like many businessmen of this time, Socasa was also deeply involved in regional government, and his loyalty to the crown prompted early rebels to sack his estates. Between 1815 and 1820, when he died, Socasa suffered tremendous losses. Like much of Potosí at this time, he found himself on the wrong side of history.

### INDEPENDENCE

When the Liberator came within a full and clear view of the famed Cerro of Potosí, the flags of Peru, Buenos Ayres, Chile, and Colombia were at the same moment unfurled upon its summit. On his excellency's entering the town, twenty-one *camaratas* or large shells, were fired off, the report of each of which was equal to that of six 24-pounders. This aerial salute had a very singular and imposing effect. The deep valleys of the surrounding country echoed and re-echoed as if with claps of thunder. This was the signal of Bolívar's having entered Potosí. The bells of every church and convent rang with an almost deafening peal.[34]

Thus did General William Miller, an Englishman who accompanied Simón Bolívar in his final battles, recall the Liberator's reception in what would henceforth no longer be called the "Imperial" Villa of Potosí. After some fifteen years of struggle, the year 1825 marked the end, once and for all, of the mita and of Spanish domination of the Cerro Rico, "king of mountains" and "envy of kings." Almost 300 years had passed since the Rich Hill's discovery by Diego Gualpa. Miller describes the overwhelming joy of potosinos of all social classes, not least the city's indigenous majority, at

Silver medal minted in Potosí for Simón Bolívar, 1825. Courtesy of Daniel Frank Sedwick, LLC, Auction #23, Lot 1479.

receiving this hero and founder of republics. But what did it mean for Potosí to be free?

Potosí's mine and mill owners may have reasonably wished to cut ties to Spain, with its incessant decrees, taxes, and moral condemnations. Likewise, the indigenous inhabitants of the vast region subject to the Potosí mita might also have imagined a brighter future without a Spanish king who ordered them to work inside a distant anthill for a pittance at great risk to their lives. But as in other parts of the Spanish empire where crown attention had been long focused, greater Potosí's inclinations—both native and Spanish—had been to remain loyal.

The merchants of Buenos Aires who declared independence in 1810 were not seen as preferable masters, and even if some other model of autonomy was on offer, it was unlikely that Potosí would retain its access to subsidized mercury. This was something only the Spanish crown seemed capable of producing. For native Andeans, the mita, despite its horrors, was to some extent offset by crown guarantees of land protection and legal aid. The prospect of a creole-run government, especially a liberal one aiming to break up communal properties, was repulsive.

From a global perspective, Potosí remained a Holy Grail–like prize, perhaps the most desired plot of real estate in all of South America. The rebels desperately wanted it—hence this triumphal arrival by Simón Bolívar and his forces in 1825. The Liberator symbolically proclaimed South American freedom from atop the Cerro Rico. Yet British investors were close on his heels, and some of their best informants—including William Miller—were among his ranks. Potosí's mining industry, all but defunct with only a dozen refining mills in operation on Bolívar's entrance, seemed ripe for innovation.

We have seen that Potosí in the eighteenth century was the focus of considerable attention from Spain's Bourbon dynasty. Facing constant military challenges worldwide, the kings of Spain were as desperate as their Habsburg predecessors for a reliable source of revenue in hard cash. In their optimism they believed the great machine of Potosí had only to be upgraded: revived by new laws, lower taxes, and technological patches. It was a question of science, of rationalization.

But why cling to the old labor system of the mita in this modernizing age? Much like slavery elsewhere in the Americas, the mita lived on and even grew in Potosí in part because enlightened eighteenth-century European thinkers could not escape the same realities faced by previous observers. Colonial America's most-prized commodities were still produced by workers more than machines, and coercion of at least a portion of the workforce had become an addiction. Paradoxically, mita service had become a point of pride among some Andeans faced with other pressures. Such were the contradictions of global commodity production.

Behind the pompous chronicle of Bourbon success and failure is a less-told story of indigenous survival and resistance. A well-armed elite may have headed off the violence of the Great Andean Rebellion of 1780–82, which engulfed major cities such as Oruro and La Paz, but there was another, older battle that continued to be fought every day. This battle was over control of the mines and more specifically the mines' best fruits or finest ores. The kajchas of the eighteenth century defined the terms of exploitation much as the alleged *corpa* thieves of Toledo's day had done. Potosí would never simply be a site of Spanish oppression and native suffering. It would accommodate both cruelty and creativity, compulsion and private or communal initiative. In the years to come, these paradoxes of life and work in the world's greatest early modern boomtown did not disappear. But they would be transformed by a new, industrial wave of globalization.

# EIGHT

# Summing Up

In three centuries Potosí's Cerro Rico consumed eight million
lives.

—EDUARDO GALEANO, *Open Veins
of Latin America*[1]

POTOSÍ MINEWORKERS AND TOUR guides repeat this phrase as a truism. Is it true? As we have seen, the *mita* and other labor arrangements killed thousands of indigenous miners inside the Cerro Rico over the long colonial period, and many thousands more, including women and children, died from disease, malnutrition, and forced marches. The mountain that "ate men" cast a long and deadly shadow, showering the Imperial Villa with mercury vapor, lead, zinc, and other toxins. Added to the mix was foul water, silent killer of many more. We have also seen that the polemics against the horrors of mine work and the mita date almost to the Cerro Rico's discovery in 1545, and they continued to Independence and final abolition of the mita in 1825.

Yet rich as it is, the colonial record provides no tally of total deaths inside the Cerro Rico. It provides a sense of the scale of the mita and of highland demography, plus a clear record of registered silver output and mercury consumption. Piles of documents in Bolivia, Argentina, Chile, Peru, the United States, Spain, France, and the United Kingdom also describe the silver mines and their many dangers in detail. Yet all that we know from surviving records renders the number eight million "consumed" by the Cerro Rico all but impossible to imagine given the scale of colonial Andean societies.

For polemicists going back to Bartolomé de las Casas, numbers in the millions got people's attention and raised consciousness. When Eduardo Galeano was writing in the early 1970s, he was no doubt thinking of the number of then-known victims of the Holocaust, and also perhaps of the number of Africans known to have been transported by the transatlantic slave trade. In the late twentieth century, Potosí's colonial past became a new kind of moral exemplum: the world's worst case of imperialist greed.

For Galeano, whose *Open Veins of Latin America* remains a source of popular knowledge in many parts of Latin America, Potosí's Cerro Rico was the first and most glaring example of "five centuries of the pillage of a continent." Galeano gave the horror of the Cerro Rico's mines a number, a truly stunning figure to enshrine and quote, but he was tapping into a long festering and widely shared anger over foreign resource extraction, "third world" underdevelopment, and enduring racism. He was not telling Potosí's militant miners something they did not already know.

The story of Potosí's alleged eight million colonial mineworker victims reminds us of the many controversies that have swirled around this world-famous mining town and its iconic red hill since 1545. Rather than pick a fight with Galeano, whose burning sense of injustice and penetrating intellect are sorely missed, this book has approached the long history of Potosí as an exemplum of another, more ambivalent kind. When one examines the details of Potosí's rich historical record in light of its increasingly calculable global economic and political significance, it becomes evident that the city and its mines encapsulated and cast into sharp relief many of the paradoxes of global modernity.

World interconnectedness after 1492, pushed by plunder and pulled by trade, made the discovery and transformation of the Cerro Rico of Potosí possible, probably unavoidable. If it had not been Diego Gualpa who tripped in the wind and stumbled onto pay dirt, it would have been somebody else. Once harnessed to the world economy, Potosí's inimitable silver bonanza and its many unintended consequences could only be seen as perplexing, at turns horrifying and entertaining, a constant source of awe and disbelief. Even as its rival ethnic factions gunned each other down in the streets, the Cerro Rico and its "Imperial Villa" together constituted a modern marvel, a new phenomenon, an "eighth wonder of the world."

The many and often controversial social processes described in this book may not have been new, but the scale and terms of argument were, and this was as evident to early visitors like Diego de Ocaña as it was to eighteenth-century locals such as Bartolomé Arzáns. Forced to compete in tight proximity, a wildly diverse mix of people battled it out and came up with new and hybrid solutions to a host of problems, technical and social. As they smelted and amalgamated silver ores known by their colors, they forged new identities that defied old categories. Potosí killed, but it also revitalized. All this took place in the great mixing bowl of the Imperial Villa, whose obscene wealth and challenging environment created unique opportunities as well as temptations.

Potosí was rife with paradox from the start, a site of human depravity and ingenuity, oppression and opportunity, piety and profligacy, race mixture and ethnic retrenchment. The list could go on. As we have seen, the city was a swirl of contradictory impulses. Was it different from other Spanish American mining towns, for example Zacatecas or Guanajuato, twin pillars of Mexico's great silver industry? Certainly these cities shared features, but the sheer scale and isolation of Potosí's early mines and refineries stood out in prefiguring industrial systems long before they existed, hinting at the environmental consequences of unbridled resource extraction long before industrial wastelands became commonplace. Zacatecas and Guanajuato did this as well in the eighteenth century, as a kind of American Silver: Act II.[2]

One may agree with Eduardo Galeano that the seeming paradoxes of colonial Potosí fit perfectly well inside the lopsided drama of Western imperialism and the global spread of capitalism, or the creation of an unfair world-system that sucked peripheries like highland Bolivia dry, but when taken too literally or as polemic these grand narratives of exploitation compress and oversimplify history, strengthening the strong and weakening the weak. I have not sought to flip the script or ignore the shifting locus and flow of imperial power, but I have tried to emphasize how Potosí has always been a site of struggle and innovation, a dense concentration of predictable losses and unpredictable successes, an indigenous space and also a complex African and European one, a woman-centered world despite powerful men's best efforts.

Thousands of peasants were torn from their means of subsistence to extract silver for others, yet many forced migrants adapted to city life, a new and modern phenomenon that some considered an improvement. Some indigenous migrants became renowned artisans and sponsors of religious confraternities, periodically returning to their native villages to inject needed capital, much as Iberian migrants remitted silver to needy relatives in Spain. Catholic priests sought to snuff out indigenous religious practices amidst this great migration, but many such practices survived and mutated, often going underground. Enslaved African women and men from Angola, Congo, and elsewhere created their own religious and economic spaces as well, challenging repeated attempts by Spanish elites and officials to keep them subservient, silent, and immobile. Traces of their agency litter the record.

Potosí's environmental legacy is much harder to balance. In fact it looks like sheer destruction and wanton pollution from every angle. The Cerro Rico provided the world with untold tons of silver as successive waves of

El Tío, guardian of the underworld, 1995. Photo by author.

miners transformed it into an unstable anthill surrounded by toxic waste dumps. Even Potosí's pristine mountain air was ruined by noxious fumes and the constant din of mill stamps. As part of the paradox, the Imperial Villa got fat and pretentious at the turn of the seventeenth century just as its vast hinterland was stripped of every stick of timber and clump of moss, wiping out even marginal pasturelands. The struggle for water mirrored the struggle for silver.

By the end of the colonial period, Potosí seemed to be stuck in a rut, inching forward but lurching back and forth between quasi-industrial and folk models of mining and refining. Customary practices like *kajcheo* were tenaciously resilient, revitalized when challenged by outsiders. Even the mita, that old bugbear, persisted in spite of repeated calls for abolition. Simón Bolívar ended the mita for good in 1825, but as Kendall Brown aptly put it: "The psychological burden of the colonial mita did not die quickly in the Andes."[3] Villagers in the Potosí hinterland remember "Blood Mountain."

As anthropologist Pascale Absi has shown, Potosí's mostly indigenous mineworkers continue to speak with ambivalence about their fate even as they display deep awareness of global influences on their lives, from commodity price fluctuations to international trade pacts to climate change. What we learn from listening to today's miners of the Red Mountain is not that mining is evil or that global capitalism is evil or that socialist solutions to Bolivian poverty and dependency might be easily implemented with the right political alignments. Few are so naive.

Rather, most Potosí miners say that mining is and always was reciprocal, a tense exchange that is never fixed or certain because we human beings are never satisfied and we can never know the will of the gods. Like children we test Pachamama, our Mother Earth, we test El Tío, lord of the underworld. We start out terrified, acting humble before these deities who determine or at least know our fate, seeking balance, attempting to be "good" not for its own sake but out of self-preservation, making certain to offer the proper sacrifices and obeisance. We ought to be satisfied with a small but steady income paid for with blood and sweat.

But instead of taking only what we need and nothing more, and giving back, especially in times of bounty, we humans get greedy and desperate, resorting to all-or-nothing pacts. Yet one cannot really make a pact with Pachamama, who is the Matrix, the giver of all life. She may weep for you or show you pity but she is not the one who will crush you or show you the way to bonanza. For the miners who lose control and get desperate, there is but one choice. "To make a pact with El Tío is like selling yourself to him body and soul, as if to say 'Give me riches and I'll give you my soul.' You give your soul not to God but to El Tío."[4] These stories of Faustian pacts inside the mountain invariably end badly for humans. Perhaps before the Cerro Rico collapses upon itself in a plume of red dust and the former Imperial Villa shrivels and dies for lack of water, we may ask ourselves, collectively, if we have made such a pact.

# *Epilogue*

POTOSÍ SINCE INDEPENDENCE

FOLLOWING NAPOLEON'S OCCUPATION of the Iberian Peninsula in 1807–08, Great Britain heeded the cry for Latin American independence. In part this was because British imperialists were happy to see the rival Spanish and Portuguese Empires fall apart, but British capital was also accumulating amid the Industrial Revolution. By the late 1810s, British firms and banks sought investment opportunities and new markets in Mexico and South America. In the home of the pound sterling, precious metals mines were rare. Newly independent Bolivia in 1825 had numerous mines wanting fresh capital from abroad, and first to capture investors' imagination was the fabled Cerro Rico of Potosí.[1]

With the aim of resuscitating the Cerro Rico, British investors formed the Potosí, La Paz, and Peruvian Mining Association in April 1825. Blessed by none other than Alexander von Humboldt, the superstar scientist and most respected mining engineer of the day, the company's crew sailed for South America in the good ship *Potosí,* stocked with mercury, mining tools, and sundry supplies. At the expedition's head was former Peruvian diplomat and key investor General Diego Paroissien, along with technical expert Baron Hermann von Czettritz und Neuhaus. Secretary Edmond Temple kept a colorful diary of the company's labors high in the mountains of Bolivia.[2] As in the days of Nordenflicht, modern European science was expected to save the day. Yet Potosí remained a perfect reef upon which to wreck a company ship.

The adventurers left England in September 1825 and reached Buenos Aires in November. They arrived in Potosí in March 1826. The company had arranged to rent a major mill along with its associated mines from an exiled

Scene in front of the new Potosí cathedral, ca. 1825, Edmond Temple, *Travels in Various Parts of Peru*. Courtesy of the John Carter Brown Library at Brown University.

Potosí noble, the marquis of Casa Palacio, along with two part-owners living in the old Imperial Villa, the sisters María Josefa and Bernarda de la Quintana. Their Laguacayo mill was not a bad choice, and the company had sent materials to help upgrade it and also to build Born-style tumblers. Unfortunately, financial trouble back in London doomed the venture before work could begin. The company's stock value crashed amid a speculation bubble. The company's letters of credit were suddenly worthless, and to pay transport costs its factors had to sell their precious supply of mercury.

Would the Potosí Company have succeeded otherwise? We cannot know, but Von Czettritz and Temple both offered discouraging descriptions of the mining situation in Potosí as they struggled to get their mills rolling.[3] A major factor was the high cost of labor. Without the *mita,* workers were more than twice as costly as before, consuming nearly a quarter of gross product. In lieu of higher quality ores, which the Cerro Rico was unlikely to yield, or a major technological breakthrough, which the Potosí Company seems unlikely to have developed on its own, mining in liberated Potosí was not going to "take off" any time soon. It would in fact be many decades before scientists developed radically new methods for silver beneficiation.

As Tristan Platt has shown, the mine owners and refiners of Potosí and its hinterland did not give up after the failure of foreign technological missions and capital-intensive projects.[4] Instead, several of them focused on improving refining technologies to adapt to the new lack of mita labor and higher mercury prices. The mining guild of Potosí still clamored for mita workers, but in lieu of getting them they shifted to methods pioneered by Padre Alvaro Alonso Barba in the early seventeenth century. Barba's method of boiling pulverized silver ore with salt in copper caldrons, invented in 1609, never caught on in colonial times. Salt and copper were readily available, but fuel costs in Potosí's heyday were restrictive.

As Platt demonstrates, Barba's method, which was informed by his alchemical learning, was essentially reinvented in the 1780s by Ignaz von Born (whom we met in chapter 7), according to Enlightenment-era theoretical assumptions. Even so, it was not Born's version of "hot" amalgamation that was tried in Potosí in the 1790s but rather his "cold" rotating barrel method. It was in the 1810s (or earlier) that Bolivian refiners in and around Potosí developed the older "hot" method and applied it to various types of ores, just as Barba had done while moving among mining camps before settling in the Imperial Villa.

Fuel remained a problem in a barren land without coal deposits, but Bolivian mine and refinery owners encouraged native Andeans to collect wood, dung, and other combustibles in exchange for tribute exemption (the mita was abolished, but not "Indian" tribute, which gave rise to what Platt calls a "crypto-mita"). Bolivia's great copper mines of Corocoro, not far from La Paz, were also developed in these years, providing substantial material for the construction of caldrons, which wore out quickly due to the actions of salt, mercury, and friction. In essence, Bolivian metallurgy found its own path to modernity in part by reviving seventeenth-century technological innovations.

After 1850, major cinnabar discoveries near San Jose, California, led to a drop in mercury prices and greater availability, further stimulating the return of amalgamation. Curiously, Bolivian miners and refiners continued to describe amalgamation in terms of alchemical principles inherited from colonial times and expressed most fully in print by Álvaro Alonso Barba, whose work was reissued. Production figures were in their favor. Local methods matched local needs for many years despite claims of Bolivia's backwardness and ignorance. Notably, Barba's old "hot boiling amalgamation" method was used by small-scale indigenous miners working at the base of the Cerro Rico in the 1890s. It had become as Bolivian as *chuño*. And at the same time, the old wind furnaces of pre-Columbian days continued to burn not far from Potosí at Porco, where the Incas had once extracted the silver of Tawantinsuyu.[5] *Kajcheo,* yet another colonial practice, continued in tandem with industrial mining.

Perhaps in part because of these seeming tricks of time or colonial continuities, silver mining boomed in and around Potosí from 1873 to 1895, and unlike in many other parts of Latin America at the time, it was largely local mining elites, men like Aniceto Arce (president of the republic from 1888–92) and Gregorio Pacheco, who benefited. The biggest local investors in the Cerro Rico were members of the Aramayo family. As a result, political power remained concentrated in Bolivia's southern highlands, as it had in colonial times.

Rigid state fiscal policies up to the early 1870s had severely constrained the silver sector, and when they were finally relaxed, coupled with changes in world silver demand, the industry expanded rapidly.[6] Creole mining magnates prospered, and with them so did the old city of Potosí, increasingly modernized if still behind the major capitals. Even as mining itself was largely concentrated in Potosí's peripheral camps like Pulacayo or Colquechaca, the role of the ex–Imperial Villa remained key as home to the national silver exchange bank and the mint. All roads still led to Potosí.

Foreign mining interests were never absent in these heady years of global industrial investment, and as protectionist policies faded, outsiders seized upon Bolivia's undeveloped nitrate zone in the Atacama Desert in the early 1870s. A series of intrigues and betrayals led to the War of the Pacific in 1879, which ended with Bolivia losing its coastal provinces by 1880. Nevertheless, Bolivian silver mining continued to flourish and modernize even as world prices slumped.

Investments in technology helped keep silver flowing in and out of Potosí, and by the turn of the twentieth century the city was finally linked to the world by rail and its major mines electrified thanks to a new hydroelectric plant in the Cayara gorge. The city boasted a brewery by 1907, a new industrial competitor for indigenous *chicheras*. After silver prices collapsed, the country turned to tin. The Department of Potosí was rich in tin mines and the Cerro Rico contained significant deposits as well. Unfortunately, the new silver industry infrastructure, including a rail line to the now-Chilean coast, enabled foreign companies to export raw mineral, killing Bolivia's venerable refining sector. A new era of foreign dependency was under way that would last until 1952.

<br>

## DAMNED YANKEES

As we saw at the opening of this book, American explorer Hiram Bingham visited Potosí on his way north from Buenos Aires in 1909. Bingham was stunned by the grandeur of the ruined Imperial Villa, but he was also captivated by the Cerro Rico,

> the beautifully colored cone that raises itself fifteen hundred feet above the city. It is impossible to describe adequately the beauty of its colors and the marvelous way in which they change as the sun sinks behind the western Andes. I hope that someday a great painter will come here and put on canvas the marvelous hues of this world-renowned hill. Pink, purple, lavender, brown, gray, and yellow streaks make it look as though the gods, having finished painting the universe, had used this as a dumping ground for their surplus pigments.[7]

At the time of Bingham's visit several dozen mines were working, along with twenty-eight refineries, all foreign-owned. Informal mining and refining continued as in colonial times, and the miners' lot seemed to Bingham little changed: "They wear thick knitted caps which save their heads from the bumps and shield them from falling rocks. Their knees are protected by strong leather caps. Their feet they bind in huge moccasins. Those that carry out the ore frequently wear leather aprons tied on their backs. The workmen are a sordid, rough-looking lot who earn and deserve very good wages."[8] And at the refineries: "The workmen are mostly Quichuas. Some of them are evidently not city bred, for they dress with the same pigtails and small clothes that they wore when Spanish conquistadores forced them to take the precious metal out of the hill without any thought of reward other than the fact that they were likely to die sooner and reach heaven earlier than if they stayed quietly at home."[9]

The son of Protestant missionaries to Hawai'i, Bingham could not resist reference to the Black Legend, and throughout his visit to Potosí it appears he scarcely spoke to anyone from Bolivia except the departmental prefect. His hotel was run by an Austrian, and his comments on native Bolivians were interspersed with his musings on llamas. On market vendors selling porridge:

> The women dress in innumerable petticoats of many-colored materials and wear warm, heavy, colored shawls, brought together over the shoulders and secured with two large pins, occasionally of handsome workmanship, but more often in the shape of spoons. Generally they are content with uninteresting felt hats, but now and then one will have a specimen of a different design, the principal material of which is black velveteen, ornamented with red worsted and colored beads. On their feet the women usually wear the simplest kind of rawhide sandals, although when they can afford it, they affect an extraordinary footgear, a sandal with a French heel an inch and a half high, and shod with a leather device resembling a horse shoe.[10]

For the American explorer, Potosí was picturesque, its inhabitants exotic, almost Oriental. Potosí had long been a tourist destination, albeit a rarely visited one. About a decade before Bingham's stop in Potosí, there arrived in town an American travel writer, Marie Robinson Wright, who offered her own description of Potosí mineworkers:

> There is something quite picturesque in the appearance of the Potosí miner, whose garb is a mixture of European and Indian dress, and even the little tallow dip which he wears in his cap attracts attention, not only by its shape, which is like a tiny tin jug with the wick lying over the spout, but because it is invariably ornamented by a small cross which stands up from the rim as a conspicuous ornament.[11]

Wright also cited a common ditty: "Te diera, si me dieras, De tu linda boca un sí, Las aromas de la Arabia, El Cerro de Potosí" (roughly: "I would give you, if you gave me, from your pretty mouth a 'yes,' the aromas of Arabia, the Cerro Rico of Potosí").[12]

Turn-of-the-century Potosí was thus folded into the romantic imagination, and almost predicting the reaction of Bingham, Wright gushed:

> A brilliant past still casts its glamour over the historic city of Potosí. Romance lingers about its wonderful old palaces, fascinating in their antiquated style, with their exquisitely carved doorways and curiously wrought *miradores* [balconies]. Unwritten history is suggested in every varying design, and in a thousand indefinable touches of the elaborate art that constructed them in centuries gone by . . . There is an attractiveness about it all which few cities in the New World possess.[13]

These are the views of outsiders, like Accarette du Biscay and Elias al-Mûsili two and a half centuries before them, at once naive and perceptive. Wright and Bingham were in fact following a well-worn path in exoticizing Potosí's colonial past pioneered by the Argentine writers Vicente Quesada and Juana Manuela Gorriti, along with Peru's Ricardo Palma. For them Potosí was a kind of stage for "Andean gothic" tales. Potosí's industrial reality after 1910 or so was perhaps not so fantastic.

## TIN AND THE REVOLUTIONARY STATE

The quaint and exotic Potosí described by Wright and Bingham over a century ago was as superficial as many short-term travelers' impressions are today. The city and Cerro Rico were not frozen in time, even if the colonial past seemed to haunt the present. Indeed, the reality of life in Potosí after the introduction of cyanide processing, pneumatic drills, and electric ore carts was undoubtedly modern, not stuck in a colonial, much less a pre-Columbian, time warp.

Average Bolivians were often poor and undernourished despite the silver and later tin booms, and workers' lives were tough, but as Robert Smale and others have shown, the turn from silver to tin starting in the 1890s revolutionized Bolivian mining and also made revolutionaries of many miners.[14] The fiercely militant political sensibility of the Potosí miner so evident today was largely forged in the struggles of the first half of the twentieth century.

Most of Bolivia's major tin mines were closer to Oruro, in the old colonial province of Chayanta. Some tin mines such as those at Colquechaca fell within the northern district of Potosí Department, and miners migrated throughout the south-central highlands in search of work. The city of Potosí counted 2,230 mineworkers in a 1900 census, the highest single concentration of any Bolivian city or town, followed by Oruro (1,913) and Pulacayo (1,720).[15] By the first decade of the twentieth century, the city of Potosí became a hotbed of political agitation as anarcho-syndicalists and other radical labor organizers emerged to preach a new gospel.

The shift to tin after 1900 was reflected in national politics as the old silver elite and their Conservative Party fell from grace. Liberal rule made way for new entrepreneurs, most spectacularly Simón Patiño, whose fortune ballooned in the 1910s and 1920s as he expanded his portfolio of tin mines as well as transport networks and even processing plants in Europe. Patiño's treatment of workers was by contrast dismal, and several violent episodes in his and other mines in the Departments of Potosí and Oruro revealed a rising awareness of shared exploitation.

Dangerous working conditions, foul camps and disease, and above all low wages (in the 1910s averaging a boliviano or well under a dollar, for a long day's work) led miners to consider organizing and striking. Some were radicalized in Chile, where they had migrated to work in the nitrate fields during World War I.

The tin town of Uncía, in northern Potosí Department, became a flashpoint when workers struck against Patiño in 1919. A 1920 contract and parallel rise of the Republican Party, which wanted mineworkers as voters, muted the conflict temporarily, but on 4 June 1923, in the aftermath of May Day protests, Bolivian soldiers gunned down several mineworkers. The Republicans showed which side they were on, mixing harsh repression with attempts to divide miners and railworkers in Potosí and Oruro.

Republican Party leaders tried to mollify miners with new laws protecting them from abuses, but enforcement was another matter. A worker's congress was to be held in Potosí in June 1928 to commemorate the Uncía Massacre, but it was postponed by repression of a massive peasant uprising in Chayanta that included the ritualized murders of several hacienda owners. Mineworker and peasant consciousness was fusing in a new amalgam of nativist revivalism and international socialist ideals.

Potosí remained a hotbed of radical dissent, sometimes including university-educated youths, but bickering among anarcho-syndicalists and socialists, plus a new pull from workers in La Paz, helped stall reform in the mining sector. Other global and regional events would also intervene. The stock market crash of 1929 led to a collapse of world demand for tin, and the Bolivian government found a distraction in the disastrous Chaco War with Paraguay from 1932–34. Many soldiers and officers who survived returned to Potosí as amputees. For the first time, mine owners, including Simón Patiño, employed women underground.[16]

Only during World War II, when tin prices rebounded, did Potosí return to center stage in Bolivia's political economy. In 1942, workers at Simón Patiño's Catavi mines were fired on by soldiers in response to their demands for a holiday bonus. Outraged family members were subsequently shot as well. This massacre, huge compared to the killings at Uncía in 1923, led to the widespread reorganization of miners throughout Potosí Department, including those at Pulacayo, in the mountains between Potosí and Uyuni. The

*Thesis of Pulacayo,* drafted in 1946, became a partial blueprint for the revolution that swept Bolivia in 1952. Mineworkers, heirs of the *mitayos* and *kajchas* of the Cerro Rico, were finally in the lead.

## POTOSÍ FROM THE 1952 REVOLUTION TO
## THE ERA OF EVO MORALES

Although overshadowed by the rise of La Paz after 1900, Potosí remained a vitally important city, capital of the nation's richest department. Regionalist tensions were displaced somewhat after 1952 with the creation of COMIBOL, or the Corporación Minera de Bolivia. Mines belonging to the Patiño, Aramayo, and other families were now state property, and mineworkers were state employees. Economic nationalism was the order of the day. Despite a rough start, COMIBOL managed to earn profits by the mid-1960s and mineworkers enjoyed a rare era of prosperity or at least social security. They appeared to be a privileged working class. Bolivia's governing party, the MNR or Movimiento Nacionalista Revolucionario, cleverly played the United States and Soviet Union off of each other in the 1960s, which also aided the mining sector.

Although mineworkers seemed like a privileged class compared to Bolivia's peasant majority, the reality was more complex. As Kendall Brown points out, a complicated "pyramidal hierarchy" developed among mineworkers under COMIBOL, with those holding official posts exploiting a number of subcontracted underlings.[17] With colorful names like *buhos* (owls) and *jukus* (ore thieves), those at the bottom survived by scrounging abandoned mines for bits of marketable ore. These men got none of the benefits of state employees. *Lameros* or "slimers" reworked old tailings or muds, many of them saturated with mercury, cadmium, and other toxins. Women continued to work as freelance *palliris* or high-grade ore sorters, most of them earning a pittance.

A far-left swing in 1969 was negated by the bloody coup led by General Hugo Banzer in 1971. Banzer was buoyed by high commodity prices as he renegotiated U.S. trade relations. Mineworkers continued to benefit from global demand for Bolivia's minerals and Potosí remained a political and economic hub of significance, although the eastern lowlands, especially the capital of Santa Cruz de la Sierra, had also gained political clout with the success of oil and gas exploration. In seeking to remain in power in 1977,

Banzer provoked widespread dissent, and the Bolivian political system that would give rise to Evo Morales was born.[18] Demographic changes had essentially eroded the power once held by the mining unions. The mining sector, and with it COMIBOL and thus Potosí, were also headed for a dark period.

After a series of coups, Bolivia's democratic regimes broke up COMIBOL and fired thousands of workers in the later 1980s. Strikes proved useless. This was not simply a case of state mismanagement: world demand for tin had died. For small and medium miners in Potosí and elsewhere, zinc was a poor substitute for tin, but if you knew where to look in the old COMIBOL mines, silver could once again yield a living, if only barely. By 1990, mining on the Cerro Rico reverted to kajcheo-style cooperatives, some of them using equipment sold off cheaply by COMIBOL. Cooperatives were organized by seniority and they claimed mines largely by occupation rather than through formal legal mechanisms.

After a long slump, mineral prices rose at the start of the twenty-first century as China became an industrial powerhouse, with South Korea, India, and other Asian countries not far behind. With COMIBOL all but defunct, Bolivia opened up to foreign mining companies and revived some of its own state holdings. Small-scale cooperative miners squared off with foreign companies, although some found work with them. Free-market fever caught hold, and neoliberal concessions, mostly in the energy sector, were among the causes of President Gonzalo Sánchez's fall from power in 2003. The proximate cause was a massacre of protesters in El Alto, next to La Paz. The people could not be silenced.

Mineworkers, indigenous activists, and coca growers, including Evo Morales, pushed hard against Sánchez's pro-U.S., neoliberal agenda, ultimately driving him from power and into exile. Evo Morales was elected president with broad support from Potosí miners in 2005, perhaps with the hope of a revived COMIBOL. Morales's relationship with the miners of Potosí quickly grew troubled, however, steadily worsening in the dozen years following his first election. Relying on state energy revenues, Morales toyed with Bolivia's mineral sector, courting foreign investment and keeping mineworkers off balance by supporting some union actions and blocking others.

Morales's seeming ambivalence toward mining and miners thus sharpened divisions in Potosí, both within the city and across the department, one of Bolivia's largest and still one of its richest in terms of minerals. The Cerro Rico's dozens of cooperatives became powerful with high commodity prices despite the global financial crisis of 2008, but they remained vulnerable to expropriation without government guarantees. Their periodic protests after 2010 turned violent both in Potosí and La Paz, with dynamite their preferred means of getting everyone's attention.

As of this writing (2018) Potosí is a much larger and shinier city than the one I first visited in 1995. What was then a depressed mining town is now a thriving metropolis, spilling down from the Cerro Rico and into neighboring canyons and valleys not inhabited since colonial times. The city council is working desperately to increase tourism as the mines peter out and other economic opportunities fade. Now home to over 300,000 people, the city is facing a water crisis. Climate change has exacerbated highland desertification, and the reservoirs built on order of Viceroy Toledo are drying up. Water piped in from other highland basins cannot reach the upper half of the city, and today poor citizens fight with mill owners over access to every precious drop, especially in the dry winter months. In September 2017 a Potosí mayor was deposed for allegedly selling municipal drinking water to silver and zinc refiners at the edge of the city's old colonial sector.

Andean mineworkers, meanwhile, continue to labor inside the Cerro Rico day and night, cheeks jammed with coca leaves and lungs full of silica dust. Many work for the equivalent of a few dollars a day. Some are mere boys, others are broken men coughing blood before the age of forty. Tall ore trucks rumble regularly down the mountain toward dozens of refineries whose tailings fill inadequate sediment ponds below the city. With each rainy season the Pilcomayo River gets a dose of Potosí's accumulated heavy metals, cyanide, acidic sludge, and other contaminants. In August, the Tomahave winds still howl against the spirit of St. Bartholomew, obscuring the sun with particulates and plastic bags.

Patient as ever with human folly in the face of indifferent nature, the great red Cerro Rico, scarred and collapsing but dressed up with festive night lights, stares down on the once Imperial Villa, now a pastiche of mirrored glass and garishly painted concrete. She was never the "king of mountains" as the Holy Roman Emperor Charles V had declared, but she may have been the Queen of the Andes, a singular manifestation of Pachamama and the Virgin Mary. It may seem a distant memory now, but this unique assemblage of mountain, town, and hinterland in the remote highlands of Bolivia was for over a century the undisputed "treasury of the world."

# APPENDIX: VOICES

Potosí in its colonial heyday inspired many commentators, not all of them reliable. Below is a small selection of eyewitness accounts in translation that are intended to add flavor to the main text. The first item relates Diego Gualpa's alleged discovery of the Cerro Rico in 1545 as recalled on his deathbed before a priest in 1572. Second is Dominican friar Domingo de Santo Tomás's famous quote describing Potosí as a "mouth of hell" during his visit in 1550. Next is Jeronymite alms collector Diego de Ocaña's description of a very wealthy native Andean or mestizo man, Pedro de Mondragón, whose house he visited in the year 1600. Fourth is a series of descriptions of minework and accidents provided by Potosí refinery owner Luis Capoche, composed and sent to Spain in 1585. Capoche's work greatly influenced that of the famous Jesuit naturalist José de Acosta, who published his description of Potosí a few years later. Next is an anonymous 1603 report on Potosí's tremendous consumption of wood and dressed timber, a reminder of the environmental consequences of the great boom. Last is an awestruck description of a Potosí festival as remembered by French eyewitness Accarette du Biscay in 1658. Even in hard times, the Imperial Villa could put on a heck of a show.

## DESCRIPTION OF THE CERRO DE POTOSÍ
### AND ITS DISCOVERY, 1572

"This Indian Gualpa climbed the mountain with another Indian whom they ordered to accompany him, as the climb was substantial and rough, a distance of more than 2,000 paces. Going along on their errand with difficulty, both Indians arrived at the very summit of the mountain of Potosí, the same which has a mesa at its very top about a hundred feet across, more or less, and spreading out equally in all directions. There they discovered a shrine [pertaining to] the surrounding Indians and there were a few offered things of little importance to the *huaca* that was there, all which this said Indian don Diego Gualpa gathered up, and he loaded it onto [the back of] his companion and sent him to the four Spaniards who were down at the sites they named for Gonzalo Pizarro. This Indian Gualpa stayed there alone on the mountain of Potosí after having sent his companion with the booty of the *huaca* that was on the highest point of the peak to the four Christians who had sent him … He said that upon descending from the highest part of the mountain, there came a wind so great that it knocked him to the ground, a common occurrence on this mountain of Potosí as it has great gusts, being scoured on all sides and as nature has created it in the shape of a point of a diamond, where he lost his senses and remained for a space of time after coming to, without being able to get up. He looked all around to see if his companion he had sent to the four Christians had returned … Upon rolling over to lift himself up, he put his hands on the ground, and they made a mark in it as if he were passing his hands over well smoothed clay, and it marked his hands; and as the hour had arrived in which God Our Lord took as right for his service that such an immeasurable treasure should be made known to humanity, he opened the eyes of understanding of this Indian and he recognized that it was silver ore upon which he had placed his hands, as he had seen in the camp of Porco another ore like this, and he took of it a quantity of eight or ten marks [4–5 lbs.] and he descended the mountain in search of the four Christians who had been sent, the same which did not wait for him but had returned to Porco." (Source: Rodrigo de la Fuente Santangel, *clérigo presbítero*. In *Biblioteca de Autores Españoles* No. 185 (Madrid: Atlas, 1965), 357–61, orig. in Biblioteca Nacional Madrid, ms. vol. J.58., 6ff., my translation.)

## FRAY DOMINGO DE SANTO TOMÁS ON POTOSÍ AS "MOUTH OF HELL," CA. 1550

"It must have been about four years during which this land was about to be lost [i.e., during the Gonzalo Pizarro rebellion] that there was discovered a *mouth of hell,* into which have entered, as I say within that time, a great quantity of people, which by the greed of the Spaniards they sacrifice to their god, and these are some silver mines that they call Potosí. And so that your highness may understand that it truly is a mouth of hell, that in order to swallow up souls God permitted to be discovered in this land, I will here paint something of it. It is a hill in an extremely cold wasteland, around which for six leagues in all directions not a single plant grows that can sustain beasts, nor is there firewood to cook food. Indians bring these things on their backs or on llamas, those who have them, and the same is true for all that is necessary for the sustenance of the Spaniards and Indians who reside and remain there. The closest source for these things is 12, 15, or 30 leagues away, and the farthest is Collao, a hundred leagues [557 km] away. A bushel of wheat commonly costs 30 *castellanos* [ca. 60 silver pesos] in that place, and most often more; the bushel of maize, which is the food of the Indians, from 15 to 20 *castellanos;* the bushel of other foods of theirs called *chuño* and potatoes, which are roots of plants, at 12 or 15 *castellanos.* They take the ore from that mountain I mentioned with all the labor one could imagine could be taken out of them, both because it is a great task to remove the ore from so deep among so many rocks and with such danger of frequent mine collapses, as well as what happens to them from the cold and distemper of the land. The charcoal to smelt [the ore] they bring from six leagues away and more. The firewood with which to warm themselves and to cook their food from the same distance to the fame of this hill and its richness from 200 leagues and more; from here 250, from there 230. From 180 leagues away they send the poor Indians by the force of each draft allotment according to its rules. From one allotment fifty, from another sixty, from another 100, from another 200, and so on in greater numbers. However contrary to reason and the laws of free persons this may be, anyone who knows what freedom is ignores it, because sending off souls by force is either the condition of slaves or of condemned men to such a great penalty for grave crimes, and not the law of the free which your highness in his provisions and ordinances claims these poor folk to be." (Source: José María Vargas, *Fr. Domingo de Santo Tomás, defensor y apostol de los indios del Perú: Su vida y sus escritos* (Quito: Editorial Santo Domingo, 1937), 15–21, my translation, my emphasis (orig. ms. in AGI Lima 113). The *castellano* was an accounting unit equivalent to 4.6 grams of 22-karat gold.)

## DIEGO DE OCAÑA ON A "RICH INDIAN" IN POTOSÍ, CA. 1600

"There are in Potosí very rich Indians, in particular one they call [Pedro de] Mondragón. One day I went to the house of this Indian, who holds the office of inspector of weights and measures [*fiel ejecutor*] in perpetuity, just to see him and his house; and from Spain one may come to see this one's house. And I found him eating on the floor, on a low table, as the Indians typically eat on the floor without a table at all, nor do they use even a chair, but rather always sit squatting like broody hens. And this one, being hispanized in dress, had a table, but very low like a small stool. And he has all of his capital in his house at all times, before his eyes. He has a room filled with silver, in one part the bars, in another the ingots ['pinecones'], and in another, in some jugs, the coins [reals]. I was quite stunned to see so much silver in one place and I asked him how much was there, that I was seeing, and he replied to me: 'There are 300,000 pesos of assayed silver.' This one loans to the king every year 100,000 or 200,000 pesos for the fleet to take; and later they go discounting from the fifths that he has to give the king from the bars he makes, because the business he has is to buy 'pinecones' and make bars and hammer them into coins [via the royal mint]. And in each one of these things he earns in all at such and such a percent, and little by little it gets to be more as he does not engage in other exchanges where he might risk his estate, but only this which he has constantly going on in his house. He is a man who must make many secret pious donations, but public ones, no, and the general opinion is that he makes none." (Source: Diego de Ocaña, *Viaje por el Nuevo Mundo de Guadalupe a Potosí, 1599–1605,* ed. Blanca López de Mariscal and Abraham Madroñal (Madrid: Iberoamericana/Vervuert, 2010), 270–71, my translation. Kenneth Mills, in "Ocaña's Mondragón in the Eighth Wonder of the World" (forthcoming, 2019), explains Ocaña's fascination with indigenous and mestizo strivers, a persistent cause for wonder among visitors from Spain.)

## LUIS CAPOCHE ON THE CERRO RICO, MINING METHODS
## AND ACCIDENTS, 1585

"The [*mita*] Indians take out the ore, [each load] amounting to some two *arrobas* [approx. 50 lbs. or 22.7 kg] in blankets belonging to them, and I do not know by what obligation they bring these, tied around the chest and the ore [borne] across their shoulders, and they climb up three by three, and the one in front carries a candle in one hand by which they see where they are climbing and descending, as the mines are dark and without any visibility, and the candle providing little light and quite often it is extinguished by the wind, and between their two hands they come grasping and helping, and climbing with great effort 150 statures [5.5 ft. each, total 825 ft. or approx. 251 m] and so many more in descending; and in mines over 400 statures [2,200 ft. or approx. 671 m deep]—a distance that on a flat surface would tire a man thus encumbered, much less descending and climbing with much risk—the Indians reach the exit sweating and breathless, and robbed of heat, and the refreshment they generally encounter in order to assuage their fatigue is to be called a dog, and to be given a round [of blows] for bringing too little ore or for taking too long, or being told it was only dirt they had brought out, or that they had stolen something. And not four months ago it so happened that a mine owner, wanting to get into it with an Indian over this, and [the Indian] fearing the stick with which he was to be injured he sought refuge in the mine itself, and in the confusion he fell and was dashed into 100,000 pieces."

"The *minga* Indians have some advantages and are better treated, since they are contracted with some freedom and they have the right to take away some *corpa* of ore, which is to say a large piece, as their daily wage, and if this were in some way limited they would not return to the mines. And those [mines] that make most frequent use of *minga* Indians are the rich ones, where they encounter profit and can take away ores for mercury [refining] and rich ones [ores to be refined in wind furnaces] should they be close at hand, and if they are there, there is no hiding them. Those [mines] with poor ores cause their owners to suffer, as the Indians allotted to them are so few that they are practically ineffectual . . . "

"Also huge is the trade in this villa of European cloth, and it is so great that each year it amounts to more than 1,200,000 pesos that is consumed and enters by sea from the port of Arica as well as that which comes from Cuzco, not counting some 500,000 pesos' worth of woolen stuff, baize, and grogram from Quito, from Huánuco, and La Paz, and 100,000 pesos' worth of local cloth, and 25,000 in cloth from Tucumán, which is a lot of cotton linen, carpets and ornamental cloths, honey, wax, and Indian cloth. The iron they consume in the equipment of the mills adds up to more than 300,000 quintals; the wine of Ica, Camaná, and Arequipa, which are wines from the [Pacific] coast and its valleys, and that of Caracato, which is in the district of La Paz, it is great the quantity that enters, which must come to more than 15,000 jugs, which are sold for 8 ½ to 9 assayed pesos. From Castile there enter more than 8,000 jugs worth 15 or 16 assayed pesos each; the conserves and sugar consumed is tremendous."

"Some time ago, it happened that a Portuguese entered with seven Indians to work a mine, shifting the labor from one part to another. And reaching the deepest part, where they sought to start working again, rocks began to fall away in the mine beneath them and earth came down from above, and to shelter themselves from this, five of them put themselves in a cave and the other two pressed themselves into another smaller space, where they could defend themselves against all that was falling, which was so much that it filled the better part of the mine, leaving them alive in those cavities left by the rubble. Once news reached the town, Diego Bravo, magistrate of mines, and also the inspectors, made a great effort to rescue these people, sending many Indians up the mountain to pull apart and remove the earth that had fallen, but it was to no effect, because no sooner did they remove some when more began to fall. And the next day, somewhat late, they pulled out the two Indians who were not enclosed by so much earth. The Indians who went in to clear the mine by day and by night did so at no small risk to their lives, due to the earth that continued to fall, and as the space in which they had to work could not accommodate many people; those who worked did all they could but it was to no avail. The Portuguese and the five Indians had space to move around, as the cave they were in was rather large. This encouraged those outside, giving them hope that they would surely defeat the earth, and [from the cave] the Portuguese told them not to abandon them nor tire out, as God would be served to free them from that anguish and tribulation, and they were controlling themselves to resist hunger, although the cold had left them fatigued, and to sustain themselves they had eaten their shoes. And the Indians also spoke. And in this way they passed four or five days, with people always arriving with refreshments so that they could work with more effort. And once it became clear that it would not be possible to remove them, a Jesuit father went down to confess them, and the Portuguese made a will, and thus they bid farewell to them with many sighs on both sides, the Indians saying some silly, rustic things to pass along to their wives and children, and thus they died without any means of remedy. The one who lived longest was a somewhat Latinized Indian, who said that the Portuguese was no longer speaking, that he had decided to go to sleep, and that the rest of his companions were there dead beside him." (Source: Luis Capoche, *Relación general de la Villa Imperial de Potosí,* ed. Lewis Hanke, Biblioteca de Autores Españoles 122 (Madrid: Atlas, 1959), 109, 159, 179, my translations.)

## POTOSÍ'S DEMAND FOR TIMBER IN THE ANONYMOUS 1603 RELACIÓN

"This town has a huge expenditure on wood, such that the amount consumed cannot be determined, as there are so many dealers in it; but so that one may get an idea of how large the expenditure is, I will say that one beam that they call an axle, which is 22 feet long and two feet square in width, is worth 900 and even 1,000 assayed pesos; and a beam they call a mortar [for crushing ore], of the same width but ten feet long, is worth 400 assayed pesos, and a beam they call a mallet, two and a quarter yards long and one palm wide is worth 14 pesos; and an ordinary plank 10 pesos; and following from this one can imagine the great expenditure there has to be in wood for the 128 stamp-mill heads there are here; leaving aside all the houses of Spaniards with their doors, windows, and recessed cabinets of cedar, most finely finished in every way. And the ceilings of the houses are of some staves they call *agaves,* which although hollow inside are incorruptible, and are three or four yards long, and about the thickness of an arm, and each one is worth 4 reales." (Source: "Description of the Villa and Mines de Potosí in the year 1603." Anonymous—in José Urbano Martínez, ed., *Relaciones geográficas de Indias—Peru,* Biblioteca de Autores Españoles, vol. 185 (Madrid: Atlas, 1965), 372–85, my translation.)

## ACCARETTE DU BISCAY ON A POTOSÍ CELEBRATION, 1658

"And all the people great and small, whether Spaniards, foreigners, Indians, or blacks, minded nothing else but to do something extraordinary for the solemnizing of this festival. It began with a cavalcade made by the corregidor, the twenty-four magistrates of the city, the other officers, the principal of the nobility and gentry, and the most eminent merchants of the city, all richly clothed; all the rest of the people, and particularly the ladies, being at the windows and casting down abundance of perfumed waters, and great quantities of dry sweetmeats. The following days they had several plays, some of which they call *juegos de toros,* others *juegos de cañas,* several sorts of masquerades, comedies, balls, with vocal and instrumental music, and other divertissements, which were carried on one day by the gentlemen, another day by the citizens; one while by the goldsmiths, one while by the miners; some by the people of diverse nations; others by the Indians, and all with great magnificence and a prodigious expense."

After commenting on a special show put on by native residents, Acarrete describes the finale:

"The last day save one surpassed all the rest, and that was a race at the ring, which was performed at the charge of the city with very surprising machines. First there appeared a ship towed along by savages [*sic*] of the bulk and burden of 100 tons, with her guns and equipage of men clothed in curious habit, her anchors, ropes, and sails swelling with the wind, which very luckily blew along the street through which they drew her to the great public place, where, as soon as she arrived, she saluted the company by the discharge of all her cannon. At the same time, a Spanish lord, representing an emperor of the East coming to congratulate the birth of the prince, came out of the vessel attended with six gentlemen and a very fine train of servants who led their horses, which they mounted and so went to salute the President of Los Charcas. And, while they were making their compliment to him, their horses kneeled down and kept in that posture, having been taught this trick before. They afterward went to salute the corregidor and the judges of the field, from whom, when they had received permission to run at the ring against the defendants, they acquitted themselves with great gallantry, and received very fine prizes distributed by the hands of the ladies." (Source: Irving Leonard, *Colonial Travelers in Latin America* (New York: Alfred A. Knopf, 1972), 141–42.)

# GLOSSARY

ADIT. horizontal mine tunnel

APIRI. indigenous ore carrier

AUDIENCIA. Spanish district or circuit court

AYLLU. Andean kin group

AZOGUE. old Spanish term for mercury (Arabic *az-zauq*)

AZOGUERO. refinery owner, guild member

CHARQUI. jerked llama flesh or beef

CHICHA. maize beer

CHICHERA. female chicha vendor

CHUÑO. freeze-dried, pressed potato

CORPA. high-grade ore for trade

CORREGIDOR. royal magistrate in charge of *corregimiento* district

ENCOMIENDA. fief-like grant of native tributaries

FORASTERO. non-ayllu member, free-floating Andean

GUAIRA. wind (also *guayra*), wind furnace (also *guairachina*)

GUAIRADOR. operator of a guaira

HUACA. sacred site (also *waka, guaca*); for Spanish a cache of treasure

ICHU. thatch-like puna grass

INGENIO. large ore-crushing mill

JUKU. "ore thief," scavenger (Aymara)

KAJCHA. "ore thief," scavenger (Quechua)

KAJCHEO. ore theft or after-hours scavenging

KURAKA. Andean native lord (also cacique)

MINERO. mine overseer, administrator

MINGADO. hired Andean mineworker

MITA. rotational labor draft

MITAYO. mita worker

PALLIRI. female ore sorter

PESO DE A OCHO. "piece of eight" or silver coin worth eight reals or 272 *maravedís*

PESO ENSAYADO. "assayed" peso or accounting unit worth 450 *maravedís*

PIÑA. pinecone-shaped silver ingot

PUNA. high Andean desert

QUINTAL. hundredweight, approx. 46 kg

RANCHERÍAS. Andean barrios or townships of Potosí

SOCAVÓN. horizontal tunnel (adit)

SOROCHE. high-altitude sickness; lead sulfide or galena

SUPAY. trickster god (see Tío)

TÍO. god of the underworld, mine interior deity

TRAPICHE. small ore-crushing mill

YANACONA. Andean servant, non-ayllu Andean

# NOTES

1. Hiram Bingham, *Across South America: An Account of a Journey from Buenos Aires to Lima by Way of Potosí* (Boston: Houghton Mifflin, 1911), 117, 121. For a recent study of Bingham, see Christopher Heaney, *Cradle of Gold: The Story of Hiram Bingham, a Real-Life Indiana Jones and the Search for Machu Picchu* (New York: Palgrave Macmillan, 2010).

2. For a new take on this mining boom, see John Tutino, *Making a New World: Founding Capitalism in the Bajío and Spanish North America* (Durham, NC: Duke University Press, 2011).

3. Originally published in 1974, see the updated edition by Immanuel Wallerstein, *The Modern World-System I: Capitalist Agriculture and the Origins of the European World-Economy in the Sixteenth Century* (Berkeley: University of California Press, 2011).

4. Steve J. Stern, "Feudalism, Capitalism, and the World-System in the Perspective of Latin America and the Caribbean," *American Historical Review* 93:4 (Oct. 1988): 829–72.

5. See James D. Tracy, ed., *The Rise of Merchant Empires: Long-Distance Trade in the Early Modern World, 1350–1750*, and *The Political Economy of Merchant Empires: State Power and World Trade, 1350–1750* (New York: Cambridge University Press, 1990, 1991).

6. A recent exception to the "brute commodity" view of Latin American silver is Carlos Marichal's superb chapter on the "piece of eight" in *From Silver to Cocaine: Latin American Commodity Chains and the Building of the World Economy, 1500–2000*, ed. Steven Topik, Carlos Marichal, and Zephyr Frank (Durham, NC: Duke University Press, 2006), 25–52.

7. See Pedro Cardim, Tamar Herzog, Jos Javier Ruiz Ibez, and Gaetano Sabatini, eds., *Polycentric Monarchies: How Did Early Modern Spain and Portugal Achieve and Maintain a Global Hegemony?* (Sussex: Sussex University Press, 2012).

8. See, for example, Femme Gaastra, *The Dutch East India Company: Expansion and Decline* (Zutphen: Walburg, 2003), and K. N. Chaudhuri, *The English East India Company: The Study of an Early Joint-Stock Company, 1600–1640,* 2nd ed. (London: Routledge, 1999). Kenneth Pomeranz and Steven Topik sparked many new and genuinely global discussions with *The World That Trade Created: Society, Culture, and the World Economy, 1400 to the Present* (Armonk, NY: M. E. Sharpe, 1999).

9. Andre Gunder Frank, *ReOrient: Global Economy in the Asian Age* (Berkeley: University of California Press, 1998). See also William Schell, "Silver Symbiosis: ReOrienting Mexican Economic History," *Hispanic American Historical Review* 81:1 (Feb. 2001): 89–133.

10. Economist Dennis O. Flynn and historian Arturo Giráldez have published a number of essays and books on American silver in Asia, arguing forcefully for a Pacific-centered globalized world dating to 1571.

11. On the Ottomans and Safavids, see Sevket Pamuk, *A Monetary History of the Ottoman Empire* (New York: Cambridge University Press, 2000); and Rudi Matthee, *Persia in Crisis: Safavid Decline and the Fall of Isfahan* (London: I. B. Tauris, 2012). For Mughal India, see, for example, Shireen Moosvi, "The Silver Influx, Money Supply, Prices and Revenue-Extraction in Mughal India," *Journal of the Economic and Social History of the Orient* 30:1 (1987): 47–94.

12. Richard Von Glahn, in *Fountain of Fortune: Money and Monetary Policy in China, 1000–1700* (Berkeley: University of California Press, 1996) and in more recent works, has reminded us of the importance of Japanese silver and also of the complex money systems operating within China amid the Potosí boom.

13. Historian Timothy Brook tells a lyrical tale of early modern globalization linking Potosí, the Netherlands, China, and much more in *Vermeer's Hat: The Seventeenth Century and the Dawn of the Global World* (New York: Viking Penguin, 2008).

14. See Giorgio Riello, *Cotton: The Fabric That Made the Modern World* (New York: Cambridge University Press, 2013).

15. A model study is Daviken Studnicki-Gizbert, "Exhausting the Sierra Madre: Mining Ecologies in Mexico over the Longue Durée," in *Mining North America: An Environmental History since 1522,* ed. John R. McNeill and George Vrtis (Berkeley: University of California Press, 2017), 19–46. In conjunction with his PhD advisee, Saúl Guerrero, Studnicki-Gizbert has commented on recent findings published by Nicholas A. Robins on mercury contamination in Potosí and Huancavelica, Peru. See Robins, *Mercury, Mining, and Empire: The Human and Ecological Cost of Colonial Silver Mining in the Andes* (Bloomington: Indiana University Press, 2011); and *Santa Barbara's Legacy: An Environmental History of Huancavelica, Peru* (Leiden: Brill, 2017). Guerrero's landmark work is *Silver by Fire, Silver by Mercury: A Chemical History of Silver Refining in New Spain and Mexico, 16th to 19th Centuries* (Leiden: Brill, 2017).

16. See, for example, Colin A. Cooke, Prentiss H. Balcom, Charles Kerfoot, Mark B. Abbott, and Alexander P. Wolfe, "Pre-Columbian Mercury Pollution

Associated with the Smelting of Argentiferous Ores in the Bolivian Andes," *Ambio* 40:1 (Feb. 2011): 18–25. Archaeologists of mining have also joined this search, for example Pablo Cruz and Jean-Joinville Vacher, eds., *Mina y metalurgía en los Andes del Sur desde la época prehispánica hasta el siglo XVII* (Sucre: IFEA, 2008), 201–29.

17. Kendall Brown, "Workers' Health and Colonial Mercury Mining at Huancavelica, Peru," *The Americas* 57:4 (Apr. 2001): 467–96.

18. See, for example, Pratigya J. Polissar, Mark B. Abbott, Alexander P. Wolfe, Mathias Vuille, and Maximiliano Bezada, "Synchronous Interoceanic Holocene Climate Trends in the Tropical Andes," *Proceedings of the National Academy of Sciences of the U. S. A.* 110:36 (Sept. 2013): 14551–56.

## INTRODUCTION

1. Miguel de Cervantes, *Don Quixote* (1605–15), trans. Edith Grossman (New York: Ecco, 2003), chap. LXXI (p. 920).

2. Nicolás Wey-Gómez, *The Tropics of Empire: Why Columbus Sailed South to the Indies* (Cambridge, MA: MIT Press, 2008), 214–24. See also Peter J. Bakewell, ed., *Mines of Silver and Gold in the Americas* (Aldershot: Variorum, 1997).

3. John J. TePaske and K. W. Brown, *A New World of Gold and Silver* (Leiden: Brill, 2010), 151. For Zacatecas, see Peter Bakewell, *Silver Mining and Society in Colonial Mexico, Zacatecas 1556–1700* (New York: Cambridge University Press, 1971). For San Luis Potosí, see Saúl Guerrero, *Silver by Fire, Silver by Mercury: A Chemical History of Silver Refining in New Spain and Mexico, 16th to 19th Centuries* (Leiden: Brill, 2017).

4. On this theory see Orlando Bentancor, *The Matter of Empire: Metaphysics and Mining in Colonial Peru* (Pittsburgh: University of Pittsburgh Press, 2017), 321–45.

5. Pedro de Cieza de León, *Crónica del Peru, Primera Parte,* ed. Franklin Pease G. Y. (Lima: PUCP Fondo Editorial, 1984), 288–93.

6. Cieza de León, *Crónica del Peru,* 292; my translation.

7. Thomas D. Goodrich, *The Ottoman Turks and the New World: A Study of Tarih-I Hind-I Garbi and Sixteenth-Century Ottoman Americana* (Wiesbaden: Otto Harrassowitz, 1990), 61–62.

8. Agustín de Zárate, *The Discovery and Conquest of Peru,* ed. and trans. J. M. Cohen (London: Penguin, 1968), 247–49.

9. Goodrich, *Ottoman Turks and the New World,* 285.

10. Ibid., 286. See also the excellent discussion of this manuscript in the context of Ottoman geopolitics by Giancarlo Casale, *The Ottoman Age of Exploration* (New York: Oxford University Press, 2010), 160–63. The caption for the Ottoman miniature of the Cerro Rico appears to be drawn directly from Cieza de León, probably in Italian translation: "The afore-mentioned group extracted the afore-mentioned mineral in the following way: first they build a great oven and later they mix the earth of the mineral with a quantity of charcoal and dung compost and they place

it within the afore-mentioned oven. They drill a hole in its side by wind and make an aperture. Later they fire the charcoal and manure. Then slowly with a fiery glow the silver and gold [*sic*] melts and leaks out by a path. It comes out from one corner of the oven. In this way the afore-mentioned Carvajal amassed 700,000 [pesos of] Peru silver."

11. Kenneth Ch'en, "Matteo Ricci's Contribution to, and Influence on, Geographical Knowledge in China," *Journal of the American Oriental Society* 59:3 (Sept. 1939): 325–59. Thanks to Prof. Brian DeMare for deciphering the characters.

12. Cieza de León, *Crónica del Perú*, 293.

13. Ibid.

14. "Relación muy particular del Cerro y minas de Potosí y de su Calidad y labores, por Nicolás del Benino, dirigida a don Francisco de Toledo, virrey del Peru, en 1573," in *Relaciones geográficas de Indias—Peru*, Biblioteca de Autores Españoles, vol. 183, ed. José Urbano Martínez Carreras (Madrid: Atlas, 1965), 362–71. Archivo y Biblioteca Nacional de Bolivia (ABNB) Escrituras Públicas (EP) 1, f.37v, ff.344–45; EP 3, ff.564–65; 673v-76.

15. Richard Kagan contrasts views of Potosí with Mexico City, Lima, and Cuzco in *Urban Images of the Hispanic World, 1493–1793* (New Haven, CT: Yale University Press, 2000), 151–97.

## CHAPTER ONE

1. In Mercedes de las Casas Grieve, ed., *Relación de las cosas acaecidas en las alteraciones del Perú después que Blasco Núñez Vela entró en él* (Lima: PUCP, 2003), 251; my translation.

2. Account of Rodrigo de la Fuente Santangel, *clérigo presbítero,* in José Urbano Martínez Carreras, ed., *Relaciones geográficas de Indias—Peru*, Biblioteca de Autores Españoles, vol. 183 (Madrid: Atlas, 1965), 357–61.

3. Juan de Matienzo, *Gobierno del Perú*, ed. Guillermo Lohmann-Villena (Paris / Lima: IFEA, 1967). See chapter 8 on Porco / Potosí *yanaconas* vs. other types.

4. See Pablo Cruz, "Huacas olvidadas y cerros santos: Apuntes metodológicos sobre la cartografía sagrada en los Andes del sur de Bolivia," *Estudios Atacameños* 38 (2009): 55–74. See also Tristan Platt and Pablo Quisbert, "Tras la huella del silencio: Potosí, los Incas y Toledo," *Runa* 31:2 (2010): 112–52.

5. Simon Lamb, *Devil in the Mountain: A Search for the Origin of the Andes* (Princeton, NJ: Princeton University Press, 2004), 143–45. See also Edward W. Berry, "Fossil Plants from Bolivia and Their Bearing on the Age of the Uplift of the Eastern Andes," *Proceedings of the U. S. National Museum* 54:2229 (1917): 103–64.

6. C. G. Cunningham, R. E. Zartman, E. H. McKee, et al., "The Age and Thermal History of Cerro Rico de Potosí, Bolivia," *Mineralium Deposita* 31 (1996): 374–85.

7. Such has been the fate of the fabled Cerro San Pedro, the "Cerro Rico" of the namesake San Luis Potosí, in Mexico. It is now a huge pit. See Daviken

Studnicki-Gizbert, "Exhausting the Sierra Madre," in *Mining North America: An Environmental History since 1522,* ed. John R. McNeill and George Vrtis (Berkeley: University of California Press, 2017), 1–46.

8. Colin A. Cooke et al., "Pre-Colombian Mercury Pollution Associated with the Smelting of Argentiferous Ores in the Bolivian Andes," *Ambio* 40:1 (Feb. 2011): 18–25.

9. John V. Murra coined the term "vertical archipelago." See chapter 1 of Murra, *Reciprocity and Redistribution in Andean Civilizations: The 1969 Henry Morgan Lectures,* ed. Freda Yancy Wolf and Heather Lechtman (Chicago: University of Chicago Press, 2017). On the Chiriguanaes, see Thierry Saignes, *Historia del pueblo Chiriguano,* ed. Isabelle Combès (La Paz: IFEA, 2007).

10. Ana María Presta, "La primera joya de la corona en el Altiplano Surandino: Descubrimiento y explotación de un yacimiento minero inicial: Porco, 1538–1576," in *Mina y metalurgía en los Andes del Sur desde la época prehispánica hasta el siglo XVII,* ed. Pablo Cruz and Jean-Joinville Vacher (Sucre: IFEA, 2008), 201–29.

11. Tristan Platt, Thérèse Bouysse-Cassagne, Olivia Harris, con el aliento de Thierry Saignes, *Qaraqara-Charka: Mallku, Inka y Rey en la provincia de Charcas (siglos XVI–XVII): Historia antropológica de una confederación aymara* (La Paz: IFEA / Plural, 2006), 162.

12. Platt et al., *Qaraqara-Charka,* 151. For the larger campaign, see Kenneth Mills, *Idolatry and Its Enemies: Colonial Andean Religion and Extirpation, 1640–1750* (Princeton, NJ: Princeton University Press, 1997).

13. Platt et al., *Qaraqara-Charka,* 151.

14. Sonia Alconini, *Southeast Inca Frontiers: Boundaries and Interactions* (Gainesville: University Press of Florida, 2016).

15. The story is well told in John Hemming, *The Conquest of the Incas* (New York: Harcourt, Brace, Jovanovich, 1970), 31–45.

16. John J. TePaske, *A New World of Gold and Silver,* ed. Kendall W. Brown (Leiden and Boston: Brill, 2010), 111.

17. Thomas Dandelet, *The Renaissance of Empire in Early Modern Europe* (New York: Cambridge University Press, 2014), 111–15.

18. See Kenneth Andrien, *Andean Worlds: Indigenous History, Culture, and Consciousness* (Albuquerque: University of New Mexico Press, 2001), 43–45.

19. José María Vargas, *Fr. Domingo de Santo Tomás, defensor y apostol de los indios del Perú: Su vida y sus escritos* (Quito: Editorial Santo Domingo, 1937), 15–21; my translation and my emphasis.

20. Archivo y Biblioteca Nacional de Bolivia (ABNB) Escrituras Públicas (EP) 1, ff.27v-30; 32v-35 (both 1548). By 1549 there appear royal decrees outlawing *servicio personal* (e.g., ABNB Rück 1 / 1, ff.359–62).

21. Peter J. Bakewell, *Miners of the Red Mountain: Indian Labor in Potosí, 1545–1650* (Albuquerque: University of New Mexico Press, 1984), 40–45.

22. ABNB Minas EP 3, ff.367–67v (1559); EP 1, f.106 (1549); EP 1, ff.4–5 (1549).

23. This section relies heavily on my translation of Luis Capoche's 1585 account, available in Spanish in Lewis Hanke, ed., *Relación general de la Villa Imperial*

*de Potosí,* Biblioteca de Autores Españoles 122 (Madrid: Atlas, 1959), 1–221, and Bakewell, *Miners of the Red Mountain.*

24. Ximena Medinacelli G., *Sariri: Los llameros y la construcción de la sociedad colonial* (La Paz: IFEA / Plural, 2010); ABNB EP 1, f.38, ff.76–76v; 103v-104.

25. Reference to Benino's works appears in early notary records, e.g., ABNB EP 3, ff.238v-39v, 452v-53 (both 1559). He was still making contracts to extract ore from his adits in 1576, e.g., ABNB EP 25, ff.210v-11v.

26. See for example "Relación muy particular del Cerro y minas de Potosí y de su calidad y labores, por Nicolás del Benino, dirigida a don Francisco de Toledo, virrey del Peru, en 1573," in José Urbano Martínez Carreras, ed., *Relaciones geográficas de Indias—Peru,* Biblioteca de Autores Españoles, vol. 183 (Madrid: Atlas, 1965), 363: "The mountain has a height of half a league and is quite steep and rough to climb, and in climbing it one is short of breath, not only humans but also the beasts and cavalcades, and thus they have been seen to be much winded" (my translation).

27. "Relación muy particular," 362–71. For earlier mention of a *socavón* on the Cerro Rico see, for example, ABNB EP 5, ff.467–48 (1563). Other tunnels are mentioned in contracts for neighboring Porco.

28. The debate over high grading was fierce and lasting. See, for example, Josep M. Barnadas, "Una polémica colonial: Potosí, 1579–1684," *Jarbuch für Geschichte von Staat, Wirtschaft un Gessellschaft Lateinamerikas* 10 (1973): 16–70.

29. Jane E. Mangan, *Trading Roles: Gender, Ethnicity, and the Urban Economy in Colonial Potosí* (Durham, NC: Duke University Press, 2005); and Paulina Numhauser, *Mujeres indias y señores de la coca: Potosí y Cusco en el siglo XVI* (Madrid: Cátedra, 2005).

30. ABNB Rück 3, ff.98–105.

31. ABNB Manuscritos No Librarios (MNL) 52 / 7. "Que en vista de los inconvenientes y vejaciones que se siguen de pasar españoles, mestizos y mulatos a las rancherías de indios, se guarde la ordenanza hecha y los alguaciles tengan cuidado de ella ... que ningun negro ni negra viva ni ande en las rancherías de indios, ni trate con estos, por el daño que les hacen ... que no vendan pan en las rancherías de indios ... que habiendo entre los indios e indias de las rancherías niños y niñas mestizos huérfanos que adquieren las costumbres de los indios, cualquier español pueda tomarlos a su servicio con conocimiento de la justicia, o se provea lo necesario en beneficio de ellos."

32. Bakewell also doubts Toledo's responsibility for the grid in *Miners of the Red Mountain,* 12.

33. ABNB EP 1, ff.92v-93.

34. ABNB EP 3, f.79v-80.

35. Pedro de Cieza de León, *Crónica del Peru, Primera Parte,* ed. Franklin Pease G. Y. (Lima: PUCE Fondo Editorial, 1984), 288–93; my translation.

36. Enrique Otte, ed., *Cartas privadas de emigrantes a Indias, 1540–1616* (Mexico City: FCE, 1993), 518; my translation.

37. Garcilaso de la Vega, El Inca, *Royal Commentaries of the Incas and General History of Peru,* trans. H. V. Livermore (Austin: University of Texas Press, 1966),

525–26 (8:21). Garcilaso relates a similar story from Seville regarding parrots exposing quack doctors.

38. Archivo Histórico de Potosí (AHP) Escrituras Notariales (EN) 19, f.1536.

39. Diego de Ocaña, *Viaje por el Nuevo Mundo: De Guadalupe a Potosí, 1599–1605,* ed. Blanca López de Mariscal and Abraham Madroñal (Madrid: Iberoamericana / Vervuert, 2010), 270–71; my translation. For more on Pedro de Mondragón, see Paulina Numhauser, "Un asunto banal: Las luchas de Vicuñas y Vascongados en Potosí (siglo XVII)," *Illes i Imperis* 14 (2011): 113–38. Kenneth Mills, in "Ocaña's Mondragón in the Eighth Wonder of the World" (forthcoming, 2019), explains Ocaña's fascination with indigenous and mestizo strivers, a persistent cause for wonder among visitors from Spain.

40. Cieza de León, *Crónica del Perú,* 288–93; my translation.

41. Mangan, *Trading Roles,* 48–75.

CHAPTER TWO

1. Luis Capoche, *Relación general de la Villa Imperial de Potosí,* Biblioteca de Autores Españoles 122, ed. Lewis Hanke (Madrid: Atlas, [1585] 1959), 109–10; my translation.

2. Pedro de Cieza de León, *Crónica del Peru, Primera Parte,* ed. Franklin Pease G. Y. (Lima: PUCE Fondo Editorial, 1984), 288–93; my translation.

3. Mary Van Buren and B. Mills, "Huayrachinas and Tocochimbos: Traditional Smelting Technology of the Southern Andes," *Latin American Antiquity* 16:1 (2005): 2–25. See also T. Cohen, T. Rehren, and M. Van Buren, "La huayrachina por dentro y por fuera: Un estudio arqueo-metalúrgico de la tecnología de fundición de plomo en Porco-Potosí, Bolivia," in *Mina y metalurgía en los Andes del Sur desde la época prehispánica hasta el siglo XVII,* ed. Pablo Cruz and Jean-Joinville Vacher (Sucre: IFEA, 2008), 29–56.

4. Capoche, *Relación,* 110; my translation.

5. For the prevalence of smelting in colonial Mexico and its likely environmental costs, see Saúl Guerrero, *Silver by Fire, Silver by Mercury: A Chemical History of Silver Refining in New Spain and Mexico, 16th to 19th Centuries* (Leiden: Brill, 2017), chap. 3.

6. Capoche, *Relación,* 111; my translation.

7. Archivo y Biblioteca Nacional de Bolivia (ABNB) Escrituras Públicas (EP) 3, ff.88–88v.

8. ABNB EP 3, ff. 390v-91v, 473v-74. See also ff.692v-694, in which a Potosí blacksmith sells a mine belonging to his mestiza daughter, apparently inherited from her mother, Inés "yndia de Yucay." Similar cases are on ff.860–61, 927v-28v, 1116–16v, 1147v-48v. Also in 1559, one Pedro de Cabrera "de color moreno" sold ten yards of a mine on the Cerro Rico for 60 pesos (ibid., ff.140v-41). The same Cabrera "libre" later purchased forty llamas at 10 pesos each (ibid., ff.523–24).

9. ABNB EP 3, ff.717–18v.

10. ABNB EP 1, ff.142–43; 21v-22.

11. ABNB EP 3, ff.849–49v.

12. ABNB EP 1, ff.343–44; ff.11v-18v; EP 3, ff352v-54v. Tools were "picos, aza-dones, barras y almádanas." A contract from 1561 refers to workers in general as peons, but also lists obligations to feed, clothe, and indoctrinate yanaconas in the mines of Aullagas, in what is today Norte de Potosí. Some tools were provided as well. ABNB EP 4, ff.1154v-55.

13. Capoche, *Relación*, 108; my translation.

14. Peter J. Bakewell, *Miners of the Red Mountain: Indian Labor in Potosí, 1545–1650* (Albuquerque: University of New Mexico Press, 1984), 50–60.

15. Capoche, *Relación*, 109; my translation.

16. Ibid.

17. ABNB EP 10, ff.301–12v; MNL 52 / 17.

18. Capoche, *Relación*, 109; my translation.

19. ABNB Manuscritos No Librarios (MNL) 52 / 17. The La Plata audiencia ordered the use of horses and llamas outfitted with leather bags. Acosta describes mine work in Potosí in his 1589 *Natural and Moral History of the Indies,* ed. Jane E. Mangan (Durham, NC: Duke University Press, 2002), 179–81.

20. Capoche, *Relación*, 109; my translation.

21. ABNB Minas 1 / 1.

22. ABNB MNL 52 / 17. The terms given are "romadizo y dolor de costado" (rheumatism and side aches).

23. ABNB EP 24, ff.247–48. Heidi Scott examines clerical mine investments in detail in "Mining Places and Subterranean Spaces in Colonial Spanish America: Nature, Government, and Moral Debate in the Exploitation of the Underground" (unpublished manuscript, 2018).

24. Archivo Histórico de Potosí (AHP) Escrituras Notariales (EN) 9, f.546: lists of goods imported to Potosí in 1578 by members of the wealthy Corso merchant family, including iron.

25. ABNB EP 3, ff.516–16v, 509–509v.

26. Kris Lane, *Quito 1599: City and Colony in Transition* (Albuquerque: University of New Mexico Press, 2002), 178–88. See also Rachel Corr, *Interwoven: Andean Lives in Colonial Ecuador's Textile Economy* (Tucson: University of Arizona Press, 2018).

27. Carlos Sempat Assadourian, *El sistema de la economía colonial: El mercado interior—regiones y espacio económico* (Mexico City: Nueva Imágen, 1983). Sempat Assadourian reproduces rare merchant correspondence from the 1590s (pp. 91–126) demonstrating the complex webs of trade linking Santiago de Chile to Mendoza and Córdoba, Argentina, with side trips to Paraguay and Buenos Aires but all oriented toward running livestock and dry goods through Tucumán to Potosí.

28. Capoche, *Relación*, 179, my translation.

29. AHP EN 12, f.473. A debt obligation from 3 April 1587 includes a long list of Chinese fabrics, along with "painted boxes" and fans. EN 13, f.791. Another obligation includes a variety of European, Mexican, and Chinese fabrics, including "Chinese linen" (*lienzo de la China*).

30. AHP EN 13, ff.1653–60. "vestido de cumbi antiguo del tiempo del Ynga," "unas mangas de tela plata blanca que es del dicho vestido," "una manta de Trujillo que parece de la China."

31. AHP EN 13, f.3254. "tasas de vidrio de Venecia."

32. AHP EN 12, f.849.

33. AHP EN 12, f.774, 1587.

34. Capoche, *Relación,* 141; my translation.

35. ABNB EP 1, ff.57–57v. EP 3, ff.263–64.

36. ABNB MNL 52 / 17; EP 9, ff.598–98v (1567).

37. Jane E. Mangan, *Trading Roles: Gender, Ethnicity, and the Urban Economy in Colonial Potosí* (Durham, NC: Duke University Press, 2005), 76.

38. ABNB EP 11, ff.337v-38 (1560); EP 6, ff.408–408v (1564).

39. ABNB MNL 52 / 17.

40. ABNB EP 3, ff.944–44v. ABNB MNL 52 / 17.

41. AHP EN 9, f.viii, notes 62 *botijas* of *vino de la tierra* to sell in 1577 for 8 pesos 2 *tomines plata ensayada* each. Arequipa wine was priced at 8 pesos per jug (f.78v). On Moquegua, see Prudence M. Rice, *Vintage Moquegua: History, Wine, and Archaeology on a Colonial Peruvian Periphery* (Austin: University of Texas Press, 2012).

42. AHP EN 14, f.3283.

43. Bartolomé Alvarez, 1588, quoted in Regina Harrison, *Sin and Confession in Early Colonial Peru* (Austin: University of Texas Press, 2016), 205.

44. Juan de Matienzo, *Gobierno del Perú,* ed. Guillermo Lohmann-Villena (Paris / Lima: IFEA, 1967), 161–89. For early coca controversy in Cuzco, see that city's first town council books in the Archivo Regional del Cusco. Thanks to Jeremy Mikecz for this lead.

45. Matienzo, *Gobierno del Perú,* 133.

46. AHP EN 12, f.780, 1587.

47. ABNB EP 1, ff.11, 13; 227v-28v.

48. Paulina Numhauser, *Mujeres indias y señores de la coca: Potosí y Cusco en el siglo XVI* (Madrid: Cátedra, 2005). See also Mangan, *Trading Roles.* An early wholesale contract is in CNM AH EN 9, f.519, involving 4,500 pesos worth of coca imported by one of Potosí's town councilmen.

49. AHP EN 13, f.2236, codicil. Numhauser reads the surname as "Carna": *Mujeres indias,* 272–73.

50. Mangan, *Trading Roles,* 113.

51. A sale contract from 1588 notes Nicaraguan tobacco selling wholesale for 6 reales per manoja. AHP EN 13, f.511.

52. Sarsparilla appears in a 1589 wholesale merchandise list selling for 3 *tomines* per pound, or 14 pesos for half an *arroba,* AHP EN 9, f.645v. See also Linda A. Newson, *Making Medicines in Early Colonial Lima, Peru: Apothecaries, Science and Society* (Leiden: Brill, 2017).

53. Cited in Andrés I. Prieto, *Missionary Scientists: Jesuit Science in Spanish South America, 1570–1810* (Nashville: Vanderbilt University Press, 2011), 107. The

original description is in Bernabé Cobo, *Historia del Nuevo Mundo,* Pt. I, BAE 91 (Madrid: Atlas, 1956), 1: 128–31.

54. AHP EN 12, f.914.

55. ABNB EP 1, f.226–26v.

56. James Lockhart, *Spanish Peru, 1532–1560: A Colonial Society* (Madison: University of Wisconsin Press, 1968), 178.

57. AHP EN 9, f.182.

58. Capoche purchased 24-year-old Francisca for 800 pesos on 2 November 1589, AHP EN 14, f.3488.

59. Lolita Brockington, *Blacks, Indians, and Spaniards in the Eastern Andes: Reclaiming the Forgotten in Colonial Mizque, 1550–1782* (Lincoln: University of Nebraska Press, 2006).

60. AHP EN 12, f.768, "jugador ínfamo"; EN 13, f.1515.

61. ABNB EP 23, f.13.

62. AHP EN 9, scribe Luis de la Torre, ff.17v-18, 35v, 58, 78v, 157, 210; EN 12, f.29v. At 450 maravedis versus 272, the *peso ensayado* was worth about 40 percent more than a piece of eight, or *patacón.*

CHAPTER THREE

1. Felipe Guaman Poma de Ayala (ca. 1615), *Primer Nueva Corónica y buen gobierno,* f.1065, Danish Royal Library, www.kb.dk/permalink/2006/poma/1065/en /text.

2. The literature on Toledo is vast. The best recent study is by Jeremy Ravi Mumford, *Vertical Empire: The General Resettlement of Indians in the Colonial Andes* (Durham, NC: Duke University Press, 2012). On the bureaucratic "reconquest" see Peter J. Bakewell, "Conquest after the Conquest: The Rise of Spanish Domination in America," in *Spain, Europe, and the Atlantic World: Essays in Honour of John H. Elliott,* ed. Richard Kagan and Geoffrey Parker (Cambridge: Cambridge University Press, 1995), 296–315.

3. Archivo Histórico de Potosí (AHP) Escrituras Notariales (EN) 12, ff.350–54, 1587, EN 13, f.1554v, 1588. For specifics, see Jeffrey A. Cole, *The Potosí Mita, 1573–1700: Compulsory Indian Labor in the Andes* (Stanford, CA: Stanford University Press, 1985), 1–22; Peter J. Bakewell, *Miners of the Red Mountain: Indian Labor in Potosí, 1545–1650* (Albuquerque: University of New Mexico Press, 1984); and Rossana Barragán, "Working Silver for the World: Mining Labor and Popular Economy in Colonial Potosí," *Hispanic American Historical Review* 97:2 (May 2017): 193–222. For variations in work practice amid mita demands, see Paula C. Zagalsky, "Trabajadores indígenas mineros en el Cerro Rico de Potosí: tras los rastros de sus prácticas laborales (siglos XVI y XVII)," *Revista Mundos do Trabalho* 6:12 (July–December 2014): 55–82.

4. Nicholas A. Robins, *Santa Bárbara's Legacy: An Environmental History of Huancavelica, Peru* (Leiden: Brill, 2017); Kendall Brown, *A History of Mining in*

*Latin America from the Colonial Era to the Present* (Albuquerque: University of New Mexico Press, 2012), 19–20. See also the classic study by Guillermo Lohmann Villena, *Las minas de Huancavelica en los siglos XVI y XVII* (Seville: EEHA, 1949).

5. Kris Lane, *Quito 1599: City and Colony in Transition* (Albuquerque: University of New Mexico Press, 2002), 128–29.

6. On the polemic, see especially Cole, *Potosí Mita.* For the eighteenth century, see Enrique Tandeter, *Coercion and Market: Silver Mining in Colonial Potosí, 1692–1826,* trans. Richard Warren (Albuquerque: University of New Mexico Press, 1993 [1st Span. ed. 1992]).

7. Bakewell, *Miners of the Red Mountain,* chap. 4.

8. Ann Zulawski, *They Eat from Their Labor: Work and Social Change in Colonial Bolivia* (Pittsburgh: Pittsburgh University Press, 1995), 69; prices drawn from Antonio de Ayáns, "Breve relación de los agravios que reciben los indios que ay desde cerca del Cuzco hasta Potosí," in *Pareceres en asuntos de indios,* ed. Rubén Vargas Ugarte (Lima, 1951), 38.

9. Luis Capoche, *Relación general de la Villa Imperial de Potosí,* Biblioteca de Autores Españoles 122, ed. Lewis Hanke (Madrid: Atlas, 1959), 158; my translation.

10. See for example Archivo y Biblioteca Nacional de Bolivia (ABNB) Libros de Acuerdos Audiencia de Charcas (LAACh) 5, f.155 (1575 suit over deaths of two native Andean mineworkers). For key reflections on workers' limited legal avenues, see Paula C. Zagalsky, "Trabajo indígena, conflictos y justicia en la Villa Imperial de Potosí y su Cerro Rico, una aproximación: Virreinato del Perú, siglos XVI y XVII," *Revista Historia y Justicia* 9 (2017), online at https://journals.openedition.org/rhj/1122.

11. Capoche, *Relación,* 159; my translation.

12. Ibid.

13. Bakewell, *Miners of the Red Mountain,* 74–75.

14. Vargas Ugarte, *Pareceres,* 112; my translation.

15. Vargas Ugarte, *Pareceres,* 112–13; my translation.

16. Vargas Ugarte, *Pareceres,* 113; my translation.

17. Ibid.

18. Diego de Ocaña, *Viaje por el Nuevo Mundo de Guadalupe a Potosí, 1599–1605,* eds. Blanca López de Mariscal and Abraham Madroñal (Madrid: Iberoamericana / Vervuert, 2010), 257–58; my translation.

19. Vargas Ugarte, *Pareceres,* 116–31; my translations.

20. Thomas Abercrombie, *Pathways of Memory and Power: Ethnography and History among an Andean People* (Madison: University of Wisconsin Press, 1998), 233. See also Tristán Platt, *Estado tributario y librecambio en Potosí (siglo XIX): Mercado indígena, proyecto proteccionista y lucha de ideologías monetarias* (La Paz: Hisbol, 1986).

21. Noble D. Cook, *Demographic Collapse: Indian Peru, 1520–1620* (New York: Cambridge University Press, 1981), 242.

22. Ibid., 243.

23. Ibid., 243, 245.

24. Abercrombie, *Pathways of Memory and Power,* 230–36.

25. Ximena Medinacelli and Marcela Inch, coords., *Pleitos y riqueza. Los caciques andinos en Potosí del siglo XVII. Transcripción y estudios del expediente de don Diego Chambilla contra los bienes de su administrador* (Sucre: Ediciones Archivo y Biblioteca Nacionales de Bolivia, 2010).

26. Capoche, *Relación,* 159; my translation.

27. Peter J. Bakewell, "The First Refining Mills in Potosí: Design and Construction," in *In Quest of Mineral Wealth: Aboriginal and Colonial Mining and Metallurgy in Spanish America,* ed. Alan K. Craig and Robert C. West, Geoscience and Man Series, vol. 33 (Baton Rouge: Louisiana State University Press, 1994), 298–99.

28. AHP EN 13, f.97. Another contract to bring wood to Potosí from June 1572 is not specific, but may have been in response to Toledo's arrival; Archivo y Biblioteca Nacional de Bolivia (ABNB) EP 24, ff.207–207v.

29. ABNB Manuscritos No Librarios (MNL) 52 / 17; EP 24, ff.598v-92; ff.365–66v; 417–20v; 127v-29v; 293v-97v.

30. Robins calculates mercury emissions in *Mercury, Mining, and Empire: The Human and Ecological Cost of Colonial Silver Mining in the Andes* (Bloomington: Indiana University Press, 2011), chap. 4.

31. For example ABNB Libros de Acuerdos Audiencia de Charcas (LAACh) 5, ff.47v–49v (Nov. 1572). These decrees restrict loads carried by Andean porters, including ore and tailings (50 lbs.). The ban on *abogados* is in ABNB MNL 52 / 17.

32. See Vera Candiani, *Dreaming of Dry Land: Environmental Transformation in Colonial Mexico City* (Stanford: Stanford University Press, 2014).

33. ABNB MNL 52 / 17.

34. Calomel is a salt, mercurous chloride, $Hg_2Cl_2$. Until recently it was used in refined form as a cathartic in Western medicine. Robins suggests mercury fallout in Potosí was tremendous, and no doubt it was (*Mercury, Mining, and Empire,* 126–33). But some of Robins's findings are questioned by Saúl Guerrero in *Silver by Fire, Silver by Mercury: A Chemical History of Silver Refining in New Spain and Mexico, 16th to 19th Centuries* (Leiden: Brill, 2017), 132–43, 354.

35. Brown, *History of Mining,* 19–20.

36. Colin Cooke et al., "Use and Legacy of Mercury in the Andes," *Environmental Science and Technology* 47 (2013): 4181–88. For the colonial mines, see Kendall Brown, "Workers' Health and Colonial Mercury Mining at Huancavelica, Peru," *The Americas* 57:4 (April 2001): 467–96. On transport, see Brian S. Bauer et al., "El Camino del Mercurio de Huancavelica a Potosí," trans. Javier Flores Espinoza, in *Nuevas tendencias en el estudio de los caminos,* ed. Sofía Chacaltana, Elizabeth Arkush, and Giancarlo Marcone (Lima: Ministerio de Cultura, 2017), 380–99.

37. The original manuscript accounts, including slave purchases and equipment orders, are in Archivo General de Indias (AGI) Contaduría 1805.

38. Martín de Murúa, *Historia General del Pirú,* Facsimile of J. Paul Getty Ms. Ludwig XIII 16 [1616] (Los Angeles: Getty, 2008), ff.379r-383v.

39. Mauricio Drelichman and Hans-Joachim Voth, *Lending to the Borrower from Hell: Debt, Taxes, and Default in the Age of Philip II* (Princeton, NJ: Princeton University Press, 2014).

40. Arturo Giráldez estimates an annual average of 2 million pesos of Mexican and Peruvian silver combined in *The Age of Trade: The Manila Galleons and the Dawn of the Global Economy* (Boulder, CO: Rowman & Littlefield, 2015), 154. A valuable quantitative source is Engel Sluiter, *The Gold and Silver of Spanish America* (Berkeley, CA: Bancroft Library, 1998), 137–46.

41. AHP EN 12, f.473, 1587. On the trade to Manila, see Charles R. Boxer, "Plata es Sangre: Sidelights on the Drain of Spanish-American Silver to the Far East, 1550–1700," *Philippine Studies* 18:3 (1970): 457–78.

42. One sale appears in 1640 in AHP EN 105, ff.17–20v. The notary books will reveal more such sales. For a sense of the Asian population of Lima about this time, see N. D. Cook and Mauro Escobar Gamboa, eds., *Padrón de los indios de Lima en 1613* (Lima: Seminario de Historia Rural Andina, 1968). Thanks to Tatiana Seijas for this lead.

43. Barreto's story remains to be fully told. Her will and inventory are in the U. S. Library of Congress, Harkness Collection, documents 950–53.

44. ABNB Cabildo de Potosí Libros de Acuerdo (CPLA) 20, ff.39–44.

CHAPTER FOUR

1. Felipe Guaman Poma de Ayala, *The First New Chronicle and Good Government,* trans. David Frye (Indianapolis: Hackett, 2006), 245.

2. Archivo General de Indias (AGI) Charcas 43. It is possible that the witnesses were lying, but the details suggest a genuine affliction. For early theories and therapies, including cautery, see Jon Arrizabalaga, John Henderson, and Roger French, *The Great Pox: The French Disease in Renaissance Europe* (New Haven, CT: Yale University Press, 1997). See also Linda A. Newson, *Making Medicines in Early Colonial Lima, Peru: Apothecaries, Science and Society* (Leiden: Brill, 2017).

3. "Description of the Villa and Mines de Potosí in the year 1603." Anonymous— in José Urbano Martínez Carreras, ed., *Relaciones geográficas de Indias—Peru,* Biblioteca de Autores Españoles, vol. 183 (Madrid: Atlas, 1965), 379; my translation.

4. "Description of the Villa," 373.

5. Hispanic Society of America, "Atlas of Sea Charts K3," a partially copied ms. with accompanying images on calfskin.

6. Martin de Murúa, *Historia General del Pirú,* 1616 (Getty Manuscript), ff.379r–383v.

7. Pedro Querejazu and Elizabeth Ferrer, *Potosí: Colonial Treasures and the Bolivian City of Silver* (New York: Americas Society, 1997), 54–55; and Emma Sordo, "Our Lady of Copacabana and Her Legacy in Colonial Potosí," in *Early Modern Confraternities in Europe and the Americas: International and Interdisciplinary*

*Perspectives,* ed. Christopher Black and Pamela Gravestock (Aldershot: Ashgate, 2006), 187–203. The miracle of the mill stamps is related by Alonso Ramos Gavilán, *Historia del Santuario de Nuestra Señora de Copacabana,* ed. Ignacio Prado Pastor (Lima: P. L. Villanueva, 1988), 373–74. The original was published in Lima by Jerónimo Contreras in 1621. The woodcut appears on p. 334 of the original.

    8. Kris Lane, *Quito 1599: City and Colony in Transition* (Albuquerque: University of New Mexico Press, 2002), 178–86.

    9. On these routes, see Clara López Beltrán, *La Ruta de la Plata de Potosí al Pacífico: Caminos, comercio y caravanas en los siglos XVI al XIX* (La Paz: Plural Editores, 2016).

    10. Archivo Histórico de Potosí (AHP) Escrituras Notariales (EN) 12, f.846.

    11. Kenneth Verosub and Jake Lippman, "Global Impacts of the 1600 Eruption of Peru's Huaynaputina Volcano," *Eos* 89:15 (April 2008): 141–48.

    12. See, for example, Jane E. Mangan, *Trading Roles: Gender, Ethnicity, and the Urban Economy in Colonial Potosí* (Durham, NC: Duke University Press, 2005); Paulina Numhauser, *Mujeres indias y señores de la coca: Potosí y Cusco en el siglo XVI* (Madrid: Cátedra, 2005); Allison Bigelow, "Women, Men, and the Legal Languages of Mining in the Colonial Andes," *Ethnohistory* 63:2 (2016): 351–80; and Emma Sordo, "Civilizational Designs: The Architecture of Colonialism in the Native Parishes of Potosí" (PhD diss., University of Miami, 2000).

    13. Diego de Ocaña, *Viaje por el Nuevo Mundo de Guadalupe a Potosí, 1599–1605,* ed. Blanca López de Mariscal and Abraham Madroñal (Madrid: Iberoamericana / Vervuert, 2010), 264–65, 268.

    14. Mangan, *Trading Roles.*

    15. Bigelow, "Women, Men, and the Legal Languages of Mining."

    16. Catalina de Erauso, *Lieutenant Nun: Memoir of a Basque Transvestite in the New World,* trans. Michele and Gabriel Stepto (Boston: Beacon Press, 1996), 30–32. On Ortiz de Sotomayor, see Alberto Crespo, *La guerra entre vicuñas y vascongados: Potosí 1622–1625,* 2nd ed. (La Paz: Talleres Gráficos don Bosco, 1969), 37–42.

    17. Bartolomé Arzáns de Orsúa y Vela, *Historia de la Villa Imperial de Potosí,* 3 vols., ed. Lewis Hanke and Gunnar Mendoza (Providence, RI: Brown University Press, 1965), 1: 306–9. See also Crespo, *La guerra,* 40, and Alberto Crespo, *Historia de la Ciudad de La Paz (siglo XVII)* (Lima: Industrial Gráfica, 1961), 37–42.

    18. Bartolomé Arzáns de Orsúa y Vela, *Tales of Potosí,* ed. R. C. Padden, trans. Frances López-Morillas (Providence, RI: Brown University Press, 1975), 64–65; and for the Spanish original, Arzáns, *Historia de la Villa Imperial,* 2: 149–54. See also Gina Hermann, "Amazonic Ambivalence in Imperial Potosí," *Modern Language Notes* 114:2 (March 1999): 315–40; and Leonardo García Pabón, "Espacio andino, escritura colonial y patria criolla: La historia de Potosí en la narrativa de Bartolomé Arzáns" (PhD diss., University of Minnesota, 1990).

    19. Arzáns, *Tales of Potosí,* 70.

    20. Kara D. Schultz, " 'The Kingdom of Angola Is Not Very Far from Here': The South Atlantic Slave Port of Buenos Aires, 1585–1640," *Slavery & Abolition* 36:3 (Sept. 2015): 424–44. See also David Freeman, *A Silver River in a Silver World:*

*Dutch Trade in the Río de la Plata* (New York: Cambridge University Press, 2019). For the transformation of Córdoba, see Carlos Sempat Assadourian, *El sistema de la economía colonial,* chap. 1, and *El tráfico de esclavos en Córdoba de Angola a Potosí, siglos XVI–XVII* (Córdoba, Argentina: Universidad Nacional de Córdoba / Instituto de Estudios Americanistas, 1966).

21. C. R. Boxer, *Salvador de Sá and the Struggle for Brazil and Angola, 1602–1686* (London: Athlone, 1952).

22. Z. Moutoukias, *Contrabando y control en el siglo XVII: Buenos Aires, el Atlántico y el Espacio Peruano* (Buenos Aires: Bibliotecas Universitarias, 1988).

23. Kris Lane, "South by Southwest: Commercial Cosmopolitanism in Charles Boxer's *Salvador de Sá and the Struggle for Brazil and Angola,*" in *Commercial Cosmopolitanism? Policing Contact Zones and Governing "Multinationals" in the Early Modern World,* ed. Felicia Gottmann (forthcoming).

24. AHP EN 105, f.173.

25. Kris Lane, "The Ghost of Seventeenth-Century Potosí," *The Americas* 76:2 (April 2019). R. C. Padden excerpts the story under the problematic title "The Spook" in Arzáns, *Tales of Potosí,* 56–57.

26. Lane, "South by Southwest." It is worth noting that Alberto Crespo pointed out the importance of enslaved Africans in these years in *Esclavos negros en Bolivia* (La Paz: Academia Nacional de Ciencias de Bolivia, 1977).

27. See Kenneth Mills, "Diego de Ocaña's Hagiography of New and Renewed Devotion in Colonial Peru," in *Colonial Saints: Discovering the Holy in the Americas, 1500–1800,* ed. Allan Greer and Jodi Bilinkoff (New York: Routledge, 2003), 51–75. My translations are from the following Spanish edition: Fray Diego de Ocaña, *Viaje por el Nuevo Mundo: De Guadalupe a Potosí, 1599–1605,* ed. Blanca López de Mariscal y Abraham Madroñal (Madrid / Frankfurt: Iberoamericana / Vervuert, 2010).

28. Ocaña, *Viaje por el Nuevo Mundo,* 287–94; my translations.

29. Pedro Ramírez del Águila, *Noticias políticas de Indias y relación descriptiva de la ciudad de La Plata, metrópoli de las Provincias de Los Charcas* (Sucre: Ciencia Editores, 2017), 141, my translation. For more details, see the excellent essays in Andrés Eichmann and Marcela Inch C., eds. *La construcción de lo urbano en Potosí y la Plata (siglos XVI–XVII)* (Sucre: Ministerio de Cultura de España / Archivo y Biblioteca Nacionales de Bolivia, 2008).

30. See Marcela Inch, in Eichmann and Inch C., *La construcción.*

31. Irving A. Leonard, *Books of the Brave,* 2nd ed. (Berkeley: University of California Press, 1992), 243–47.

32. See, for example, Christopher Brooke, *Philosophic Pride: Stoicism and Political Thought from Lipsius to Rousseau* (Princeton, NJ: Princeton University Press, 2012); and Robert Birely, *The Counter-Reformation Prince: Anti-Machiavellianism or Catholic Statecraft in Early Modern Europe* (Chapel Hill: University of North Carolina Press, 1990).

33. For a modern translation, see Oliva Sabuco de Nantes Barrera, *New Philosophy of Human Nature,* ed. and trans. Mary Ellen Waithe, María Colomer Vintró, and C. Ángel Zorita (Urbana: University of Illinois Press, 2007).

34. Galindo Esquivel shows up in miscellaneous Inquisition papers in Archivo Histórico Nacional de Chile (AHNC) Inquisición, v.359, f.86. The forced comedy acting is at the start of the same batch of documents, from 1627. Guevara Hita appears in AHP EN 116, f.356.

35. Archivo y Biblioteca Nacional de Bolivia (ABNB) Correspondencia 1025.

36. AHP EN 18, ff.1015–1019v, 26-III-1590. It appears the company dissolved before this, perhaps in dispute. I translate *truques* as tricks.

37. AHNC Inquisición v.359 contains a wide range of these for the years 1627–54.

38. AHP EN 107.

39. Brian Farrelly, *Vicente Bernedo: Apóstol de Charcas* (Salamanca: Editorial San Esteban, 1986), 130–31. For an early hagiography and other documents, see Fray Juan Meléndez, *Vida del venerable padre fray Vicente Bernedo del Orden de Predicadores,* ed. Armando Alba (Potosí: Colección de la Cultura Boliviana, 1965).

40. Biblioteca Nacional Madrid Ms.11045, f.1; my translation.

41. Ana Schaposchnik, *The Lima Inquisition: The Plight of Crypto-Jews in Seventeenth-Century Peru* (Madison: University of Wisconsin Press, 2015).

42. See Paulina Numhauser, "Un asunto banal: Las luchas de vicuñas y vascongados en Potosí (siglo XVII)," *Illes I Imperis* 14 (2012): 113–38; Bernd Hausberger, "La guerra de los vicuñas contra los vascongados en Potosí y la etnicización de los vascos a principios de la edad moderna," in *Excluir para ser: Procesos identitarios y fronteras sociales en la América hispánica (xvii–xviii),* ed. Christian Büschges and Frederique Langue, 23–57 (Frankfurt: AHILA/Vervuert, 2005). My short narrative of the "war" draws from several manuscript accounts and owes great debts to Alberto Crespo Rodas, *La guerra entre vicuñas y vascongados: Potosí, 1622–1625* (La Paz: Colección Popular, 1969); and David Dressing, "Social Tensions in Early Seventeenth-Century Potosí" (PhD diss., Tulane University, 2007). Dressing makes the strongest case for long-brewing social tensions rooted in the city's delicate mining economy.

CHAPTER FIVE

1. Astete's letter to the *corregidor* is quoted by Antonio Vázquez de Espinosa, who visited Potosí soon after the disaster. See his *Compendium and Description of the West Indies,* trans. Charles Upson Clark (Washington, DC: Smithsonian Insititution, 1942), 634–35. See also the description by Friar Diego de Mendoza, *Chronica de la Provincia de San Antonio de los Charcas,* 1664, pp. 127–31.

2. Geoffrey Parker, *Global Crisis: War, Climate Change, and Catastrophe in the Seventeenth Century* (New Haven, CT: Yale University Press, 2013). The Little Ice Age stretched from the fifteenth to early nineteenth centuries, with a maximum chill ca. 1650. There has been much debate over the extent of crisis in Greater Peru and Spanish America broadly, provoked in part by Ruggiero Romano's *Coyunturas opuestas: La crisis del siglo XVII en Europa y Hispanoamérica* (Mexico City: FCE, 1993). While by some measures Greater Peru was vibrant compared to Spain, Potosí's

*mining crisis* seems to have been genuine, and this and other factors, such as drought and epidemic disease, tied the city's fate more closely to the metropolis than some have claimed, particularly in the reign of Philip IV.

3. Noble D. Cook, *Demographic Collapse: Indian Peru, 1520–1620* (New York: Cambridge University Press, 1981), 62; Ann Zulawski, *They Eat from Their Labor: Work and Social Change in Colonial Bolivia* (Pittsburgh: Pittsburgh University Press, 1995), 63–65.

4. Zulawski, *They Eat from Their Labor,* 174; for malaria in Mizque, see Daniel Gade, *Nature and Culture in the Andes* (Madison: University of Wisconsin Press, 1999), 75–101.

5. Jeffrey A. Cole, *The Potosí Mita, 1573–1700: Compulsory Indian Labor in the Andes* (Stanford: Stanford University Press, 1985), 105–22.

6. Zulawski, *They Eat from Their Labor.*

7. Luis Miguel Glave, "La petición grande de don Gabriel Fernández Guarache y el debate sobre la mita minera en el contexto de crisis colonial," in *Mita, caciques y mitayos: Gabriel Fernández Guarache—Memoriales en defensa de los indios y debate sobre la mita de Potosí (1646–1663),* ed. Roberto Choque Canqui and Luis Miguel Glave, 177–211 (Sucre: ABNB / FCBCB, 2012).

8. Anon. 1603, "Description of the Villa," 379; my translation.

9. Nicholas Robins, *Mercury, Mining, and Empire: The Human and Ecological Cost of Colonial Silver Mining in the Andes* (Bloomington: Indiana University Press, 2011).

10. Archivo Histórico de Potosí (AHP) Escrituras Notariales (EN) 13, f.367.

11. See Gade, *Nature and Culture in the Andes,* 66–69.

12. AHP EN 111, f.278v.

13. Vázquez de Espinosa, *Compendium and Description,* 637.

14. Arzáns, *Historia de la Villa Imperial,* 2:1–15; Archivo y Biblioteca Nacional de Bolivia (ABNB) Cabildo de Potosí Libros de Acuerdos (CPLA)15, ff.2–16.

15. Vázquez de Espinosa, *Compendium and Description,* 637.

16. ABNB CPLA 15, ff.2–16.

17. Vázquez de Espinosa, *Compendium and Description,* 636.

18. ABNB CPLA 15, ff. 59v–61.

19. ABNB CPLA 15, ff. 276–78v.

20. Vázquez de Espinosa, *Compendium and Description,* 638–39.

21. AHP EN 104, f.718.

22. See Josep Barnadas, *Alvaro Alonso Barba (1569–1662): Investigaciones sobre su vida y obra* (La Paz: Biblioteca Minera Boliviana, 1986). A portion of Barba's 1657 petition is in Archivo General de Indias (AGI) Charcas 416, L.5, ff.152v–54v.

23. See Tristan Platt, "The Alchemy of Modernity: Alonso Barba's Copper Cauldrons and the Independence of Bolivian Metallurgy, 1790–1890," *Journal of Latin American Studies* 32:1 (Feb. 2000): 1–54; and Joaquín Pérez Melero, "From Alchemy to Science: The Scientific Revolution and Enlightenment in Spanish American Mining and Metallurgy," in *The Revolution in Geology from the Renaissance to the Enlightenment,* ed. Gary D. Rosenberg, 51–61 (Boulder, CO: Geological Society of

America, 2009). See also my discussion in the epilogue of this book. On why Barba may have foundered in Spain, see Saúl Guerrero, *Silver by Fire, Silver by Mercury: A Chemical History of Silver Refining in New Spain and Mexico, 16th to 19th Centuries* (Leiden: Brill, 2017), 45–47.

24. J. H. Elliott, *Spain, Europe and the Wider World, 1500–1800* (New Haven, CT: Yale University Press, 2009), 146. In this section I am summarizing ongoing work on the great mint fraud. See Kris Lane, "From Corrupt to Criminal: Reflections on the Great Potosí mint fraud of 1649," in *Corruption in the Iberian Empires: Greed, Custom, and Colonial Networks,* ed. Christoph Rosenmüller, 33–62 (Albuquerque: University of New Mexico Press, 2017).

25. María Antonia Garcés, ed., *An Early Modern Dialogue with Islam: Antonio de Sosa's Topography of Algiers (1612),* trans. Diana de Armas Wilson (Notre Dame, IN: Notre Dame University Press, 2011), 188.

26. Kris Lane, "Slavery and the Casa de la Moneda in Seventeenth-Century Potosí," in *Teritorios de lo cotidiano, siglos XVI–XX: Del antiguo virreinato del Perú a la Argentina contemporánea,* ed. Mónica Ghirardi, 101–14 (Rosario: Prohistoria, 2014). See also Eugenia Bridikhina, "Desafiando los límites del espacio colonial: La población negra en Potosí," *Estudios Bolivianos* 13 (La Paz: Universidad Mayor de San Andrés, 2007): 169–216.

27. Carlo Cipolla, *Conquistadores, piratas, mercaderes: La saga de la plata española,* trans. Ricardo González (Buenos Aires: FCE, 1999), 67–72.

28. A partial confession survives in AGI Escribanía 871D, 2:1, ff.205v-209, but the larger *proceso* has not been located. Special thanks to Masaki Sato for clarifying.

29. The quote is in Richard Von Glahn, *Fountain of Fortune: Money and Monetary Policy in China, 1000–1700* (Berkeley: University of California Press, 1996), 217: "I still remember that in 1649–50, before maritime trade was proscribed, the marketplaces were filled with foreign goods. Buyers and sellers primarily used foreign silver coins as the medium of exchange, and thus these coins circulated widely in every province. But nowadays not a single foreign coin is to be had. This is clear evidence that the fountain of fortune has been sealed up"—provincial governor of Jiangning (China), Mu Tianyan.

## CHAPTER SIX

1. Caesar E. Farah, ed. and trans., *An Arab's Journey to Colonial Spanish America: The Travels of Elias al-Mûsili in the Seventeenth Century* (Syracuse: Syracuse University Press, 2003), 59. For more, see John-Paul A. Ghobrial, "The Secret Life of Elias of Babylon and the Uses of Global Microhistory," *Past & Present* 222:1 (February 2014): 51–93.

2. Ibid., 92. R. J. Barendse, in *The Arabian Seas: The Indian Ocean World of the Seventeenth Century* (Armonk, NY: M. E. Sharpe Press, 2002), notes that taxes were collected in Baghdad in reales in the late 1640s (p. 223).

3. Farah, *Arab's Journey,* 59.

4. Ibid., 62.

5. Archivo y Biblioteca Nacional de Bolivia (ABNB) Cabildo de Potosí Libros de Acuerdo (CPLA) 31, ff.162v–63v.

6. In Irving Leonard, *Colonial Travelers in Latin America* (New York: Alfred A. Knopf, 1972, 125–43), 136, 138. See also Accarette du Biscay, *Viajes al Río de la Plata y a Potosí (1657–1660),* trans. and ed. Jean-Paul Duviols (Doral, FL: Stockero, 2008). The French original with the invasion plan was edited by Duviols and published in *Travaux de l'Institut d'Etudes Latino-Américaines de l'Université de Strasbourg* (TILAS X, 1970): 575–626.

7. Leonard, *Colonial Travelers,* 141.

8. Ibid., 142–43.

9. Lisa Voigt, *Spectacular Wealth: The Festivals of Colonial South American Mining Towns* (Austin: University of Texas Press, 2016), 95–96. The poem was published as *Relación de la grandiosa fiesta que el Señor D. Luis de Andrade y Sotomayor alcalde ordinario de la Imperial Villa de Potosí hizo a la renovación del Santísimo Sacramento a 4 de marzo de 1663* (Seville: E. Rasco, 1899).

10. Voigt's translation, *Spectacular Wealth,* 96.

11. Rubén Vargas Ugarte, ed., *Pareceres jurídicos en asuntos de Indias* (Lima, 1951), 152; my translation.

12. Peter T. Bradley, *Society, Economy and Defence in Seventeenth-Century Peru: The Administration of the Count of Alba de Liste (1655–61)* (Liverpool: University of Liverpool Institute of Latin American Studies, 1992), 58–60. See also Luis Miguel Glave, *Trajinantes: Caminos indígenas en la sociedad colonial, siglos XVI–XVII* (Lima: Instituto de Apoyo Agrario, 1989), 194–98.

13. Jeffrey Cole, "An Abolitionism Born of Frustration: The Conde de Lemos and the Potosí Mita, 1667–73," *Hispanic American Historical Review* 63:2 (May 1983): 307–33. A somewhat expanded version of this story is in Cole's *The Potosí Mita, 1573–1700: Compulsory Indian Labor in the Andes* (Stanford: Stanford University Press, 1985), 91–94.

14. Vargas Ugarte, *Pareceres,* 154.

15. Ignacio González Casasnovas, *Las dudas de la corona: La política de repartimientos para la minería de Potosí (1680–1732)* (Madrid: CSIC, 2000).

16. On Mexico under the late Habsburgs, Alejandro Cañeque has described a Baroque turn to the "rhetoric of wretchedness." See *The King's Living Image: The Culture and Politics of Viceregal Power in Colonial Mexico* (New York: Routledge, 2004), 186–91.

17. Vargas Ugarte, *Pareceres,* 168–83.

18. Ibid., 178.

19. Pedro Ramírez del Águila, *Noticias políticas de Indias y relación descriptiva de la ciudad de La Plata, metrópoli de las Provincias de Los Charcas* (Sucre: Ciencia Editores, 2017), 94.

20. This section relies on the masterful study by Peter J. Bakewell, *Silver and Entrepreneurship in Seventeenth-Century Potosí: The Life and Times of Antonio López de Quiroga* (Albuquerque: University of New Mexico Press, 1987).

21. Nicanor Domínguez Faura, "Rebels of Laicacota: Spaniards, Indians, and Andean Mestizos in Southern Peru during the Mid-Colonial Crisis, 1650–1680" (PhD diss., University of Illinois, Urbana-Champaign, 2007). See also the classic work of Alberto Crespo, *Historia de la Ciudad de La Paz, siglo XVII* (Lima: Industrial Gráfica, 1961), 63–95.

22. Gregorio de Robles, *América a fines del siglo XVII: Noticia de lugares de contrabando,* ed. Victor Tau Anzoátegui (Valladolid, Spain: Casa-Museo de Colón, 1980), 52–53. Raquel Gil Montero, *Ciudades efímeras. El ciclo minero de la plata en Lípez (Bolivia), siglos XVI–XIX.* Lima: IFEA/Plural, 2014.

23. Enrique Tandeter, *Coercion and Market: Silver Mining in Colonial Potosí, 1692–1826,* trans. Richard Warren (Albuquerque: University of New Mexico Press, 1993 [1st Span. ed. 1992]). For a new interpretation of *kajcheo,* see Rossana Barragán, "Working Silver for the World: Mining Labor and Popular Economy in Colonial Potosí," *Hispanic American Historical Review* 97 (2017): 193–222. Colonial records refer to "cacchas."

24. Tandeter, *Coercion and Market.*

25. Adrian Pearce, "The Peruvian Population Census of 1725–1740," *Latin American Research Review* 36:3 (2001): 69–104.

26. Emma Sordo, "Our Lady of Copacabana and Her Legacy in Colonial Potosí," in *Early Modern Confraternities in Europe and the Americas: International and Interdisciplinary Perspectives,* ed. Christopher Black and Pamela Gravestock (Aldershot: Ashgate, 2006), 190.

27. Bartolomé Arzans de Orsúa y Vela, *Historia de la Villa Imperial de Potosí,* 3 vols., ed. Lewis Hanke and Gunnar Mendoza (Providence, RI: Brown University Press, 1965), 3:416.

28. See, for example, Stephanie Merrim, *The Spectacular City, Mexico, and Colonial Hispanic Literary Culture* (Austin: University of Texas Press, 2010).

29. For a recent appraisal, see Suzanne Stratton-Pruitt, *The Art of Painting in Colonial Bolivia* (Philadelphia: St. Joseph's University Press, 2017), 40–50.

30. Voigt, in *Spectacular Wealth,* 42–51, examines the painting in relation to Arzáns and other texts, including fray Juan de la Torre's *Aclamación festiva de la muy noble Imperial Villa de Potosí, en dignísima promoción del Excmo. Señor Maestro Don Fray Diego Morzillo Rubio y Auñón . . .* (Lima: Francisco Sobrino, 1716). See also Miguel Zugasti, "Teatro recuperado en Charcas: Dos loas olvidadas de fray Juan de la Torre (OSA) a la entrada del virrey Diego Morcillo en Potosí, 1716," in *El teatro en la Hispanoamérica colonial,* ed. Ignacio Arellano and José Antonio Rodríguez Garrido (Madrid: Iberoamericana/Vervuert, 2008), 295–321.

CHAPTER SEVEN

1. Alonso Carrió de la Vandera, aka Concolorcorvo, *El Lazarillo de ciegos caminantes,* BAE CXXII (Madrid: Atlas, 1959), 341; my translation. See Ruth Hill, *Hierarchy, Commerce and Fraud in Bourbon Spanish America: A Postal Inspector's Exposé* (Nashville: Vanderbilt University Press, 2005).

2. See, for example, the sale records in Archivo Histórico de Potosí (AHP) Escrituras Notariales (EN) 158 (Escribano Josef Díaz de Orellana, 1731–32). Sales of adolescents appear common (e.g., f.31), and in one sale seven men and six women were exchanged (f.40v). Slavers included Tomás Navarro, "conductor de negros bozales del Real Asiento de Inglaterra" (EN 157, 1735). Under the English, many enslaved Africans appear to have reached Potosí unbaptized.

3. Enrique Tandeter, *Coercion and Market: Silver Mining in Colonial Potosí, 1692–1826*, trans. Richard Warren (Albuquerque: University of New Mexico Press, 1993 [1st Span. ed. 1992]), 123.

4. For this and the context of the Potosí mining reforms, see Adrian J. Pearce, *The Origins of Bourbon Reform in Spanish South America, 1700–1763* (New York: Palgrave Macmillan, 2014), 89–121. For a sense of parish priest concerns in these years see Archivo y Biblioteca Nacional de Bolivia (ABNB) Expedientes Coloniales (EC) 1754:31.

5. Tandeter, *Coercion and Market*, 40, 57–58.

6. The main case in which *kajchas* were accused of damaging mine structures by extracting ore from support pillars is in ABNB Minas 28 / 1 (1751–53). See also ABNB Libros de Acuerdo Charcas (LAACh) 10:ff.351v-52 and Minas 25 / 6. Tandeter summarizes the story in *Coercion and Market*, 98–107.

7. See the long case in ABNB Minas 25 / 13 (1752). Also Minas 150 / 11.

8. Archivo General de Indias (AGI) Lima 1134. The Basque official was don Miguel Antonio de Escurrechea, Director General de Minas y Mita y Coronel de Dragones. His informative drawing of the lake system is in AGI Mapas y Planos Buenos Aires 301.

9. Tandeter, *Coercion and Market*, 108–9, 125. Rossana Barragán, in "Working Silver for the World: Mining Labor and Popular Economy in Colonial Potosí," *Hispanic American Historical Review* 97:2 (2017): 208–10, cites an inspection from 1761–62 that counted 220 *trapiches*, only 64 of them licensed. Most trapiches (73 percent) were indigenous owned.

10. Tandeter, *Coercion and Market*, 153–59.

11. For some horrific cases, see Nicholas A. Robins, *Mercury, Mining, and Empire: The Human and Ecological Cost of Colonial Silver Mining in the Andes* (Bloomington: Indiana University Press, 2011), 149–75.

12. In Roberto Querejazu C., *Chuquisaca, 1539–1825* (Sucre: Editorial Universitaria, 1987), 416. Querejazu cites his source as AGI Sublevación de Chayanta (Charcas 594).

13. Ibid.

14. A fine overview is Sergio Serulnikov, *Revolution in the Andes: The Age of Túpac Amaru* (Durham, NC: Duke University Press, 2013). See also Nicholas Robins, *Priest-Indian Conflict in Upper Peru: The Generation of Rebellion, 1750–1780* (Syracuse: Syracuse University Press, 2007).

15. María Concepción Gavira Márquez, *Minería en Chayanta: La sublevación indígena y el auge minero, 1775–1792* (La Paz: Plural, 2013); and Sergio Serulnikov, *Subverting Colonial Authority: Challenges to Spanish Rule in the Eighteenth-Century Southern Andes* (Durham, NC: Duke University Press, 2003).

16. Kendall Brown, *A History of Mining in Latin America,* 80–82, offers a concise summary. See also documents in ABNB Minas 72 / 12.

17. Charles Walker, *The Túpac Amaru Rebellion* (Cambridge, MA: Harvard University Press, 2016). See also Ward Stavig and Ella Schmidt, *The Túpac Amaru and Catarista Rebellions: An Anthology of Sources* (Indianapolis: Hackett, 2008); and Ward Stavig, *The World of Túpac Amaru: Conflict, Community, and Identity in Colonial Peru* (Lincoln: University of Nebraska Press, 1999).

18. See María Concepción Gavira Márquez, *Historia de una crisis: La minería en Oruro a fines del periodo colonial* (Lima: IFEA, 2016); and Oscar Cornblit, *Power and Violence in the Colonial City: Oruro from the Mining Renaissance to the Rebellion of Tupac Amaru (1740–1782),* trans. E. L. Glick (New York: Cambridge University Press, 1995).

19. The definitive account is Sinclair Thomson, *We Alone Will Rule: Native Andean Politics in the Age of Insurgency* (Madison: University of Wisconsin Press, 2002).

20. Even with substantial bonanzas and revivals elsewhere in the Andes, including Hualgayoc and the Cerro de Pasco, Potosí registered production of over 40 percent of all Spanish South American silver between 1750 and 1800. See John J. TePaske, *A New World of Gold and Silver,* ed. Kendall W. Brown (Leiden and Boston: Brill, 2010), 191.

21. This section relies on Tandeter, *Coercion and Market,* and Rose Marie Buechler, *The Mining Society of Potosí, 1776–1810* (Syracuse: Syracuse University Press, 1981).

22. Tandeter, *Coercion and Market,* 175.

23. This and the next section rely on John Fisher, *Silver Mines and Silver Miners in Colonial Peru, 1776–1824* (Liverpool: Center for Latin American Studies, 1977), 54–73.

24. *Mercurio Peruano* VII:216–17 (1791), 66–81 (available online).

25. A. Z. Helms, *Travels from Buenos Aires by Potosí to Lima* (London: R. Phillips, 1807).

26. This section relies heavily on Tandeter, *Coercion and Market,* 189–206. See also Concepción Gavira Márquez, "Disciplina laboral y códigos mineros en los virreinatos del Río de la Plata y Nueva España a fines del periodo colonial," *Relaciones* 26 (2005): 201–31.

27. On Villava, see José M. Portillo Valdés, ed., *Vida atlántica de Victorián de Villava* (Madrid: MAPFRE, 2009); and Ricardo Levene, ed., *Vida y escritos de Victorián de Villava* (Buenos Aires: Peuser, 1946).

28. See Fisher, *Silver Mines and Silver Miners,* 74–89.

29. Tandeter, *Coercion and Market,* 210–19.

30. Caciques and mita captains frequently complained of "inhuman" treatment to the Charcas audiencia in these years. See, for example, ABNB Minas 130 / 9.

31. See *Fiestas triunfales que consagró el 2 de agosto de 1812 la fidelísima Imperial Villa de Potosí al invicto General Americano el Sr. Mariscal de Campo don José Manuel de Goyeneche* (Lima: Imprenta de los Huérfanos, 1812). Thanks to Lisa Voigt for pointing out this valuable source. See her *Spectacular Wealth: The Festivals of*

*Colonial South American Mining Towns* (Austin: University of Texas Press, 2016), 152. The lavish reception of the "Invincible" Goyeneche is surprisingly similar to that described by General William Miller, below, on the 1825 arrival of the "Liberator" Simón Bolívar. It seems *potosinos* went whole-hog with such events regardless of the politics of the conquering leader.

32. An azogueros' protest against the 1812 decree is in ABNB Ministerio de Hacienda (MH) 29 / 9: 41–59.

33. I draw here from the excellent study by Esther Aillón Soria, *Vida, pasión y negocios: El propietario de la Viña "San Pedro Mártir" Indalecio González de Socasa (1755–1820)—Potosí y Cinti a fines de la Colonia y en la Guerra de la Independencia* (Sucre: ABNB, 2009).

34. John Miller, *Memoirs of General Miller, in the Service of the Republic of Peru,* 2 vols. (London: Longman, Rees, 1829), 2:306.

CHAPTER EIGHT

1. Eduardo Galeano, *Open Veins of Latin America: Five Centuries of the Pillage of a Continent,* trans. Cedric Belfradge (New York: Monthly Review Press, 1973), 50.

2. John Tutino effectively makes this argument in *Making a New World: Founding Capitalism in the Bajío and Spanish North America* (Durham, NC: Duke University Press, 2011).

3. Kendall Brown, *A History of Mining in Latin America from the Colonial Era to the Present* (Albuquerque: University of New Mexico Press, 2012), 102.

4. Miner don Toribio, age 44, quoted in Pascale Absi, *Los ministros del diablo: El trabajo y sus representaciones en las minas de Potosí* (La Paz: IFEA, 2009), 249; my translation.

EPILOGUE

1. See Antonio Mitre, *Los patriarcas de la plata: Estructura socioeconómica de la minería boliviana en el siglo XIX* (Lima: PUCP, 1981), 78–90; Kendall Brown, *A History of Mining in Latin America from the Colonial Era to the Present* (Albuquerque: University of New Mexico Press, 2012), 93–95, 101–5; Guillermo Ovando-Sanz, "British Interests in Potosí, 1825–1828: Unpublished Documents from the Archivo de Potosí," *Hispanic American Historical Review* 45:1 (Feb. 1965): 64–87. Notable among the investors were Sephardic merchants of Portuguese ancestry.

2. Edmond Temple, *Travels in Various Parts of Peru, Including a Year's Residence in Potosí,* 2 vols. (Philadelphia: Carey & Hart, 1833), 2:139–40.

3. Enrique Tandeter, *Coercion and Market: Silver Mining in Colonial Potosí, 1692–1826,* trans. Richard Warren (Albuquerque: University of New Mexico Press, 1993 [1st Span. ed. 1992]).

4. Tristan Platt, "The Alchemy of Modernity: Alonso Barba's Copper Cauldrons and the Independence of Bolivian Metallurgy, 1790–1890," *Journal of Latin American Studies* 32:1 (Feb. 2000): 1–54.

5. A *guaira* was photographed by U. S. mining engineer Robert Peele, "A Primitive Smelting-Furnace," *School of Mines Quarterly* 15 (1893–94): 8–10.

6. Mitre, *Los patriarcas de la plata.* Mitre defines three phases of post-Independence mining: a "protectionist" era (1830–50), a transitional period of growing flexibility (1850–73), and a boom (1873–95) owing to a confluence of factors. See also Tristan Platt, *Estado tributario y librecambio en Potosí (siglo XIX): Mercado indígena, proyecto proteccionista y lucha de ideologías monetarias* (La Paz: Hisbol, 1986).

7. Hiram Bingham, *Across South America: An Account of a Journey from Buenos Aires to Lima by Way of Potosí* (Boston: Houghton Mifflin, 1911), 120.

8. Ibid., 123.

9. Ibid.

10. Ibid., 128.

11. Marie Robinson Wright, *Bolivia: The Central Highway of South America, a Land of Rich Resources and Varied Interest* (Philadelphia: George Barrie & Sons, 1907), 324.

12. Ibid., 321.

13. Ibid., 337.

14. Robert L. Smale, *"I Sweat the Flavor of Tin": Labor Activism in Early Twentieth-Century Bolivia* (Pittsburgh: University of Pittsburgh Press, 2010). For the parallel story of Bolivia's indigenous peasantry, see Laura Gotkowitz, *A Revolution for Our Rights: Indigenous Struggles for Land and Justice in Bolivia, 1880–1952* (Durham, NC: Duke University Press, 2007).

15. Smale, *I Sweat the Flavor of Tin,* 29.

16. Brown, *History of Mining,* 146.

17. Brown, *History of Mining,* 155–60. Anthropologist June Nash recorded the stories of many Oruro-area miners in *We Eat the Mines and the Mines Eat Us: Dependency and Exploitation in Bolivian Tin Mines* (New York: Columbia University Press, 1979). See also the classic testimonial by Domitila Barros de Chungara with Moema Viezzer, *Let Me Speak! Testimony of Domitila, a Woman of the Bolivian Mines* (New York: Monthly Review Press, 1978). Anthropologist Michael Taussig popularized some of this work in *The Devil and Commodity Fetishism in South America* (Chapel Hill: University of North Carolina Press, 1980).

18. Herbert Klein, *A Concise History of Bolivia,* 2nd ed. (New York: Cambridge University Press, 2011), 234–36.

# BIBLIOGRAPHICAL ESSAY

Potosí's colonial historiography is rich and varied, but generally recent. Between the 1940s and 1960s, historians Gwendolin Cobb, Lewis Hanke, Gunnar Mendoza, and Alberto Crespo published important work on interregional trade and social conflict in early colonial Potosí. Although their studies were narrowly focused, Cobb and Crespo relied on primary sources to build their narratives. Cobb used published sources, such as Juan de Matienzo's *Gobierno del Peru* (ca. 1570) and Roberto Levillier's massive collections of materials relating to Viceroy Francisco de Toledo, and Crespo worked with items in the Bolivian National Archive in Sucre annotated by Gunnar Mendoza, and then with items from the Archivo General de Indias (AGI). Another part of the Potosí puzzle was solved by Peruvian historian Guillermo Lohmann Villena, whose 1949 history of the mercury mines of Huancavelica—Potosí's lifeblood—remained standard until Nicholas Robins's 2017 book on the city and its mines.

In 1956, the North American historian Lewis Hanke pointed to potential lines of inquiry in a short book. He pursued a few of these lines in brief articles, but mostly he focused on publishing manuscript sources. In 1959, Hanke and Mendoza collaborated on an annotated transcription of Luis Capoche's 1585 description of the mountain, city, and hinterland (heavily cited in this book). Published in the popular Biblioteca de Autores Españoles series, this volume was followed by another in 1965 including fragmentary descriptions of Potosí from the AGI and other Spanish archives. It was also in 1965 that Hanke and Mendoza published the massive, three-volume *Historia de la Villa Imperial de Potosí,* by Bartolomé Arzáns de Orsúa y Vela, ending centuries of mystery but also prompting new questions about historical veracity.

Also in the early 1960s, the Argentinian historian Carlos Sempat Assadourian pursued Potosí's trade linkages to Buenos Aires via Córdoba, an important Atlantic-interior South American corridor by 1590 and also to Santiago de Chile. He was already formulating his theory of mining-centered colonial development, a counterpoint to then-fashionable models of underdevelopment derived from dependency theory. The Brazilian historian Alice Canabrava and French historian Marie Helmer were also working out Potosí's South Atlantic connections, illuminating Luso-Brazilian trade ties and developing aspirations following the 1580 Luso-Hispanic union. Inge Wolff offered an early look at Potosí's enslaved African population.

The English historian Charles Boxer also approached the Cerro Rico from Brazilian territory with his extraordinary biography of Rio de Janeiro governor Salvador Correia de Sá e Benavides (1952). Economic historians were also at work, inspired by Earl Hamilton's seminal studies of Spain's early modern price revolution. U. S.-born Brazilianist Bailey Diffie was among the first to attempt a summing up of early Potosí silver production using smeltery ledgers housed in Seville, a task carried forward in Potosí's own archives and other repositories by Peter Bakewell, whose figures are now standard. Potosí mine and mint output has been treated on a larger scale by John J. TePaske, Herbert Klein, Kendall Brown, Ward Barrett, Engel Sluiter, and others—taken to the global sphere by Arturo Giráldez and Dennis Flynn. Registered silver production and its relation to global trends can now be fathomed thanks to these scholars.

Hanke and Mendoza's monumental 1965 publication of Arzáns's *History of the Imperial Villa of Potosí* (ca. 1736) perhaps epitomizes the first great wave of scholarship, focused as it was on getting important raw material and basic facts published while also sketching the general contours of Potosí's heyday in a regional if not quite global context. R. C. Padden was inspired by the huge 1965 three-volume Arzáns to translate and annotate some of his most picturesque stories in 1975 under the title *Tales of Potosí.* The cultural and literary history of Potosí seemed to be budding, but there were as yet few takers. Stephanie Merrim and Lisa Voigt have recently revived this line of inquiry. Voigt (2016) uses Arzáns and corroborating sources to illuminate the Imperial Villa's die-hard festival culture, comparing it with the near-namesake Vila Rica in Minas Gerais, Brazil.

In the next wave of historical studies (1970s–80s), Peter Bakewell, Mario Chacón Torres, Jeffrey Cole, Enrique Tandeter, Josep Barnadas, and Rosemarie Buechler published landmark studies based on extensive archival research. Bakewell and Cole focused on the Habsburg-era *mita,* and Tandeter and Buechler examined this infamous labor draft alongside *kajcheo* and other economic practices in the Bourbon era, when the mines underwent a substantial revival. Chacón, an art historian, mined Potosí's notary books for the first time. Bakewell used Luis Capoche as a key source for how mining and refining were carried out by free as well as drafted indigenous workers and traders in the early years, whereas Cole examined the vast polemical literature surrounding the mita for insights into Habsburg colonial governance.

The key players in Cole's narrative were not the Andean workers or the "activist" viceroys (nor the priests) who routinely claimed to seek their protection, but rather the refiners, or *azogueros*. Soon after the arrival of Viceroy Toledo in 1572, Potosí's silver refiners came to constitute a new and powerful class, one that persisted to the end of colonial times. The other institution established by Toledo, the Potosi mint, was first studied in depth by Arnaldo Cunietti-Ferrando, although various numismatists before him had written about it. He set a standard for numismatic studies based on archival materials as well as printed matter. Meanwhile, historian Clara López Beltrán opened a new kind of historical geography with Potosí at its center.

Labor and bureaucracy were indeed not the only things of interest in Potosí, and in 1987 Peter Bakewell published a biography of seventeenth-century mining and commercial magnate Antonio López de Quiroga. The thrust of Bakewell's work was colonial entrepreneurship, another counterpoint to dependency theorists' claims of underdevelopment and backwardness at the so-called periphery of the modern world-system. Meanwhile, Sempat Assadourian continued to use studies of commerce and innovation in Potosí to challenge claims of underdevelopment throughout the Andes and eventually much of colonial Spanish America. He argued that silver mining was a reliable motor for economic development even as most silver, including coin, left the continent.

In treating the indigenous world, one of the most significant contributions to the history of Potosí was the collaborative work of Tristan Platt, Olivia Harris, and Thérèse Bouysse-Cassagne: *Qaraqara Charka*. These authors built on years of fieldwork and archival work to offer an alternative history of the entire region, placing the Cerro Rico and Imperial Villa in a new context. Also key in this vital endeavor were Thierry Saignes, Xavier Albó, Tom Abercrombie, Luis Miguel Glave, Ricardo Godoy, and Carmen Salazar Soler, among others. For the city and Cerro Rico, the work of ethnographer Pascale Absi is now essential.

Aside from the work of art historians such as Teresa Gisbert, José Mesa, Mario Chacón, and a few numismatists, no monographic study of colonial Potosí appeared until 2005, when historian Jane Mangan published a breakthrough book on small-scale trade and food production in the Habsburg era. It was the first book-length work since Chacón's study of artisans to exploit Potosí's own notary records in depth, and also the first to go beyond the "tall tales" of Arzáns in treating the history of women. Mangan brought to life a city whose majority indigenous population pulsed with commercial activity, much of it involving the trading of raw silver ore for maize beer as well as bread, soup, and other victuals. Women of indigenous and mixed background fed the laboring masses, but they also made strides toward capital accumulation as entrepreneurs and social advancement as members of religious confraternities.

Another monumental contribution to the history of Baroque Potosí is Ignacio Gonzalez Casasnovas's *Las dudas de la corona* (2000), in some ways a sequel to the 1980s studies of Bakewell and Cole, tracing the evolution of the mita as well as the city's azoguero elite in the later seventeenth century. In the realm of cultural history, a superb 2008 volume of essays edited by Andrés Eichmann and Marcela Inch compares urban society in Potosí and nearby La Plata (today Sucre). Studies of the latter city's elites have always made the work of Ana María Presta vitally important to anyone interested in colonial Potosí, and her current work on Porco is even more revealing. In a similar vein, the voluminous and innovative work of Rossana Barragán, Raquel Gil-Montero, Sergio Serulnikov, Paula Zagalsky, and Eugenia Bridhikina has amplified our knowledge of indigenous as well as African-descended protagonists in and around the Imperial Villa. They represent the abiding and growing interest of Argentine scholars in several disciplines in the colonial history of Potosí.

Despite this considerable body of work, supplemented recently by Kenneth Mills, Kendall Brown, Consuelo Varela, Alan Craig, Nicholas Robins, Emma Sordo, and David Dressing, there remains a general ignorance of the basic history of Potosí—a chronological narrative to compare with the fanciful work of Arzáns. This is hardly the fault of the several generations of historians and other scholars just listed, and I urge readers to consult their invaluable work for the "real" story. As a newcomer and interloper who got seduced by the gold and emeralds of New Granada and Quito, I stand on their shoulders.

It may come as no surprise that fictional works on colonial Potosí often trace their genesis to Arzáns as well. I have mentioned the "Andean gothic" works of Juana Manuela Gorriti, Vicente Quesada, and Ricardo Palma, to which we should add the Bolivian writer "Brocha Gorda" (J. L. Jaimes) and the great Potosí compiler of history and folklore Modesto Omiste. A mid-twentieth-century novel set during the 1620s war of Basques and Vicuñas is José Enrique Viaña's vivid *Cuando vibraba la entraña de plata* (1948; an annotated edition by Alba María Paz Soldán appeared in 2016). Viaña lamented the shortage of "real" histories of Potosí, relying on the fragmentary portions of Arzáns then available. Bolivian writer Ramón Rocha Monroy mined the expanded Arzáns in his novella *Potosí 1600* (2002). American writer Annamaria Alfieri set a mystery in seventeenth-century Potosí, *City of Silver* (2009), also inspired by Arzáns. With respect to these authors, I recommend Arzáns.

# SELECT BIBLIOGRAPHY

Abercrombie, Thomas A. "Q'aqchas and La Plebe in 'Rebellion': Carnival vs. Lent in 18th-Century Potosí." *Journal of Latin American Anthropology* 2:1 (1996): 62–111.

———. *Pathways of Memory and Power: Ethnography and History among an Andean People.* Madison: University of Wisconsin Press, 1998.

Absi, Pascale. *Los ministros del diablo: El trabajo y sus representaciones en las minas de Potosí.* La Paz: IFEA, 2009.

Acosta, José de. *Natural and Moral History of the Indies.* Edited by Jane E. Mangan, trans. Frances López-Morillas Durham, NC: Duke University Press, 2002.

Acosta de Arias Schreiber, Rosa María. *Fiestas coloniales urbanas: Lima, Cuzco, Potosí.* Lima: Otorongos, 1997.

Aillón Soria, Esther. *Vida, pasión y negocios: El propietario de la Viña "San Pedro Mártir" Indalecio González de Socasa (1755–1820). Potosí y Cinti a fines de la Colonia y en la Guerra de la Independencia.* Sucre: ABNB, 2009.

Arellano, Ignacio, and Andrés Eichmann, eds. *Enremeses, loas y coloquios de Potosí (Colección del Convento de Santa Teresa).* Madrid: Iberoamericana / Vervuert, 2005.

Arzáns de Orsúa y Vela Bartolomé. *Historia de la Villa Imperial de Potosí.* 3 vols. Edited by Lewis Hanke and Gunnar Mendoza. Providence, RI: Brown University Press, 1965.

———. *Tales of Potosí.* Edited by R. C. Padden. Translated by Frances López-Morillas. Providence, RI: Brown University Press, 1975.

Assadourian, Carlos Sempat. "La producción de la mercancía dinero en la formación del mercado interno colonial: El caso del espacio peruano en el siglo XVI." In *Ensayos sobre el desarrollo económico de México y América Latina (1500–1975),* edited by Enrique Florescano, 223–92. México, D. F.: FCE, 1979.

———. *El sistema de la economía colonial: El mercado interior, regiones y espacio económico.* Mexico City: Nueva Imagen, 1983.

Bakewell, Peter J. "Registered Silver Production in the Potosí District, 1550–1735." *Jahrbuch für Geschichte von Staat, Wirtschaft und Gesellschaft Lateinamerikas* 12 (1975): 67–103.

———. "Technological Change in Potosí: The Silver Boom of the 1570s." *Jahrbuch für Geschichte von Staat, Wirtschaft und Gesellschaft Lateinamerikas* 14 (1977): 60–77.

———. *Miners of the Red Mountain: Indian Labor in Potosí, 1545–1650.* Albuquerque: University of New Mexico Press, 1985.

———. *Silver and Entrepreneurship in Seventeenth-Century Potosí: The Life and Times of Antonio López de Quiroga.* Albuquerque: University of New Mexico Press, 1987.

———, ed. *Mines of Silver and Gold in the Americas.* Aldershot: Variorum, 1997.

Ballesteros Gabrois, Manuel. *Descubrimiento y fundación del Potosí.* Zaragoza, Spain: Delegación de Distrito de Educación Nacional, 1950.

Barba, Alvaro Alonso. *Arte de los Metales.* Madrid: Imprenta del Reyno, 1640.

Barnadas, Josep M. *Charcas: Orígenes históricos de una sociedad colonial.* La Paz: Centro de Investigación y Promoción del Campesinado, 1973.

———. "Una polémica colonial: Potosí, 1579–1684." *Jarbuch für Geschichte von Staat, Wirtschaft un Gessellschaft Lateinamerikas* 10 (1973): 16–70.

———. *Alvaro Alonso Barba (1569–1662): Investigaciones sobre su vida y obra.* La Paz: Biblioteca Minera Boliviana, 1986.

Barragán, Rossana. "Ladrones, pequeños empresarios o trabajadores independientes? K'ajchas, trapiches y plata en el Cerro Rico de Potosí en el siglo XVIII." *Nuevo Mundo / Mundos Nuevos* (2015): online.

———. "Working Silver for the World: Mining Labor and Popular Economy in Colonial Potosí." *Hispanic American Historical Review* 97:2 (2017): 193–222.

Bauer, Brian S., et al. "El Camino del Mercurio de Huancavelica a Potosí," trans. Javier Flores Espinoza. In *Nuevas tendencias en el estudio de los caminos,* ed. Sofía Chacaltana, Elizabeth Arkush, and Giancarlo Marcone, 380–99. Lima: Ministerio de Cultura, 2017.

Bentancor, Orlando. *The Matter of Empire: Metaphysics and Mining in Colonial Peru.* Pittsburgh: University of Pittsburgh Press, 2017.

Bigelow, Allison. "Women, Men, and the Legal Languages of Mining in the Colonial Andes." *Ethnohistory* 63:2 (2016): 351–80.

———. *Cultural Touchstones: Mining, Refining, and the Languages of Empire in the Early Americas.* Chapel Hill: University of North Carolina Press, 2019.

Bingham, Hiram. *Across South America: An Account of a Journey from Buenos Aires to Lima by Way of Potosí.* Boston: Houghton Mifflin, 1911.

Boxer, Charles. *Salvador de Sá and the Struggle for Brazil and Angola, 1602–1686.* London: Athlone Press, 1952.

Brading, David, and Harry Cross. "Colonial Silver Mining: Mexico and Peru." *Hispanic American Historical Review* 52:4 (Nov. 1972): 545–79.

Brook, Timothy. *Vermeer's Hat: The Seventeenth Century and the Dawn of the Global World.* New York: Viking Penguin, 2008.

Brown, Kendall. "Workers' Health and Colonial Mercury Mining at Huancavelica, Peru." *The Americas* 57:4 (Apr. 2001): 467–96.

————. *A History of Mining in Latin America from the Colonial Era to the Present.* Albuquerque: University of New Mexico Press, 2012.

Buechler, Rose Marie. *The Mining Society of Potosí, 1776–1810.* Syracuse: Syracuse University Press, 1981.

Burzio, Humberto. *La ceca de la Villa Imperial de Potosí y la moneda colonial.* Buenos Aires, 1945.

Cañete y Domínguez, Pedro Vicente. *Guía histórica, geográfica, física, política y legal del govierno e intendencia de la Provincia de Potosí.* Potosí: Editorial Potosí, 1952.

Capoche, Luis. *Relación general de la Villa Imperial de Potosí* BAE CXXII. Edited by Lewis Hanke. Madrid: Atlas, [1585] 1959.

Cardim, Pedro, Tamar Herzog, Jos Javier Ruiz Ibez, and Gaetano Sabatini. *Polycentric Monarchies: How Did Early Modern Spain and Portugal Achieve and Maintain a Global Hegemony?* Sussex: Sussex University Press, 2012.

Castelnau, Francis de. *Expédition dans les parties centrales de l'Amérique du Sud: De Rio de Janeiro à Lima, et de Lima au Para,* vol. 2. Paris: P. Bertrand, 1851.

Ch'en, Kenneth. "Matteo Ricci's Contribution to, and Influence on, Geographical Knowledge in China." *Journal of the American Oriental Society* 59:3 (Sept. 1939): 325–59.

Cieza de León, Pedro de. "Crónica del Perú," Primera Parte [1553-56], ed. Franklin Pease G.Y. Lima: PUCP Fondo Editorial, 1984.

Cobb, Gwendolin B. "Potosí and Huancavelica: Economic Bases of Peru, 1545–1640." PhD diss., University of California, Berkeley, 1947.

————. "Supply and Transportation for the Potosí Mines, 1545–1640." *Hispanic American Historical Review* 29:1 (Feb. 1949): 25–45.

Cole, Jeffrey. "An Abolitionism Born of Frustration: The Conde de Lemos and the Potosí Mita, 1667–73." *Hispanic American Historical Review* 63:2 (May 1983): 307–33.

————. *The Potosí Mita, 1573–1700: Compulsory Indian Labor in the Andes.* Stanford: Stanford University Press, 1985.

Cook, Noble David. *Demographic Collapse: Indian Peru, 1520–1620.* Cambridge: Cambridge University Press, 1981.

Cooke, Colin A., et al. "Pre-Colombian Mercury Pollution Associated with the Smelting of Argentiferous Ores in the Bolivian Andes." *Ambio* 40:1 (Feb. 2011): 18–25.

Cornblit, Oscar. *Power and Violence in the Colonial City: Oruro from the Mining Renaissance to the Rebellion of Tupac Amaru (1740–1782).* Translated by E.L. Glick. New York: Cambridge University Press, 1995.

Craig, Alan K., and Robert C. West, eds. *In Quest of Mineral Wealth: Aboriginal and Colonial Mining and Metallurgy in Spanish America.* Geoscience and Man Series, vol. 33. Baton Rouge: Louisiana State University Press, 1994.

Crespo Rodas, Alberto. "La 'mita' de Potosí." *Revista Histórica* 22 (Lima, 1955): 169–82.

————. *La guerra entre vicuñas y vascongados: Potosí, 1622–1625,* 2nd ed. La Paz: Colección Popular, 1969.

Cruz, Pablo. "Huacas olvidadas y cerros santos: Apuntes metodológicos sobre la cartografía sagrada en los Andes del sur de Bolivia." *Estudios Atacameños* 38 (2009): 55–74.

――― and Jean-Joinville Vacher, eds. *Mina y metalurgía en los Andes del Sur entre la época pre-hispánica y el siglo XVII.* Sucre: Instituto Francés de Estudios Andinos, 2008.

Cummins, Thomas B. F., and Barbara Anderson, eds. *The Getty Murúa: Essays on the Making of Martín de Murúa's* Historia General del Piru, *J. Paul Getty Museum Ms. Ludwig XIII 16.* Los Angeles: Getty Research Institute, 2008.

Cunietti-Ferrando, Arnaldo J. *Historia de la Real Casa de Moneda de Potosí durante la dominación hispánica, 1573–1652.* Buenos Aires: Pellegrini, 1995.

Cunningham, C. G., et al. "The Age and Thermal History of Cerro Rico de Potosí, Bolivia." *Mineralium Deposita* 31 (1996): 374–85.

Dressing, David. "Social Tensions in Early Seventeenth-Century Potosí." PhD diss., Tulane University, 2007.

Eichmann, Andrés, and Marcela Inch C., eds. *La construcción de lo urbano en Potosí y la Plata (siglos XVI–XVII).* Sucre: Ministerio de Cultura de España / Archivo y Biblioteca Nacionales de Bolivia, 2008.

Elliott, John H. *Spain, Europe and the Wider World, 1500–1800.* New Haven, CT: Yale University Press, 2009.

Erauso, Catalina de. *Lieutenant Nun: Memoir of a Basque Transvestite in the New World.* Translated by Michele and Gabriel Stepto. Boston: Beacon Press, 1996.

Escobari de Querejazu, Laura. *Caciques, yanaconas y extravagantes: La sociedad colonial en Charcas s. XVI–XVIII,* 3rd ed. La Paz: Plural Editores / Embajada de España en Bolivia, 2012 [1st ed. 2001].

Ezquerra Abadía, Ramón. "Problemas de la mita de Potosí en el siglo XVIII." In *La minería hispana e iberoamericana,* vol. 1, 483–511. León, Spain, 1970.

Farah, Caesar E., ed. and trans. *An Arab's Journey to Colonial Spanish America: The Travels of Elias al-Mûsili in the Seventeenth Century.* Syracuse: Syracuse University Press, 2003.

Farrelly, Brian. *Vicente Bernedo: Apóstol de Charcas.* Salamanca: Editorial San Esteban, 1986.

Gade, Daniel W. *Nature and Culture in the Andes.* Madison: University of Wisconsin Press, 1999.

Galeano, Eduardo. *Open Veins of Latin America: Five Centuries of the Pillage of a Continent.* Translated by Cedric Belfrage. New York: Monthly Review Press, 1973.

Gamucio, Mariano Baptista, ed. *La ciudad de Potosí vista por viajeros y autores nacionales del siglo XVI al XXI.* Potosí: Casa Nacional de Moneda, 2011.

Gil Montero, Raquel. *Ciudades efímeras. El ciclo minero de la plata de la plata en Lípez (Bolivia), siglos XVI-XIX.* Lima: IFEA, 2014.

Gisbert, Teresa. "El Cerro de Potosí y el dios Pachacámac." *Chungara, Revista de Antropología Chilena* 42:1 (2010): 169–80.

――― and Luis Prado, eds. *Potosí: Catalogación de su patrimonio urbano y arquitectónico.* La Paz: Instituto Boliviano de la Cultura, 1990.

Glave, Luis Miguel. *Trajinantes: Caminos indígenas en la sociedad colonial, siglos XVI/XVII*. Lima: Instituto de Apoyo Agrario, 1989.

Godoy, Ricardo A. *Mining and Agriculture in Highland Bolivia: Ecology, History, and Commerce among the Jukumanis*. Tucson: University of Arizona Press, 1990.

González Casasnovas, Ignacio. *Las dudas de la corona: La política de repartimientos para la minería de Potosí (1680–1732)*. Madrid: CSIC, 2000.

Goodrich, Thomas D. *The Ottoman Turks and the New World: A Study of Tarih-I Hind-I Garbi and Sixteenth-Century Ottoman Americana*. Wiesbaden: Otto Harrassowitz, 1990.

Guaman Poma de Ayala, Felipe. *The First New Chronicle and Good Government*, abridged. Translated by David Frye. Indianapolis: Hackett, 2006.

Guerrero, Saúl. *Silver by Fire, Silver by Mercury: A Chemical History of Silver Refining in New Spain and Mexico, 16th to 19th Centuries*. Leiden: Brill, 2017.

Gunder Frank, Andre. *ReOrient: Global Economy in the Asian Age*. Berkeley: University of California Press, 1998.

Hanke, Lewis. *The Imperial City of Potosí: An Unwritten Chapter in the History of Spanish America*. The Hague: Martinus Nijhof, 1956.

———. "The Portuguese in Spanish America, with special reference to the Villa Imperial de Potosí." *Revista de Historia de América* 51 (June 1961): 1–48.

Hausberger, Bernd. "La guerra de los vicuñas contra los vascongados en Potosí y la etnicización de los vascos a principios de la edad moderna." In *Excluir para ser: Procesos identitarios y fronteras sociales en la America hispánica (xvii–xviii)*, edited by Christian Büschges and Frederique Langue, 23–57. Frankfurt: AHILA/Vervuert, 2005.

Helmer, Marie. "Comercio e contrabando entre Bahia e Potosí no século XVI." *Revista de Historia* 15 (São Paulo, 1953): 195–212.

———. "Un tipo social: El 'minero' de Potosí." *Revista de Indias* 16 (1956): 85–92.

———. *Cantuta: Recueil d'articles, 1949–1987*. Madrid: Casa de Velázquez, 1993.

Honores, Renzo. "Una sociedad legalista: Abogados, procuradores de causas y la creación de una cultura legal colonial en Lima y Potosí, 1540–1670." PhD diss., Florida International University, 2007.

Kagan, Richard. *Urban Images of the Hispanic World, 1493–1793*. New Haven, CT: Yale University Press, 2000.

Kindleberger, Charles P. *Spenders and Hoarders: The World Distribution of Spanish American Silver, 1550–1750*. Singapore: Institute of Southeast Asian Studies, 1989.

Klein, Herbert. *A Concise History of Bolivia*, 2nd ed. New York: Cambridge University Press, 2011.

*La minería hispana e iberoamericana: Contribución a su investigación histórica*. Vol. 1 of *Ponencias del VI Congreso Internacional de Minería*. León, Spain, 1970.

Langer, Erick D. *Rural Society and the Mining Economy in Southern Bolivia: Agrarian Resistance in Chuquisaca, 1880–1930*. Stanford: Stanford University Press, 1987.

León Portocarrero, Pedro de. *Descripción del virreinato del Perú*. Edited by Eduardo Huarag Alvarez. Lima: Editorial Universitaria, 2009 [bilingual ed., orig. Portuguese ms. ca. 1620].

Llanos, García de. *Diccionario y maneras de hablar que se usan en las minas y sus labores en los ingenios y beneficios de los metales (1609).* La Paz: Banco Central de Bolivia, 1983.

Lohmann Villena, Guillermo. *Las minas de Huancavelica en los siglos XVI y XVII.* Seville: EEHA, 1949.

López Beltran, Clara. *Estructura económica de una sociedad colonial: Charcas en el siglo XVII.* La Paz: Centro de Estudios de la Realidad Económica y Social, 1988.

———. *La Ruta de la Plata de Potosí al Pacífico: Caminos, comercio y caravanas en los siglos XVI al XIX.* La Paz: Plural Editores, 2016.

Mangan, Jane E. *Trading Roles: Gender, Ethnicity, and the Urban Economy in Colonial Potosí.* Durham, NC: Duke University Press, 2005.

Manrique, Juan del Pino. *Descripción de la Villa de Potosí.* Buenos Aires: Imprenta del Estado, 1836.

Martínez Carreras, José Urbano. *Relaciones geográficas de Indias—Peru.* Biblioteca de Autores Españoles, vols. 183–85. Madrid: Atlas, 1965.

Martiré, Eduardo, ed. *El Código Carolino de ordenanzas reales de las minas de Potosí y demás provincias del Río de la Plata (1794) de Pedro Vicente Cañete.* Buenos Aires: n. p., 1973–74.

Matienzo, Juan. *Gobierno del Perú.* Edited by Guillermo Lohmann-Villena. Paris / Lima: IFEA, 1967.

McNeill, John R., and George Vrtis, eds. *Mining North America: An Environmental History since 1522.* Berkeley and Los Angeles: University of California Press, 2017.

Mendoza, Gunnar. *Catálogo de los recursos documentales sobre la minería en el distrito de la Audiencia de La Plata, 1548–1826.* Sucre: Banco Central / ABNB, 2005.

Miller, John. *Memoirs of General Miller in the Service of the Republic of Peru,* 2nd ed. 2 vols. London: Longman, Rees, et al., 1829.

Mills, Kenneth, "Diego de Ocaña's Hagiography of New and Renewed Devotion in Colonial Peru." In *Colonial Saints: Discovering the Holy in the Americas, 1500–1800,* edited by Allan Greer and Jodi Bilinkoff, 51–75. New York: Routledge, 2003.

Mira Delli-Zotti, Guillermo. "El Real Banco de San Carlos de Potosí y la minería altoperuana colonial, 1779–1825." In Julio Sánchez Gómez et al., *La savia del imperio: Tres estudios de economía colonial,* 265–399. Salamanca: Universidad de Salamanca, 1997.

Mitre, Antonio. *Los patriarcas de la plata: Estructura socioeconómica de la minería boliviana en el siglo XIX.* Lima: PUCP, 1981.

Moore, Jason. " 'This Lofty Mountain of Silver Could Conquer the Whole World': Potosí and the Political Ecology of Underdevelopment, 1545–1800." *Journal of Philosophical Economics* 4:1 (2010): 58–103.

Mumford, Jeremy Ravi. *Vertical Empire: The General Resettlement of Indians in the Colonial Andes.* Durham, NC: Duke University Press, 2012.

Murra, John V. "La correspondencia entre un 'capitán de la mita' y su apoderado en Potosí." *Historia y Cultura* 3 (La Paz, 1978): 45–58.

Murray Fantom, Glenn Stephen. *Guía de las cantidades acuñadas, cecas de Potosí y Lima.* Segovia (Spain): Amigos de la Casa de la Moneda de Segovia, 2016.

Nash, June. *We Eat the Mines and the Mines Eat Us.* New York: Columbia University Press, 1979.

Numhauser, Paulina. *Mujeres indias y señores de la coca: Potosí y Cusco en el siglo XVI.* Madrid: Cátedra, 2005.

———. "Un asunto banal: Las luchas de Vicuñas y Vascongados en Potosí (siglo XVII)." *Illes i Imperis* 14 (2012): 113–38.

Ocaña, Fray Diego de. *Viaje por el Nuevo Mundo: de Guadalupe a Potosí, 1599–1605.* Edited by Blanca Lopez de Mariscal and Abraham Madroñal. Madrid / Frankfurt: Iberoamericana / Vervuert, 2010.

Otte, Enrique. *Cartas privadas de emigrantes a Indias, 1540–1616.* 2nd ed. México: FCE, 1996.

Parker, Geoffrey. *Global Crisis: War, Climate Change and Catastrophe in the Seventeenth Century.* New Haven, CT: Yale University Press, 2013.

Pearce, Adrian J. *The Origins of Bourbon Reform in Spanish South America, 1700–1763.* New York: Palgrave Macmillan, 2014.

Pentland, Joseph Barclay. "Report on the Republic of Bolivia, 1827." *Camden Miscellany* 25: 169–267. London: Offices of the Royal Historical Society, 1974.

Pérez Melero, Joaquín. "From Alchemy to Science: The Scientific Revolution and Enlightenment in Spanish American Mining and Metallurgy." In *The Revolution in Geology from the Renaissance to the Enlightenment,* ed. Gary D. Rosenberg, 51–61. Boulder, CO: Geological Society of America, 2009.

Platt, Tristan. *Estado tributario y librecambio en Potosí (siglo XIX): Mercado indígena, proyecto proteccionista y lucha de ideologías monetarias.* La Paz: Hisbol, 1986.

———. "Producción, tecnología y trabajo en la Rivera de Potosí durante la República temprana." In *El siglo XIX: Bolivia y América Latina,* edited by Rossana Barragán, Dora Cajías, and Seemin Qayum, 395–435. La Paz: IFEA, 1997.

———. "The Alchemy of Modernity: Alonso Barba's Copper Cauldrons and the Independence of Bolivian Metallurgy, 1790–1890." *Journal of Latin American Studies* 32:1 (Feb. 2000): 1–54.

Platt, Tristan, Thérèse Bouysse-Cassagne, Olivia Harris, con el aliento de Thierry Saignes. *Qaraqara-Charka: Mallku, Inka y Rey en la provincia de Charcas (siglos XVI–XVII): Historia antropológica de una confederación aymara.* La Paz: IFEA / Plural, 2006.

Platt, Tristan, and Pablo Quisbert. "Tras la huella del silencio: Potosí, Toledo y los Incas." *Runa* 31:2 (2010): 115–52.

Pomeranz, Kenneth, and Steven Topik. *The World That Trade Created: Society, Culture, and the World Economy, 1400 to the Present.* Armonk, NY: M. E. Sharpe, 1999.

Presta, Ana María. *Encomienda, familia y negocios en Charcas colonial: Los encomenderos de La Plata, 1550–1600.* 2nd ed. Sucre: ABNB, 2014.

Prieto, Andrés I. *Missionary Scientists: Jesuit Science in Spanish South America, 1570–1810.* Nashville: Vanderbilt University Press, 2011.

Querejazu, Pedro, and Elizabeth Ferrer, eds. *Potosí: Colonial Treasures and the Bolivian City of Silver.* New York: Americas Society, 1997.

Ramírez del Águila, Pedro. *Noticias políticas de Indias y relación descriptiva de la ciudad de La Plata, metrópoli de las Provincias de Los Charcas* [1639]. Sucre: Ciencia Editores, 2017.

Rice, Prudence M. *Vintage Moquegua: History, Wine, and Archaeology on a Colonial Periphery.* Austin: University of Texas Press, 2012.

Robins, Nicholas A. *Mercury, Mining, and Empire: The Human and Ecological Cost of Colonial Silver Mining in the Andes.* Bloomington: Indiana University Press, 2011.

———. *Santa Barbara's Legacy: An Environmental History of Huancavelica, Peru.* Leiden: Brill, 2017.

Robles, Gregorio de. *América a fines del siglo XVII: Noticia de lugares de contrabando.* Edited by Victor Tau Anzoátegui. Valladolid (Spain): Casa-Museo de Colón, 1980.

Rossells Montalvo, Beatriz. *La gastronomía en Potosí y Charcas, siglos XVIII, XIX y XX en torno a la historia de la cocina boliviana,* 2nd ed. La Paz: Instituto de Estudios Bolivianos, 2003.

Rudolph, William E. "The Lakes of Potosí." *Geographical Review* 26 (1936): 529–54.

Saignes, Thierry. "Notes on the Regional Contribution to the Mita in Potosí in the Early Seventeenth Century." *Bulletin of Latin American Research* 4:1 (1985): 65–76.

———. "Capoche, Potosí y la coca: El consumo popular de estimulantes en el siglo XVII." *Revista de Indias* 48:182–83 (1988): 207–35.

Salazar-Soler, Carmen. "Los 'expertos' de la Corona: Poder colonial y saber local en el Alto Perú en los siglos XVI y XVII." *De Re Metallica* 13:2 (July–Dec. 2009): 83–94.

———. "Minería y moneda en la época colonial temprana." In *Compendio de historia económica del Perú,* vol. 2, edited by Carlos Contreras, 109–228. Lima: IEP, 2009.

Sánchez Albornoz, Nicolás. *Indios y tributos en el Alto Perú.* Lima: IEP, 1978.

Sartori, Federico. "Tan a banderas desplegadas: El poder de un comisario inquisitorial americano del siglo XVII." *Colonial Latin American Review* 24:3 (July 2015) 356–82.

Sawday, Jonathan. *Engines of the Imagination: Renaissance Culture and the Rise of the Machine.* New York: Routledge, 2007.

Schell, William. "Silver Symbiosis: ReOrienting Mexican Economic History." *Hispanic American Historical Review* 81:1 (Feb. 2001): 89–133.

Scott, Heidi V. "Mining Places and Subterranean Spaces in Colonial Spanish America: Nature, Government, and Moral Debate in the Exploitation of the Underground." Forthcoming.

Serulnikov, Sergio. *Subverting Colonial Authority: Challenges to Spanish Rule in Eighteenth-Century Southern Andes.* Durham, NC: Duke University Press, 2003.

———. *Revolution in the Andes: The Age of Túpac Amaru.* Translated by David Frye. Durham, NC: Duke University Press, 2013.

Sluiter, Engel. *The Gold and Silver of Spanish America.* Berkeley: Bancroft Library, 1998.

Sordo, Emma, "Civilizational Designs: The Architecture of Colonialism in the Native Parishes of Potosí." PhD diss., University of Miami, 2000.

Stavig, Ward. *The World of Túpac Amaru: Conflict, Community, and Identity in Colonial Peru.* Lincoln: University of Nebraska Press, 1999.

Stern, Steve J. "Feudalism, Capitalism, and the World-System in the Perspective of Latin America and the Caribbean." *American Historical Review* 93:4 (Oct. 1988): 829–72.

Tandeter, Enrique. *Coercion and Market: Silver Mining in Colonial Potosí, 1692–1826.* Translated by Richard Warren. Albuquerque: University of New Mexico Press, 1993 [1st Span. ed. 1992].

Tantaleán Arbulú, Javier. *El virrey Francisco de Toledo y su tiempo: Proyecto de gobernabilidad, el imperio hispano, la plata peruana en la economía-mundo y el mercado colonial.* 2 vols. Lima: Univeresidad San Martín de Porres, 2011.

Temple, Edmond. *Travels in Various Parts of Peru, Including a Year's Residence in Potosí.* 2 vols. Philadelphia: Carey & Hart, 1833.

TePaske, John J. *A New World of Gold and Silver.* Edited by Kendall W. Brown. Leiden and Boston: Brill, 2010.

Tracy, James D., ed. *The Rise of Merchant Empires: Long-Distance Trade in the Early Modern World, 1350–1750.* New York: Cambridge University Press, 1990.

———, ed. *The Political Economy of Merchant Empires: State Power and World Trade, 1350–1750.* New York: Cambridge University Press, 1991.

Tripcevich, Nicholas, and Kevin J. Vaughn, eds. *Mining and Quarrying in the Ancient Andes: Sociopolitical, Economic and Symbolic Dimensions.* New York: Springer, 2013.

Tutino, John. *Making a New World: Founding Capitalism in the Bajío and Spanish North America.* Durham, NC: Duke University Press, 2011.

Van Buren, Mary, and B. Mills. "Huayrachinas and Tocochimbos: Traditional Smelting Technology of the Southern Andes." *Latin American Antiquity* 16:1 (2005): 2–25.

Vargas Ugarte, Rubén, ed. *Pareceres jurídicos en asuntos de Indias.* Lima, 1951.

Varón Gabai, Rafael. *Francisco Pizarro and His Brothers: The Illusion of Power in Sixteenth-Century Peru.* Translated by Javier Flores Espinoza. Norman: University of Oklahoma Press, 1997.

Vázquez de Espinosa, Antonio. *Compendium and Description of the West Indies.* Translated by C. U. Clark. Washington, DC: Smithsonian, 1942.

Viaña, José Enrique. *Cuando vibraba la entraña de plata.* Edited by Alba María Paz Soldán. La Paz: Biblioteca del Bicentenario de Bolivia, 2016.

Voigt, Lisa. *Spectacular Wealth: The Festivals of Colonial South American Mining Towns.* Austin: University of Texas Press, 2016.

Von Glahn, Richard. *Fountain of Fortune: Money and Monetary Policy in China, 1000–1700.* Berkeley: University of California Press, 1996.

Wallerstein, Immanuel. *The Modern World-System.* 3 vols. New York: Academic Press, 1974.

———. *The Modern World-System I: Capitalist Agriculture and the Origins of the European World-Economy in the Sixteenth Century,* 2nd ed. Berkeley: University of California Press, 2011.

Wiedner, David. "Forced Labor in Colonial Peru." *The Americas* 16 (1960): 357–83.

Wright, Marie Robinson. *Bolivia: The Central Highway of South America, a Land of Rich Resources and Varied Interest.* Philadelphia: George Barrie & Sons, 1907.

Zagalsky, Paula. "La mita de Potosí: Una imposición colonial invariable en un contexto de múltiples transformaciones (siglos XVI–XVII; Charcas, virreinato del Perú)." *Chungará* 46:3 (2014): 3–32.

———. "Trabajadores indígenas mineros en el Cerro Rico de Potosí: Tras los rastros de sus prácticas laborales (siglos XVI y XVII)." *Revista Mundos de Trabalho* 6:12 (July–December 2014): 55–82.

Zárate, Agustín de. *The Discovery and Conquest of Peru.* Edited and translated by J. M. Cohen. London: Penguin, 1968.

Zavala, Silvio. *El servicio personal de los indios en el Peru.* 3 vols. Mexico City: El Colegio de México, 1978–80.

Zimmer, Zac. "Bitcoin and Potosí Silver: Historical Perspectives on Cryptocurrency." *Technology and Culture* 58:2 (April 2017): 307–34.

Zugasti, Miguel. "Teatro recuperado en Charcas: Dos loas olvidadas de fray Juan de la Torre (OSA) a la entrada del virrey Diego Morcillo en Potosí, 1716." In *El teatro en la Hispanoamérica colonial,* edited by Ignacio Arellano and José Antonio Rodríguez Garrido, 295–321. Madrid: Iberoamericana / Vervuert, 2008.

Zulawski, Ann. *They Eat from Their Labor: Work and Social Change in Colonial Bolivia.* Pittsburgh: University of Pittsburgh Press, 1995.

# INDEX

British, 139, 160, 179, 186–187
Buenos Aires, 3, 95, 103–104, 126, 140, 151, 229; as viceregal capital, 166–170, 177; and independence, 177, 179

cabildo. See town council
Cajamarca, 21, 24, 30
cajas reales. See treasury, royal
California, xiii, 15, 188
canals, 81, 116, 163
Canas y Canchis, 168
candles, candle making, 52, 56, 77, 98, 200
Cañete y Domínguez, Pedro Vicente, 170–171, 174–175
Capoche, Luis, 65, 79, 197, 199–201, 214n58; and accidents, 73–74; and guairas, 46–48; and labor, 52–54, 99, 230
Carabaya, 7, 29, 64
cards, card games, 108–10, 131
Caricari. See Kari Kari
Caroline Code, 171, 173–175
Carvajal, Francisco de, 11, 208 fn10
Carvajal y Sande, Juan de, 115
Casa Real de Moneda. See mint, royal
censuses, 71, 75, 77, 120–121, 145, 192
Centeno, Diego, 31, 37
Cervantes, Miguel de, 107, 127
Chambilla, Diego, 79
Charcas, Audiencia of, (aka La Plata), 27, 51, 130–131
charcoal, 46, 50, 55, 199, 207–208n10
Charkas (and Qaraqaras), 27–28
Charles V (Charles I of Spain), 5, 8, 30–32, 37, 196
Charles (Carlos) II, 19, 150
Charles III, 168–169, 171
Charles IV, 174
charqui, 34, 60
Chayanta, 166–68, 192–93
chicha, 43, 58–61, 72, 76, 98–99, 142
chicheras, 58, 100, 189
Los Chichas, 27, 38
children, 37, 73, 100–101, 104, 201
Chile, 7, 60, 64, 129, 170, 193, 212n27
chilis (capsicum peppers or ají), 27, 79, 98, 161
China, xiv-xv, 6, 14, 57, 89–90, 127, 134, 195

Chinchón, Viceroy Count of, 128
Chiriguanaes (Chiriwana), 27, 29, 87, 101, 112, 209n9
Chocaya, 125
Chucuito, 8, 78
chuño, 72, 78, 98, 189, 198
Chuquisaca, 21, 27, 59, 101, 103, 168
churches, 2, 9, 38, 54, 67, 79, 142, 156; indigenous parish, 40, 95–96; in Babylon, 137–138
Cieza de León, Pedro de, 9–11, 15, 31, 44, 46, 207n10
Cinti Valley, 59, 178
civil wars, 11, 31–32, 112, 114
cloth, xiv-v, 15, 29, 34, 56–57, 61, 96, 98, 156, 200; cotton, xv, 56–57, 96, 200; silk, xv, 1, 14, 57, 90, 93, 96, 116; woolen, 56, 200
Cobo, Bernabé, 63
cobos, 133
coca, 27–29, 60–63, 62fig, 131, 140; trade, 38, 131, 168–169; volume, 98; current use, 195–196
Cochabamba, 61, 64–65, 71, 101, 156, 168
coins. See also mint, royal; 43, 84–85, 127–135, 132fig, 137, 199
Colbert, Jean-Baptiste, 140–141
Colquechaca, 172, 189, 192
comedies (comedias), 106, 108, 202
COMIBOL, 194–195
confraternities, religious, 61, 105, 152, 183, 231
Congo, 104, 183
conquistadors, 7, 21–22, 31, 44, 64, 113
consulados (merchant guilds), 57, 88–90
contraband, 3, 8, 42, 89, 151, 158
convents, 40, 101, 178
Copacabana, Our Lady of, 61, 96–97
copper, 5, 22, 46, 55–56, 85, 125, 130, 188
Córdoba (Argentina), 103–04, 133, 140, 170, 212n27, 229
corn. See maize
corpa, 36–38, 52, 54, 85, 180, 200
corregidores, 95, 121, 130–31, 133, 168
Council of the Indies, 32, 121, 129–130, 134
creoles, 113–114, 179
Cruz, Fray Francisco de la, 143, 161
cupellation, 47–48
Cuzco, 29–30, 43, 56–57, 61, 108, 152, 168

THE CALIFORNIA WORLD HISTORY LIBRARY

*Edited by Edmund Burke III, Kenneth Pomeranz, and Patricia Seed*